FAIRBAIRN'S OBJECT RELATIONS THEORY
IN THE CLINICAL SETTING

David P. Celani

FAIRBAIRN'S OBJECT RELATIONS THEORY IN THE CLINICAL SETTING

COLUMBIA UNIVERSITY PRESS ■ NEW YORK

COLUMBIA UNIVERSITY PRESS

Publishers Since 1893

New York   Chichester, West Sussex

Copyright © 2010 Columbia University Press

Library of Congress Cataloging-in-Publication Data

Celani, David P.

Fairbairn's object relations theory in the clinical setting / David P. Celani.

p. cm.

Includes bibliographical references and index.

ISBN 978-0-231-14906-8 (cloth : alk. paper)

ISBN 978-0-231-14907-5 (pbk : alk. paper)

1. Object relations (Psychoanalysis) 2. Fairbairn, W. Ronald D. (William Ronald Dodds)
I. Title. II. Title: Object relations theory in the clinical setting. [DNLM: 1. Fairbairn, W.
Ronald D. (William Ronald Dodds) 2. Object Attachment. 3. Models, Psychological.
4. Personality Disorders—therapy. WM 460.5.02 C392f 2010]

RC455.4.O23C45   2010

616.89'17—dc22   2009041197

Columbia University Press books are printed on permanent and durable acid-free paper.
This book is printed on paper with recycled content.

Printed in the United States of America

To Bob Barasch, Ph.D., and Stephen Krupa

It is because a fellow is more afraid of the trouble he might have than he ever is of the trouble he's already got. He'll cling to trouble he's used to before he'll risk a change. Yes. A man will talk about how he'd like to escape from living folks. But it's the dead folks that do him the damage. It's the dead ones that lay quiet in one place and dont try to hold him, that he cant escape from.

—WILLIAM FAULKNER, *LIGHT IN AUGUST*

CONTENTS

FAIRBAIRN'S OBJECT RELATIONS THEORY
IN THE CLINICAL SETTING

INTRODUCTION

THIS BOOK IS a complete rewrite and expansion to almost double the size of my previous book *The Treatment of the Borderline Patient: Applying Fairbairn's Object Relations Theory in the Clinical Setting*, which was first issued in 1993. Sixteen years have passed since the publication of that book, and in the ensuing years I have deepened my understanding and appreciation of W. R. D. Fairbairn's psychoanalytic model. During that time, many new developments in the field of "relational psychoanalysis" have emerged, and many of these recent concepts are absent from the earlier text. This enlarged text offers the reader far greater detail in the analysis of Fairbairn's papers, and includes for the first time his paper "On the Nature and Aims of Psychoanalytical Treatment" (1958), in which he described his radical vision of the process of psychoanalysis. There is an increased focus on interpretation of transference and a new emphasis on the development of a co-created narrative of the patient's developmental history in his or her family of origin. The creation of this narrative, which is understood and interpreted in terms of Fairbairn's metapsychology, is seen as central to the developing relationship between the therapist and the patient, and serves as the vehicle for reassessing the relational influences that originally formed the patient's character. It is also within the context of the emerging narrative that transferences develop and are interpreted, again, within the context of Fairbairn's metapsychology. The original text focused on the borderline personality, but this edition includes a chapter on applying Fairbairn's model to the historically and clinically significant disorders of the histrionic and the obsessional personality disorders.

My clinical experience with Fairbairn's model came from twenty-six years of full-time independent practice as a clinical psychologist specializing in the treatment of battered women and patients with borderline personality disorders or anorexia. As a clinician, I was struck by the fact that my patients were preoccupied (if not consumed) either by the rejection they were receiving from their "new" relational objects or by past rejections they had received from their parents, and yet they were unable to separate from the people who were rejecting them. In many cases, their sole purpose in life was focused on winning the love of people who appeared to hurt them endlessly. From my perspective, my patients were being rejected by parents or new relational partners who, compared with them, were blatantly manipulative and intellectually inferior. Despite this, these individuals seemed to have an almost magical grip over my patients. The most common and most frustrating clinical event that I saw in my practice (and one largely ignored in the psychoanalytic literature) was the borderline patient's hope-filled, frantic return to the rejecting object, despite having been rejected dozens of times previously. It appeared that emotional fixation and the resulting primitive dependency on frustrating and rejecting object(s) was the very core of many characterological disorders. Many of my patients' self-defeating and self-destructive behaviors were secondary consequences to intolerable frustration from long-term unmet dependency needs that were exclusively focused on the parental object(s) who failed the patients in their childhood. Despite endless discouragement, my patients returned again and again, filled with false (and sometimes almost delusional) hope that with enough effort on their part their parents (or their new relational objects) would somehow learn to appreciate them. In patients who had managed to separate from their original objects, their "new" objects proved to be as ungratifying, yet at other times as promising, as were their original objects.

My understanding of the borderline condition, as well as related characterological disorders, was advanced by the publication of Greenberg and Mitchell's *Object Relations in Psychoanalytic Theory* (1983). My reaction to their chapter describing Fairbairn's model was electric, as many of the clinical observations regarding the endless attachment to abusive objects that had puzzled me were addressed in their discussion of his model. I then immersed myself in Fairbairn's one and only text, *Psychoanalytic Studies of the Personality* (1952), which is a collection of fourteen of his papers. These papers are notoriously difficult to read, but they offer the persistent reader a complete and complex psychoanalytic model that addresses the reasons behind the powerful allure that the parental objects have on their dependent children (and later adults), as well as the dissociative mechanisms that allow patients to blindly pursue endlessly frustrating objects. As I read his papers, I was amazed that this obscure Scottish analyst had observed in the slums and orphanages of Edinburgh in 1940 exactly what I was seeing in the United States forty years later. His model, based on the innate dependency needs of humans, tied together many of the unexplained clinical observations that had been glaring at me year after year.

My patients' absolute inability to see the faults of the objects of their desire was explained by Fairbairn's central concept of the splitting defense, which allows patients to dissociate painful parts of their experience and repress intolerable memories of past rejections in their unconscious. Often the most severe examples of splitting would occur just before a patient was about to return to his or her rejecting object. Thus splitting appeared to be a defense that served the patients' unmet dependency needs, allowing them to continue to hold out hope in the goodness of their objects and simultaneously ignore the innumerable memories of abandonment they had experienced during their developmental years. The reciprocal behavior also seemed to occur in borderline patients: they ignored, fled from, or misread the intentions of helpful individuals who offered them the support they ostensibly craved. Instead, they seemed to prefer the excitement and frustration inherent in the pursuit of an object that proved, repeatedly, unable to meet their needs.

Fairbairn's model sees that unmet developmental needs within patients are the source of motivation that keeps them enslaved and attached to their original objects, or to similarly frustrating displaced objects. This hopeless, stubborn attachment was universally rationalized by my patients with the simplistic belief that massive work and effort on their part would cause the alluring but rejecting objects to ultimately love and accept them. I found it futile and counterproductive to attempt to prevent severely deprived patients from returning to their abusive objects, and so I learned to tolerate this self-destructive behavior while I worked toward the goal of offering my patients an attachment to an alternative object that eventually would replace their dependency on their rejecting objects.

Today Fairbairn's work remains obscure for a number of reasons. First, he originally published during the psychoanalytic "war" between the followers of Anna Freud and of Melanie Klein (Rayner 1991). He had no students, nor did he attract enough followers to establish a school of thought that supported his work, and so he was ignored while seemingly larger issues between the two established schools were debated. Second, the field of psychoanalysis has tended to see Fairbairn's work as a mere philosophical challenge to Freud's model, one that eliminated instinct theory, which is the very core of classical psychoanalysis. Fairbairn's replacement of drive theory with a theory of human attachment was simply unacceptable to the field of psychoanalysis in his time. He is often remembered as the originator of the simple phrase "libido is object seeking" rather than for producing a complex and complete model of human psychological functioning. It is as if Fairbairn had produced an exquisite, fully functional automobile that was mistaken for a clay model, placed in a museum, and promptly forgotten. Fairbairn's greatest contribution is not his indirect influence on other "relational" models but the creation of a complex and unique metapsychology that can be used every day in the consulting room as a "nuts and bolts" model of psychopathology and psychotherapy. It is unexcelled in treating the borderline patient as well as a wide variety of character disorders. Careful reading of Fairbairn reveals him to have been a keen observer who precisely, and most perfectly, described and explained the dynamics and structure of the borderline personality, and yet today he is overshadowed by lesser theorists even in the area of his greatest strength.

■ ■ ■

This book is designed, first and foremost, to be used by clinicians in their daily practice with patients suffering from characterological disorders. It proposes a simple and straightforward theoretical strategy for clinicians to follow: that of separating borderline patients from their bad objects (both internal and external) and replacing those bad objects with introjects from the good-object therapist. Fairbairn recognized that personality disorders are based on an internal world founded on an attachment to destructive yet desperately needed objects. It is this problem the psychotherapist must address from the first clinical interview on with all characterological patients. The therapist's focus on separating the patient from the bad objects never changes over time, even though the patient will move through various stages during the therapeutic process.

The chapters are organized in a manner designed to help clinicians grasp this fundamental therapeutic strategy. Chapter 1 offers the reader an overview of Fairbairn's work and begins with a brief biography emphasizing the developmental events in his personal history that influenced the direction and contents of his model. This is followed by a review of his first three theoretical papers, focusing on aspects of his model that have the greatest clinical applicability. Many of Fairbairn's discussions in these papers are rebuttals of Freudian doctrine, which, as mentioned, kept him locked in the category of a metapsychologist, and these debates have been largely omitted here. By selectively focusing on the clinically relevant aspects of these papers, I hope to illustrate how potent and complete Fairbairn's model is as a clinical tool, and how it can be applied today, with very few modifications, to patients with a wide array character disorders.

Fairbairn's first theoretical paper, "Schizoid Factors in the Personality" (1940), is a relatively brief article that expands the concept of "schizoid" to include disorders that are based on splitting of the ego. Fairbairn saw the schizoid personality as a direct result of emotional deprivation and as characterized by three factors: omnipotence, detachment, and a focus on the interior world. A second significant consequence of emotional deprivation on the child's emotional development is a loss of faith in whole-object relationships and a reliance on "partial" objects. The child's turn toward part-objects is seen as a regressive retreat that protects the child from further disappointment in his objects, while salvaging some semblance of contact and gratification. The third significant contribution of this paper is Fairbairn's counterintuitive observation that emotional deprivation is the source of *increased* attachment (developmental-emotional fixation without the concept of libido) to the rejecting object. Finally, he recognized that the child who experiences rejection assumes that his own love is worthless and that his hostility toward others is a reaction to feelings of inferiority and worthlessness. This paper begins the process of establishing Fairbairn's model as one of the first two relational models in the field of psychoanalysis, as his work was developed independently and simultaneously with Sullivan's model of Interpersonal Psychoanalysis in the United States.

Fairbairn's second great theoretical paper, "A Revised Psychopathology of the Psychoses and Psychoneuroses" (1941), continues the development of his theory with the introduction of a clear but incomplete developmental sequence based on the child's progressive differentiation from the object, with the child moving from a stage of complete identification with the object to a transitional stage, and ending up as a young adult completely differentiated from his or her objects. Fairbairn clearly stated that emotional support of the child by the objects was the engine of differentiation and, without it, the child would remain fixated and undifferentiated. He also continued to challenge Freud's instinct theory, saying that libidinal pleasure was a "sign-post to the object" (1941:33) and thus demoting the pleasure principle and replacing it with the primacy of attachment to objects. The lack of emotional support for the child's legitimate developmental needs not only prolongs the child's dependency on his objects, but it also turns him toward "substitutive satisfactions" (1941:40), which in today's world would translate into addictions of one type or another. The most surprising and bold clinical example in the paper is of a young female patient who thought of offering to sleep with her father, an "obvious" example of Freud's Oedipal conflict. However, Fairbairn interprets this example strictly in terms of object relations and offers the reader a surprising and viable alternative to one of Freud's central psychoanalytic constructs.

Fairbairn's monumental third theoretical paper, "The Repression and the Return of Bad Objects (with Special Reference to the 'War Neuroses')" (1943), begins with his redefinition of the human unconscious, which up to this point had been the province of Freudian and Kleinian theory. Fairbairn's unconscious contains no source of objectless energy equivalent to Freud's Id; rather, it is populated by dissociated relational events that originally took place in the external world between the child and his objects. These relational events were too intolerable and disruptive for the child to integrate into his conscious, central ego, yet too powerful and structure producing to be permanently banished. Thus Fairbairn's unconscious is filled with dissociated events from actual interpersonal interactions, and this unique "accrued" unconscious replaces the Freudian unconscious of inherited instinctual drives that are assumed to constantly pressure the ego for expression. Fairbairn's unconscious had a different source, a very different set of internal structures (which were later described in his 1944 paper), and a different purpose compared with the unconscious in classical analytic theory. This bold act of proposing a unique unconscious that has absolutely no commonality with Freud's inherited drives eliminated much of the support he might have had from the analytic community, as the models were mutually exclusive and his colleagues had to choose one model or the other. No one chose Fairbairn.

Fairbairn then turned to the issue of shame and recognized that neglected and abused children were ashamed of themselves for two separate reasons. First, because they felt demeaned by their parents, who behaved as if they were unworthy of being cared for, and, second, because they were identified with (undifferentiated) bad objects from whom they could not flee, and therefore they shared in the "badness" of their parents. From this, he developed his first major defense, "The Moral Defense Against Bad Objects," which manifests itself by the rationalization often heard from abused children that their violent parents are actually "good" but they themselves are "bad" and therefore deserving of punishment. My discussion of this defense is extremely critical of Fairbairn's analysis of the dynamics of this defense, and I offer the reader an alternative view. Fairbairn also noticed that the children who were keeping their parents "good" were quite eager to blame themselves. He recognized that by blaming themselves, the children kept the illusion alive that they lived in an orderly, predictable, and "good" world. Fairbairn recognized that it would have been devastating to the emotional equilibrium of these children to acknowledge that their objects were randomly hateful and eternally frustrating, as this would dash their hope for love and support in the future. The "Moral Defense"—that is, blaming the self for the failures of the object—is the fundamental cognitive defense that every therapist who works with this patient group must be prepared to encounter.

Fairbairn also offers the reader a clear and succinct definition of psychopathology in this paper, based on both the "badness" of the objects that the child internalized and the extent that the child identifies with these bad internalized objects. These are the internalizations that create the structures (self- and object-representations) in the Fairbairnian unconscious. The actual structures were not described in this paper but in his next paper, which followed one year later (1944). Another significant aspect of this major paper is Fairbairn's discussion of the source of the power that the bad object has over the dependent child. He recognized that the more a parent rejected the child, the deeper the reservoir of residual need that would remain unsatisfied in the child and therefore the greater the child's dependency and fixation on that object. Finally, Fairbairn (1943) used metaphors from his religious training to identify the major source of resistance to the derepression of unconscious memories of internalized bad objects, which was the fear of being overwhelmed by them: "When such bad object are released the world around the patient becomes peopled with devils which are too terrifying to face" (69).

Chapter 2 begins with a detailed review of Fairbairn's paper "Endopsychic Structure Considered in Terms of Object Relationships" (1944), which compliments his 1943 paper and introduced his structural model. He solved the problem of the toxicity of the internalized bad objects with the introduction of the splitting defense and the resulting internal structures. The splitting defense uses dissociation to force intolerable material into the unconscious, and the resulting internal structures "package" similar perceptions into a single vision of the self in relation to the object. Once dissociated, the structures protect the child's conscious central ego from awareness of how badly his objects treated him during his development. Fairbairn described six ego-and-object structures, four comprising the unconscious and two remaining conscious. The four unconscious structures form two self-and-object pairs that remain dissociated from each other, and therefore safely isolate the bad objects in the child's interior world. The two (mostly) unconscious self structures are the libidinal and antilibidinal egos that relate exclusively to the exciting or rejecting parts of the object, which have also been dissociated in the unconscious. The relational "bond" between the antilibidinal ego and the rejecting object is hate, with the antilibidinal ego hectoring the rejecting object in an attempt to force it to change and improve, while the rejecting object retaliates with uninhibited aggression and condemnation of the antilibidinal ego. Conversely, the libidinal ego knows nothing about the antilibidinal ego and sees another dissociated facet of the very same parental object as containing the promise of unlimited love. Fairbairn labeled this reciprocal part-object the "exciting object" because of the excitement engendered in the child's libidinal ego by the hope of being loved. The libidinal ego allows the child to safely love his object and hold on to the hope that he will be cherished, thus preserving the attachment to the object who is, in reality, neglectful, even abusive. The libidinal ego's love is uncontaminated by any feelings of hate, as the antilibidinal ego keeps the hate-filled relationship with the rejecting part-object sealed, separate, and apart from the libidinal ego–exciting object relationship. Thus Fairbairn's structural model solves the problem of bad objects in the unconscious by keeping them dissociated and unaware of the opposite structures. My discussion of the structures expands the previously unexplored relationship between the conscious central ego and its ideal object, a relationship in which Fairbairn had little interest, as his focus was on psychopathology.

The final paper reviewed in this chapter is Fairbairn's "On the Nature and Aims of Psycho-Analytical Treatment" (1958), in which he challenged every aspect of classical psychoanalysis, from using the couch to providing a "real" relationship for the patient outside the transference relationship that was designed to reactivate the patient's stalled development. Fairbairn's concepts put him outside the boundaries of nearly every important assumption of classical analysis, and this paper ensured that his contemporaries would ignore his work. He boldly redefined "analysis" as "synthesis," which follows from his model of dissociated selves populating the unconscious. Fairbairn saw the recovery of mental health as synonymous with the concept of integration. The therapist's task is to help the patient integrate the memories encased in his antilibidinal ego into his central ego and accept the reality that he was poorly treated as a child. Conversely, the patient must also accept that his fantasies of unlimited love residing in his libidinal ego's view of the exciting object are only a compensatory attempt to keep himself attached to his object, which is necessary to prevent his collapse into depression and despair. Unfortunately, integration of these substructures into the realm of the central ego meets resistance from the patient's inner world, which Fairbairn (1958) termed a "closed system" that tries to "press-gang" (335) the therapist into appearing to be a familiar object equivalent to the objects in the patient's unconscious.

Chapter 3, the first to address the "application" of Fairbairn's concepts, offers a detailed "user-manual" for the therapist with regard to the characteristics of the four unconscious structures. The chapter is designed to help the clinician understand the patient's productions in the clinical interview. When using this model, therapists must know which of the partially dissociated structures is dominant so that they understand "to whom" they are speaking. The four, mostly dissociated structures are the antilibidinal ego, which is in a fiercely competitive and aggressive relationship with the internalized rejecting object, and the libidinal ego, which longs for and hopes for love from the exciting aspect of the object. The two ego structures know nothing about each other or the other's associated object; thus the therapist can expect extreme shifts in behavior when one of these subegos is dissociated and replaced by the other. This split ego structure *prevents* ambivalence, as both internal and external objects are seen as all-exciting or completely rejecting, and this allows the child (or later the adult) to pour out his love toward an apparently loving object while his hate attacks a completely rejecting object. Premature, or forced, integration of these two opposing realities will create extreme ambivalence that can destroy the needed attachment and invite a psychological collapse. The developmentally fixated patient cannot afford to integrate the opposite facets of the object, because the rejecting aspects of the object would completely overwhelm the smaller fantasy-enhanced loving aspects, and the patient would see that he was dependent on an intolerably unloving, hostile, or indifferent object.

The antilibidinal ego was originally part of the central ego, but it must be dissociated because it has experienced intolerably rejecting aspects of the neglectful and abusive parental object. It is filled with impotent rage toward the rejecting object and can be accusatory, self-righteous, and filled with a desire for revenge. Because the antilibidinal ego is fixated at an earlier age owing to the lack of developmental support, it is enormously impressed with the power and importance of the rejecting object, even though the rejecting object is often (in reality) a failed, impotent, and unsuccessful person. The rejecting internalized object is composed of the intolerable aspects of the parent that could not be tolerated by the central ego and thus had to be dissociated. It attacks and demeans the child's self (antilibidinal ego) with impunity. At times, the individual with a powerful internal rejecting object can identify with that ego structure and will play out the role of the abuser with others who appear to be weaker, just as he was abused in childhood.

The libidinal ego is a dissociated ego structure that contains all the hope and unmet need for love that results from a deprived emotional history. The child's need for a loving attentive object is satisfied by the promise from the exciting part of the parental object that did occasionally meet the child's needs. The amplification of these rare relational events, along with pure fantasy, saves the child from facing an intolerably bleak reality. The exciting object creates excitement in the child, because it promises the libidinal ego that love is just around the corner.

Each of these ego structures can dominate the patient's central ego and become the executive ego, which then misperceives the therapist in predictable ways. The four transference possibilities include the patient operating out of his antilibidinal ego misperceiving the therapist as a rejecting object, as well as the reciprocal relational scenario of the patient relating to the therapist as a rejecting object with the therapist pressured into the antilibidinal ego role. On the other side of the split, the patient can relate to the therapist from the perspective of the libidinal ego and assume that he or she has been promised love in the future, or the reciprocal relational scenario in which the patient presents himself as an exciting object and tempts the therapist into the libidinal ego position. Fairbairn's structural theory offers therapists an enormously powerful model of the inner world of their patients that can be used in the consulting room as a guide when making transference interpretations.

The next section of chapter 3 focuses on the sudden and dramatic derepression of dissociated material from patients' dreams that had been contained in their antilibidinal egos. Several examples are presented and appropriate therapeutic responses are recommended that buffer the shock of this material, while not allowing the material to be dissociated once again. Again, Fairbairn saw the goal of treatment as helping patients integrate material that had been split off and held in their unconscious back into the conscious central ego. As more of this material is assimilated into the central ego, the subegos loose their potency and the central ego expands into "territories" previously under dissociation. The final section of the chapter looks at the negative therapeutic reaction, which is an extended transference where the therapist is perceived as a rejecting object and the patient tries to thwart progress to both directly frustrate the therapist and prevent the therapist from taking any satisfaction in his work

Chapter 4, which continues the theme of intervention, begins with the concept of "narrative truth," which sees psychoanalytic truth as not absolute but as relative to the model from which it comes. The co-creation of a narrative between the therapist and the patient, based on Fairbairn's metapsychology, is the fundamental relational matrix that is used to explain the processes of Fairbairnian analysis. The primary goal of this narrative is to review the patient's life story and apply Fairbairn's model to the events that are then interpreted in terms of attachment to bad objects. This process is facilitated by the maintenance of a tight and private framework. Despite the therapist's best efforts, his good intentions will be distorted by the patient's unconscious, which will see the therapist as identical to one of the structures in the patient's inner world (rejecting object, exciting object, antili-bidinal ego, or libidinal ego). The therapist must repeatedly interpret his way out of the negative transformations until he is perceived as the person he really is—a good object. I offer a number of examples of transference interpretations using Fairbairn's metapsychology. Transference interpretations are an essential part of treatment, particularly with borderline patients who often split the therapist from an exciting to a rejecting object in the very first session.

The co-created narrative is a vehicle for interaction, and during the process small bits of dissociated material will emerge. This material is seldom as dramatic as derepressed material from dreams, discussed in chapter 3, but the process is the same. The therapist must identify and keep the dissociated material in the narrative while helping the patient integrate what was once intolerable into his conscious central ego, without causing panic of abandonment. Fairbairn (1943) noted that the therapy was contingent on the patient facing an "unwantonly good object" (69), though I repeatedly remind the reader that Fairbairn (paradoxically) never believed that good objects were internalized. The fundament mutative factor in my revision of his model is an emphasis on the internalization of a new good object, which allows the patient to relinquish attachments to the internalized exciting and rejecting objects. Not only is the therapist internalized as a good object, but his or her ways of thinking, organizing, problem solving, and understanding the world are internalized as well.

Fairbairn noted that the "real" (non-transference) relationship with the patient is part of its mutative power, a position firmly rejected by the field of psychoanaly-sis. He saw patients as developmentally stunted and fixated at an earlier age, and one of the therapist's tasks is to restart the patient's developmental progress through the therapist's emotional support of the patient's real efforts in the world. Support-ing and strengthening the patient's central ego is critical to reducing the illusory power of the bad objects, and a number of examples of this process are offered. Also playing a role in enhancing the patient's ego is "positive projective identification," in which the therapist projects his love onto the patient and the patient, in turn, is influenced by the projection.

Chapter 4 ends with the patient's achievement of mature grief, as the divided aspects of his unconscious become integrated into his central ego. No longer can the patient hide from the reality that his objects were limited, and disinterested, and that he was an overlooked, even discarded, child. This once unacceptable perception, which was fragmented and dissociated, now becomes a core aspect of the patient's central ego. The therapist's role, once again, is to support the patient's perceptions. Fairbairn (1943) noted that soldiers in the field would break down with "war neuroses" when their dissociated memories emerged raw, because they were completely unable to cope with the frightening and overwhelming material without the support of a relationship with a good object.

Chapter 5 continues with the application of Fairbairn's model to patients with a borderline personality disorder and to battered women. Rich in clinical examples, the chapter focuses on issues of technique and the management of characterological patients. It begins with a Fairbairnian twist on Sullivan's concept of the "detailed inquiry." In my view, the most significant factors to explore when using Fairbairn's metapsychology are the various manifestations of the patient's dependency on external objects or, equally important, on internal objects. As the therapist works with the patient to co-create a developmental narrative, the issue of patient "badness" and guilt is often central to the discussion. As the narrative is interpreted and understood in terms of Fairbairn's model, new possibilities once thought unimaginable are introduced into the discussion regarding who was actually "bad" during the patient's development. Clinical suggestions are offered with respect to managing the patient's guilt regarding separating from his needy but abusive object. This is followed by a description of techniques that strengthen the patient's central ego, particularly in regard to helping the patient protect himself from further humiliation or even outright abuse. As the patient's central ego develops a stronger relationship with the therapist as an ideal object, the abuser's motives and techniques can be interpreted, further strengthening the patient's central ego. This allows the patient to learn, and to predict, the bad object's next interpersonal "move," and this process helps the patient reevaluate the strength and importance of the rejecting object. Over time, this process reduces the patient's antilibidinal ego's respect for the power and importance of the rejecting object. The discussion then moves to a related topic—guidelines for the therapist on how to support patients as rejecting objects actively attempt to re-intimidate or manipulate them back to their previously submissive interpersonal stance.

Chapter 5 continues with an examination of topics that Fairbairn wrote about that relate specifically to the borderline patient, as well as significant issues that I have repeatedly found in my work with this diagnostic group. Notably, many of Fairbairn's descriptions of typical "schizoid" psychopathology eventuate as resistance to the therapist's interventions. The first, and most obvious, is the schizoid's excessive focus on the inner world, which allows the apparently desperately dependent borderline patient to remain serenely uninfluenced by the therapist, who is still outside the "closed loop" of the patient's internal world. A second source of resistance comes from the borderline patient's ruthless unmet dependency needs that demand satisfaction in relationships with others. Many borderline patients display little regard for the (partial) objects with whom they relate and have even less regard for the therapist's effort and investment, as they see no immediate gratification of their needs in the relationship. There follows an extended example of the clinical manifestation of the core issue that Fairbairn cites repeatedly: "the obstinate attachment to the bad object." This attachment to bad external objects is a formidable source of resistance to the therapist's best efforts. The patient's self-destructive behavior in returning to the bad object simply cannot be prevented until the therapist has become firmly internalized as an alternative to the bad object in the patient's inner world. One dramatic example cited is that of a young patient who, in his efforts to differentiate from his objects, joined an organized cross-country bicycle trip with a group of other young people, but, on returning home, bought a house right next door to his parents' home! Fairbairn frequently spoke of "identification" with the object, and this, too, is a source of resistance; the undifferentiated patient cannot give up his objects for they are part of him, and, without them, he fears he will perish. I then offer a detailed clinical example of the effects of extreme dissociation, in which the contents of the antilibidinal ego and its relationship to the rejecting object were completely unavailable to the patient's central ego. The therapist's fundamental position—that the patient must separate from the bad object—made *absolutely no sense* to this patient, who had dissociated and repressed all the relational events that would have informed a normal integrated individual that his object was indeed bad.

The final section of chapter 5 is based on my previous book *The Illusion of Love: Why the Battered Woman Returns to Her Abuser* (1994). In that book, I applied Fairbairn's structural analysis to the three-stage "Cycle Theory of Violence" proposed by Walker (1979) and found that the shift from one stage to the next was based on a shift in dominance from one previously dissociated ego state to another in one or both of the participants. Fairbairn's model is the best explanation for the extreme shifts in perception that can be observed in both participants engaged in the battering scenario, which careen within minutes from maniacal rage to an opposite state, one of love and longing. Fairbairn's model of alternating attachments based on a need for love that is dissociated and replaced by vindictive hate and revenge offers the clinician the best model for working with these patients, particularly compared with the "failure to flee" model that has been used in the past.

Chapter 6, the final clinical chapter, looks at the two "classical" personality disorders: the hysteric and the obsessional. Both disorders are examined from a structural point of view, and in each Fairbairn's model offers new insights into these well-known personality styles.

The typical family constellation that produces obsessional disorders is one dominated by parents who are highly verbal and aggressive toward their children. Careful examination of these families reveals that the child's central ego is damaged by punitive and contradictory parental behavior that confuses the child about when the rules he is trying to follow apply. Winckler (1995) describes the effect on the child as "mystification," in that the child cannot tell when he will be attacked by his self-righteous parents for violating a rule he was unaware of or one that was suddenly replaced by another, opposite, but equally potent rule. The result is guilt and confusion, as the child cannot comprehend how or why he is condemned as bad when he is trying to be so good. These extremely intolerable relational events are dissociated, and the young obsessional develops an antilibidinal ego that is suffused with fear and defensiveness while his internalized rejecting object mimics his real parents as it attacks his antilibidinal ego's every move. Another feature of this family style is that the children are required to excel in the outside world at the same time that their emotional needs are ignored at home. As an adult, the obsessive individual is dependent and cynical in relating to others, and his frequent, and inappropriate, passive-aggressive behavior toward others originates in his engorged antilibidinal ego. His romantic partners are seen either as rejecting objects or, conversely, if the individual identifies with his internalized rejecting object, as devalued and worthless. The constant criticism of his choices by his parental object makes the obsessive wary of decision making in adulthood, and he seeks refuge in science, test reports, and recommendations from higher authorities. A Fairbairnian structural analysis sees the obsessive as suffused with a defensive and hypersensitive antilibidinal ego that is cowed by the bombastic, moralistic rejecting object, and, surprisingly, there is very little evidence of libidinal ego or exciting object in his inner world. His original object(s) gave him too little hope on which he could build libidinal ego fantasies. Finally, ritualistic symptoms can be understood as a dialogue between the two powerful structures in his inner world (the antilibidinal ego and the rejecting object), while the central ego looks on haplessly, unable to control the larger and more potent structures.

A structural approach to the hysteric reveals a different inner relational world formed by different family dynamics, such as a depressed, often uninvolved mother and a seductive father who trades what little attention he offers his daughter for premature and inappropriate sexualized behaviors on her part. The child, desperately needy for emotional support, complies and must dissociate the intolerable aspects of the sexualized relationship between her and her father, as these memories of such events cannot be integrated into her central ego. Her unmet emotional needs create a libidinal ego that sees her paternal object (and later all men) as an exciting object, as he offers some nurturance that is exaggerated by fantasy and hope, while her mother is ignored by both her and her father. The relational pattern she internalizes is projected onto all new relationships, and, from the perspective of her libidinal ego, men are approached as exciting objects. The hysteric's eager, sexualized approach to men is based on her hope for nurturance, and her sexualized behaviors are dissociated so that she approaches each new relationship in a state of "innocence." The male object often responds to the hysteric's displays with a sexual proposal, which outrages the hysteric; she immediately represses her libidinal ego, replacing it with her antilibidinal ego, and all the bitter antilibidinal disappointment in men emerges with force. This analysis offers new insight into the "castration scene" well known in the analytic literature.

Chapter 7, the final chapter in the book, looks at the legacy of Fairbairn's work in the larger world of psychoanalysis, both in terms of the acceptance of his ideas into concepts shared by other models and in regard to the number of specific texts that focus on the application of his model to the treatment process.

CHAPTER 1

FAIRBAIRN'S INTELLECTUAL DEVELOPMENT AND A REVIEW OF HIS EARLY PAPERS

W. R. D. FAIRBAIRN'S importance as a major contributor to object relations theory resulted from his acute clinical observations and his independent thinking. His work with abused and neglected children led him to abandon Freudian drive theory without destroying its clinical perceptions and overall perspective of the analytic approach. Fairbairn had a great deal of respect for Freud's psychoanalytic model, but this did not prevent him from differing with classical psychoanalysis regarding the role of dependency in the development of adult psychopathology. His writings, along with those of H. S. Sullivan, ushered in the modern concept of "relationality," which has become one of the major currents in psychoanalysis, as noted by Greenberg and Mitchell (1983): "In a series of dense and fertile papers written during the early 1940's, W. R. D. Fairbairn developed a theoretical perspective which, along with Sullivan's 'interpersonal psychiatry,' provides the purest and clearest expression of the shift from the drive/structure model to the relational/ structure model" (151).

The "relational" point of view that grew out of Fairbairn's and Sullivan's work holds that personality development is the result of a complete enmeshment of the child's nascent self with other human beings. The concept of drive (which was needed in classical theory to motivate the infant to seek out the object) is not necessary in relational psychoanalysis, because the individual does not develop in isolation. Meanings and experiences (such as the Oedipal conflict) are not assumed to be universal, but each individual has a unique interpersonal history and meanings are created in relationship to others in the developmental environment, as Mitchell (1998) notes:

> To argue that we need the concept of drive to describe what the individual seeks in interactions with other people presumes that the individual qua individual is the most appropriate unit of study. It assumes the individual, in his or her natural

state, is essentially alone and then drawn into interaction for some purpose or need. I believe that Fairbairn (like Sullivan) was struggling toward a different way of understanding the nature of human beings as fundamentally social, not as *drawn* into interaction, but as *embedded* in an interactive matrix with others as their natural state. . . . Fairbairn, Sullivan, and other architects of the relational model were redefining the nature of the human psyche as fundamentally social and interactive. Fairbairn was suggesting that object seeking, in its most radical form, is not the vehicle for the satisfaction of a specific need, but the expression of our very nature, the form through which we become specifically *human* beings. (117)

Fairbairn's work, along with Sullivan's, began the movement that eventuated in a new psychoanalytic perspective that views human beings as functioning not in isolation, but as inextricably intertwined with one another. This new view of human functioning as fundamentally relational has refocused the field of psychoanalysis from the individual to the self in relation to objects, both internal and external.

Despite the ultimate influence of his work, Fairbairn was an unlikely challenger to Freudian hegemony. He was a deeply conservative and fundamentally fearful man who did little to promote himself or his model, partly because he was afflicted by a neurotic symptom ("bashful kidney") that limited his ability to travel (Sutherland 1989). Despite his social conservatism, Fairbairn was dedicated to helping those who were obviously deprived. His altruism was mixed with his strong religious feeling, which he expressed in his youth by his memberships in organizations that were involved in practical projects designed to better the lives of others. According to Sutherland (1989): "His impulses to improve the lot of the deprived or the suffering, to make life more tolerable for all, were unquestionably strong and sincere. They were, however, to be expressed within the established structure of society, to which his attachment was unusually strong" (5).

Added to this mix of conservatism, religion, and a desire to help others was a fearless intellect coupled with an intense discipline and a scholarly bent. His model shows the effects of all these factors: his altruistic attempt to help others in need, the influence of his religious training, his respect for the existing structure, and, most important, his utter confidence in his intellect. This confidence allowed him to follow his clinical observations to their logical conclusion, which eventuated in his model of human development based on object relationships, a conclusion completely at odds with the model in which he was trained, as Grotstein and Rinsley (1994) have noted:

His style of writing reveals a man who was highly sensitive, educated, philosophical, logical and religious—one who had studied Latin and employed its arcane and cumbersome mode in his punctilious, complex, and highly structured sentences, which added all the more rigor to his reasoning. He was shy and uncharismatic, but revealed an inner flame of passion over the heretical views he offered to a psychoanalytic public that was unable, with a few outstanding exceptions, to comprehend their importance. (3)

Fairbairn was born in Edinburgh, Scotland, in 1889, the only child of older, middle-class parents. He was exposed to the restrictive moral standards fostered by Calvinism and enforced by an over-involved rigid mother (Sutherland 1989), sometimes supportive but often frightening, and a continually negative and punitive father. Beattie (2003), who also draws on Sutherland's biography of Fairbairn, sees a strong relationship between Fairbairn's model and developmental events in his personal history:

> Fairbairn was the only child of older parents whose unstinting efforts to foster his social and educational development in conformity with their puritanical views left him wretchedly confused. The miseries he underwent at the hands of his snobbish and hypochondriacal mother, who attacked any expression of sexual curiosity or exploration on his part are described with painful honesty in his self-analytic notes of 1939. (1175)

Beattie (2003) concludes that Fairbairn's model was strongly influenced by his own childhood experiences and suggests, further, that he had to split his mother and repress her bad aspects in his unconscious in order to remain attached to her supportive behaviors.

Conflict arose when his "narrow-minded," penny-pinching, perhaps even envious father opposed his and his mother's desire that he study at Oxford instead of Edinburgh University. Fairbairn's resentment now made it essential for him to ally with his mother, who encouraged his intellectual and social ambitions (Beattie 2003:1176). His educational history reflected both his intellectual bent and the support he received from his mother in pursuing a career of the mind. In contrast, his father was more interested in keeping Fairbairn in Scotland so he would not be exposed to liberal religious influences in London (Sutherland 1989). Fairbairn graduated from Edinburgh University in 1911 with a degree in philosophy and decided to become a clergyman. For short periods prior to enrolling in divinity school, he studied Hellenic culture at the Universities of Kiel, Strasbourg, and Manchester (Sutherland 1989). Fairbairn's study of philosophy was the fundamental intellectual support that gave him the courage and confidence to challenge Freud's drive-structure model:

> Fairbairn's analysis of Freud even before the "Project" was available centered upon the difficulties stemming from the problem in Freud's work which

Fairbairn identified as "philosophical dualism." He used this term to describe Freud's postulations of such oppositions as mind and body, life and death, energy and structure, form and content—all of which Fairbairn thought Freud had derived from a fundamentally dualistic view of natural phenomena. . . . Fairbairn countered the dualistic view of man, which can be seen to derive from Platonic conceptions of man by substituting a holistic view of man derived from Aristotelian psychology. (Scharff and Birtles 1994:xv–xvi)

After his study of philosophy, he followed up his decision to join the clergy by taking an intermediate degree in divinity at London University, returning to Edinburgh University in 1914. He enrolled to become a Presbyterian clergyman, but these plans were aborted by the outbreak of the First World War, in which Fairbairn served for three and a half years. Upon discharge, he gave up his plan of becoming a clergyman and instead took up medical training, beginning in 1919, with the clear goal of becoming a psychotherapist. During his medical training he read both Freud and Jung and underwent a personal analysis (1921–1923) with E. H. Connell, a businessman who came to psychoanalysis late in life, trained in Edinburgh, and was himself analyzed by Ernest Jones (Sutherland 1989). Fairbairn then was appointed as an assistant in the Royal Edinburgh Hospital, the major psychiatric and teaching hospital in Scotland (Sutherland 1989). His intellectual training and interests were unusually wide-ranging, and his prior training in philosophy and religion are reflected in the language he used to describe psychological phenomena. Fairbairn's freedom to shift from one field of intellectual interest to another is an indication of his broad interests and varied scholarly experiences.

As a young man of twenty-seven, Fairbairn visited a hospital for "shell-shocked" officers. This was his first exposure to severe psychopathology, and he was moved by the extent that psychological forces could destroy otherwise powerful men:

One pivotal event seems to have been his visit on 12 November 1916 to Craiglockart War Hospital for "nerve-shocked" officers in Edinburgh. Here, Fairbairn was profoundly impressed by the cases of conversion hysteria he saw (years later he told his daughter that it was the puzzle of actively displayed physical symptoms with no discernable medical cause which so intrigued him). . . . The patients at Craiglockart were not sexually frustrated women like those who had inspired Freud's creation of psychoanalysis. Rather they were strong men who had been unmanned by their shattering experiences during the endless trench warfare in France. (Beattie 2003:1177)

This powerful experience began the long intellectual process in which Fairbairn came to doubt Freud's claim that sexuality was the prime motivation for all human behavior. Fairbairn was a small man, not robust, and he admired officers who were physically larger and bolder than he was. Yet these very men were destroyed by conversion symptoms that completely diminished their power and reduced them to a childlike state. Later, a second, equally powerful influence on his intellectual development resulted from the part-time appointment that he held from 1927 to 1935 at the University Psychological Clinic for Children in Edinburgh. Many of these children had been temporarily removed from their homes because of the danger of physical violence, and they became the second focal population that he used in the development of his model. They were very unlike Freud's wealthy female hysterics. First, they were children, which allowed Fairbairn to have direct information about their family of origin; and, second, these children were experiencing levels of neglect and abuse that were more severe than Freud's obligation-bound patients had experienced. His key perception regarding these children was that despite their having been abused and neglected, they were extraordinarily attached to the very parents who abused them. This focus on the dependency of abused children was noted by Grotstein and Rindsley (1994): "He helped us understand the well-known conundrum that the worse one's internal objects are experienced to be, the less one is able to leave them" (7). Here in the children's clinic, as in the hospital for traumatized soldiers, sexuality played no apparent part in these puzzling and extremely powerful psychological phenomena. The desperately dependent children paid no heed to the danger at home and begged to return, preferring their unstable and abusive home environments to the safety of the clinic. The abused child's loyalty and focus on the rejecting parent was a topic that Fairbairn often discussed with Harry Guntrip, another analyst and object relations theorist, whom Fairbairn was treating in formal psychoanalysis. Guntrip's analysis lasted 1,014 sessions (Hughes 1994), and after one of them Fairbairn took Guntrip to the university orphanage to see one child in particular. Note that, in Fairbairn's day, analysts were unaware of the power of the psychoanalytic framework, specifically the prohibition of extra-therapeutic contact with patients, which undermines the established framework. Fairbairn proceeded to illustrate for Guntrip the "obstinate attachment" of the child to the bad object: "He asked one child whose mother thrashed her cruelly: 'Would you like me to find you a new, kind Mummy?' She said: 'No, I want my own Mummy back,' showing the intensity of the libidinal tie to the bad object. The devil you know is better than the devil you do not [know], and better than no devil at all" (Guntrip 1975:146).

Fairbairn's model was not influential in his lifetime for a number of reasons. First, he was isolated in Scotland, which had few psychoanalysts in the first place, and he was not a member of the two competing schools of "English Psychoanalysis"— the Kleinians and the followers of Anna Freud—and so he had no students of his own to influence. These two groups were engaged in their own struggle for dominance (Rayner 1991), one that completely overshadowed Fairbairn's less well-known work.

Perhaps more important, his intended audience was small, composed entirely of followers of one of the other branches of Freudianism. Sutherland, Fairbairn's biographer, noted that Fairbairn naively assumed that others in the extremely tightly knit world of psychoanalysis would embrace his thinking without resistance. However, analysts derived their identity and personal status from the classical tradition, and thus Fairbairn's complete dismissal of drive theory, the foundation of Freud's model, generated hostility rather than support. Finally, his work is difficult to follow, for his collected papers remained unrevised and inconsistent, as noted by Greenberg and Mitchell (1983): "Consequently, the reader is faced not with a single theory but with a series of different formulations, with varying focuses, circling again and again over the same territory, yet not wholly consistent with each other" (153).

Fairbairn's papers are difficult to read because they often wander off on philosophical tangents, a consequence of his continuous philosophical debate with Freud's drive model. The reader is faced with long meta-psychological digressions and debates that are often more prominent than his clinical insights. Despite the ultimate value of Fairbairn's work, his direct challenge to the basis of the classical model (drive theory) and the fact that he was not a member of an established school of thought doomed his model to forty years of obscurity. This long period of anonymity was breached, somewhat ironically, by Kernberg, a strong supporter of the drive/structure model, in two papers, the first appearing in 1966 in the *International Journal of Psychoanalysis* and the second in 1967 in the *Journal of the American Psychoanalytic Association*. Kernberg had no idea of the far-ranging consequence of his enthusiastic embrace of Fairbairn's model, which he saw as the key to understanding the borderline personality—and nothing more. In both papers, Kernberg highlighted Fairbairn's contribution to the understanding of splitting as a defense, which allowed a new understanding of the borderline patient's confusing behavior. Consider the following example, in which Kernberg (1966) describes a borderline patient alternating between periods of adoration and hatred and contempt for the therapist: "During the time in which he had expressed the intense feeling of love and longing for me he was completely unable to be aware of any negative feeling, in spite of preserving perfect memories of the days in which his feelings were completely opposite to his present state of mind" (238). Kernberg concludes that, in this patient, "splitting then appeared to be not only a defect in the ego but also an active, very powerful defensive operation" (238).

Kernberg's recognition of Fairbairn's model as the key to understanding one of the most difficult of all outpatient populations awakened interest in Fairbairn's work among many analysts. By championing Fairbairn's model, Kernberg, inadvertently, had introduced into the closed world of classical psychoanalysis an innovative way to comprehend the functions of the unconscious, human personality development, and the psychotherapeutic process. Kernberg's papers also illustrate the danger of applying two antithetical models to the same material, for he did not address the underlying metapsychological issue: that the defense mechanism of splitting in Fairbairn's model is based on the child's need to remain attached to the object, and this attachment is in no way related to instinctual, biological drives. Fairbairn's model emphasizes that parental failures create the need for the splitting defense in the child, leaving the individual with unmet (but legitimate) developmental needs that are thrust on the analyst. In later works, Kernberg (1984), in an effort to go back to the Freudian principles of treatment, attempted to return to the drive/structure model, advocating increasingly strict analytic neutrality and lack of involvement with borderline patients. Fairbairn's model, once Kernberg had brought it to the attention of the world of psychoanalysis, became a very minor, though visible, part of psychoanalytic thought.

The second, more significant event that awakened the world of psychoanalysis to Fairbairn's work was the publication, in 1983, of Greenberg and Mitchell's text, *Object Relations in Psychoanalytic Theory*. In 1989, the Scottish Institute of Human Relations celebrated the centennial of Fairbairn's birth with a conference in Edinburgh, which I attended. The organizers had expected fewer than 40 attendees, and yet more than 150 participants showed up, mostly from the United States and Canada, a direct consequence of the chapter on Fairbairn in Greenberg and Mitchell's book.

Fairbairn's theory is a psychic metaphor built on complex relationships between three hypothetical self-in-relation-to-object pairs of ego structures that build up gradually in the internal world from the child's actual memories (enhanced by fantasy) in relation to his objects. These relational pairs (each ego relates exclusively to a single part-object) are organized, first and foremost, to protect the child from experiencing abandonment as one pair of structures hides the hurt and abuse that child has experienced from his conscious, central ego, and the second pair creates an illusory sense of attachment to his objects. These internalized structures become a powerful force that distorts new external object relationships in ways that match the active and vibrant relationships in the internal world, thus causing painful repetition compulsions, particularly involving self-defeating relationships that could not easily be explained by Freud's pleasure principle. These painful repetitions become the focus of treatment in Fairbairn's model, as noted by Greenberg and Mitchell (1983):

Perhaps the most broadly characteristic feature of all psychopathology is its self-defeating quality. Pain, suffering, and defeat are structured into the patient's life and experienced again and again. This feature characterizes psychopathology across the entire continuum; from the neurotic character who chooses unresponsive or sadistic love objects again and again, or behaves toward them to ensure their lack of response or sadism, to the depressive who seems to suffer the deprivations of early mothering over and over again, to the schizophrenic whose primitive childhood terrors haunt his adult life. Why? (172)

Fairbairn's explanation for self-defeating repetitions illuminates the field of psychoanalysis in an innovative way compared with Freud's vision of humankind. Freud struggled with the issue of self-defeating behavior and offered a number of answers, including punishment for forbidden wishes and the inherent sensuality of suffering (Greenberg and Mitchell 1983:173). However, he could not resolve the issue of painful repetitions until he created the concept of the "death instinct," which, because it was assumed to be instinctual, was yet another variation of a biological drive. Freud's conceptual error was to point to an instinctual, pleasure-seeking substrate underlying interpersonal relationships. Fairbairn, on the contrary, rejected the concept of inherited biological structures; he assumed, instead, that the ego would develop and elaborate as a single unified self unless it met with parental failures that required the child to dissociate (split off) the intolerable relational events that occurred in his relationship to his desperately needed objects. Greenberg and Mitchell (1983) also saw Freud's insistence that the "pleasure principle" was the fundamental motivating factor in human behavior as the essential difference between Freud's drive-model and Fairbairn's relational-structure model:

> The essential striving of the child is not for pleasure but for contact. He *needs* the other. If the other is available for gratifying, pleasurable exchange, then the child will enter pleasurable activities. If the parent offers only painful, unfulfilling contacts, the child does not abandon the parent to search for more pleasurable opportunities. The child needs the parent so he integrates his relations with him on a suffering masochistic basis. . . . The emptier the real exchange, the greater his devotion to the promising yet depriving features of his parents which he has internalized and seeks within. In addition he preserves his childhood terror that if he disengages himself from these internal objects, he will find himself totally alone. (173)

Once these objects are firmly installed in the individual's inner world, then the individual's perception of reality is filtered through these sub-selves or part-object identifications, and all the world becomes a stage on which to act out or reenact these powerful internal object relationships. These traumatic events, though too powerful to dismiss, are simultaneously too disruptive to remain in one's consciousness, and so they are "packaged" into separate sub-structures (a view of the self in relation to a toxic aspect of the object) and dissociated, so that the child's essential dependency on his objects can continue: "In his most radical departure from the mainstream of psychoanalytic thought, Fairbairn maintained that, far from being a necessary condition for psychic growth, structural differentiation is a defensive and pathological process in human development" (Rubens 1998:161).

These split-off perceptions of intolerably traumatic events with the needed objects grow in proportion to the number of events that actually occur in reality. Each event strengthens the subego or part-object perception, and those children reared in neglectful or abusive environments develop large, well-elaborated, and intense subegos that distort external reality and compete with the child's actual relationship with his objects. Over time, the child's part-self subegos relate more consistently to the split-off part-objects in his inner world than his central ego does to actual objects in the external world. These internal attachments become the source of all psychopathology and of self-destructive repetitions that haunt so many patients throughout their lives.

Fairbairn (1958) called the projection of inner objects onto the external world "closed system" thinking that produces, repeatedly, the same self-defeating results, as noted by Greenberg and Mitchell (1983):

Psychopathology persists, old pain returns, destructive patterns of integrating relationships with others and experiencing life are perpetuated — because beneath the pain and the self defeating relations and organizations of experience lie ancient internal attachments and allegiances to early significant others. The re-creation of the sorrow, suffering and defeat are forms of renewal and devotion to these ties. (174)

This is the model that Fairbairn offered the world, but it was far too radical to be accepted in its time. Fairbairn's work was politely ignored until just after his death on December 31, 1964, just two years before Kernberg's papers brought his model the notice that began the revival of his view of human psychological functioning.

There is a second way to view Fairbairn's model in relation to Freud's, in addition to Greenberg and Mitchell's dichotomy between models that assume that drive produces structure versus models that assume that relational patterns produce structure. Davies (1996) sees the main difference between Fairbairn's model and other similar models that are based on the internalization of external traumatic events as a debate between models based on dissociation versus those based on repression. She labels Freud's early "seduction theory" as "pre-analytic," because Freud initially concluded that psychopathology was based on actual sexual trauma. This was also true of the earlier work of Janet and Charcot, who also used a model of multiple self-states that were the consequence of the child dissociating and then repressing traumatic events that he could not tolerate. Although Freud initially embraced this model, he turned away from the "seduction" theory and replaced it with what became "classical psychoanalysis," a model based on unconscious fantasies that arise from inherited, biologically based drives. Freud's new focus required that the defense mechanism of repression contain and hold primitive instinctual-based material in the unconscious because these disruptive impulses were unacceptable to the ego and superego. As a result, classical psychoanalysis deemphasized the impact of actual interpersonal events and replaced them with unconscious fantasy that arose from the drives. Fairbairn's model is based on the earlier models of dissociated self and object representations that have to be banished to the unconscious because they are too disruptive to the conscious ego. These events are elaborated with fantasy and understood at the developmental level at which they occurred. The current "relational" trend in psychoanalysis is the reemergence of Fairbairn's original model of multiple self- and object-representations held together by a more or less organized central ego.

Like all inventors of new systems, Fairbairn was caught between the model in which he was trained and the one he created. The result was a lack of specifics on how to apply his theory in clinical practice. The common fate of many innovators is that they are unable to fully appreciate all the ramifications of their inventions — nor is it their job to do so, as Guntrip (1971) noted:

> It is not the function of the pioneer to say the last word but to say the first word. That is the most difficult step. All the pioneer has to begin with is a problem which has always been there, but hitherto no one has looked at the phenomenon in this particular way. . . . Once the all important start has been made along some new line of investigation, those who come after have only to faithfully follow up every possible line of inquiry it suggests. (3)

The overall goal of this book is to examine Fairbairn's model carefully, to modify its obvious areas of weakness, and, most important, to apply his structural model in the clinical setting in ways that Fairbairn was simply unable to envision. Fairbairn's model is not an exercise in psychoanalytic theorizing; rather, it is a set of linked assumptions and observations that eventuate into a powerful and usable model that is applicable to the treatment of patients desperately in need of help. The model offers an entirely new perspective on the treatment of severely damaged and self-destructive patients.

A REVIEW OF FAIRBAIRN'S 1940, 1941, AND 1943 PAPERS

Fairbairn's thoughts on object relations theory evolved in a series of papers spanning the years 1927 to 1963. His first two published papers in 1927 and 1931 were traditional, single-case clinical reports that contained the seeds of his later ideas on splitting. In these first two papers, he noted that both patients he had analyzed had "subegos" that apparently existed independently from each other and, most important, did not conform to the Freudian concept of a three-part internal structure. He also concluded that these subegos were a consequence of failed relationships with outside objects, as Sutherland (1989) noted regarding a patient in his first papers: "It was the creation of the personalized relationships between herself and the deities in her inner world to meet her desperate needs for actual relationships that formed the original context of her neurosis. The intense conflicts amongst these incompatible relationships of several selves, like a multiple personality, reflected closely the family figures as she felt them in her childhood" (26).

This was the beginning of Fairbairn's view regarding the multiplicity of egos and of his recognition of the central role played by the splitting defense. Fairbairn was originally influenced by the work of Klein, specifically by her notions of an inner world that developed as a consequence of relationships with objects. He also adopted a schema similar to Klein's for the explanation of psychopathology early on in his model making, in that he assumed that two distinct developmental phases existed. These phases were the early and late oral phases, and the late phase was nearly identical to Klein's depressive position (Greenberg and Mitchell 1983). Fairbairn's first model of psychopathology differed significantly from Klein's in that the infant in the "early oral stage" was motivated by dependency rather than by biologically fueled aggression. Fairbairn's denial of an innate aggressive instinct, which held a central position in Klein's model, and his substitution of an internal world based on the child's actual reactions to real objects eventually led to the exclusion of Fairbairn from the Kleinian school. Later, in his 1943 paper, Fairbairn distanced himself even further from Klein with the production of his second model of psychopathology based on "The Moral Defense Against Bad Objects." This second model abandoned the notion of two oral positions and substituted the idea of the child's internalization of his parent's "badness" as the starting point for psychopathology.

Beattie (2003) sees Fairbairn's four wartime papers as his best, and the clinical population that gained his greatest attention was adults suffering from "war neuroses":

It was in this context, and framed by the events that unfolded from May 1940 (Dunkirk, the fall of France, the Battle of Britain, the Blitz) that Fairbairn's truly creative ferment began. It resulted, by November, in the first of his great theoretical papers, "Schizoid Factors in the Personality." The evolution of Fairbairn's thinking in his four major wartime papers can be seen as a running commentary on both his self-analytic notes and on his detailed assessment interviews with "war neurotics." They consist, in fact, of two pairs, in each of which a more descriptive, experientially focused piece is followed by a drier theoretical elaboration. (1182)

Beginning with the paper "Schizoid Factors in the Personality," the reader can immediately recognize Fairbairn's intellect, his concern with the devastating effects of early childhood rejection and neglect, and the psychological consequences of faulty parenting that he probably experienced himself.

"SCHIZOID FACTORS IN THE PERSONALITY" (1940)

Fairbairn's first theoretical paper, "Schizoid Factors in the Personality" (1940), included many of the basic notions that he would rework in his later papers. He changed the meaning and the relative importance of the concept "schizoid" from a narrow and specific class of disorders to a supra-category that included any patient that was afflicted by splits in his or her ego structure, effectively creating a huge category that excluded only individuals with remarkably good mental health. Many non-neurotic types were included in his definition, including those with social inhibitions, the inability to concentrate on work, problems of character, perverse sexual tendencies, and psychosexual difficulties (5). Fairbairn was not only expanding the definition of "schizoid" to include a wide variety of disorders, but also changing its status from a specific disorder to a supra-category defined by the psychic process of splitting of the ego, which he saw as the basis of all other forms of psychopathology. Fairbairn's use of the preexisting diagnostic category of "schizoid" to mean something entirely different from its use in the field of psychoanalysis was, in retrospect, a "marketing" error, as his reformation conflicted with the established meaning of the word (Celani 2001). In order to accept this new meaning, his reader (who was inevitably another psychoanalyst) had to give up his prior understanding of "schizoid" and all that it meant in relation to other disorders.

Fairbairn also noted in this earliest of his theoretical papers that the schizoid individual has three characteristics that are well known today: omnipotence, a sense of detachment, and an excessive focus on the inner world (6). All three characteristics are the consequence of various forms of developmental deprivation—that is, a failed relationship with the person's earliest objects. The infant's experience with his object sets the pattern for the structuralization of the individual's inner world. Early failures in the nurturing environment cause the child to look within himself when the outside world is extremely depriving, and this focus on internalized memories of comfort becomes an alternative to the harsh external world. A second result of early maternal deprivation is a focus on the need satisfying part of the mother rather than the whole mother. Fairbairn introduced the concept that frustration led the deprived infant to focus on the part of the object that was potentially need satisfying, a "partial object" in his words. In the following quote, Fairbairn reformulates the mother–infant nursing scenario from a Freudian drive-reduction perspective into a failed interpersonal situation:

Although the emotional relationship involved is essentially one between the child and his mother as a person, and although it must be recognized that his

libidinal object is really his mother as a whole, nevertheless his libidinal interest is essentially focused on her breast; and the result is that, in proportion as
disturbances in the relationship occur, the breast itself tends to assume the role
of libidinal object; i.e., the libidinal object tends to assume the form of a bodily
organ or *partial object* (in contrast to that of a person or whole object).   (11)

Fairbairn's redefines what Freud assumed to be an instinct-based, drive-reduction
event into a failed interpersonal relationship. Classical drive theory assumed that
the infant was not initially attached to his object but that he was motivated by
"objectless" id energy and became attached secondarily to the object only because
of tension reduction. Fairbairn turned drive theory on its head, in his assumption
that "drive" (or what appears to be "drive") is a consequence of the unsatisfied
infant giving up on the whole-object human relationship and greedily going after
gratification as a *compensation* for the loss of contact with the object.

Fairbairn spelled out his view on the source of the schizoid tendency, repeat-
ing it several times in this 1940 paper. He was convinced that the mother's lack of
attunement, indifference, and lack of emotional attachment were the fundamental
sources of all psychopathology, and the persistence of this theme in all his writing suggests that he spoke from experience. The following three quotes also demonstrate that Fairbairn was the first member of the psychoanalytic community to
advocate for the child. The first states his original formulation:

> Here it may be remarked [that] the orientation towards partial objects found
> in individuals displaying schizoid features is largely a regressive phenomenon
> determined by unsatisfactory emotional relationships with their parents, and par-
> ticularly their mothers, at a stage in childhood subsequent to the early oral phase
> in which this orientation originates. The type of mother who is specially prone
> to provoke such a regression is the mother who fails to convince her child by
> spontaneous and genuine expressions of affection that she herself loves him as a
> person. Both possessive and indifferent mothers fall into this category.   (13)

Fairbairn next introduces the idea that remains one of his greatest contributions,
which is his observation that the rejected-frustrated child is *more*, rather than *less*,
attached to the object that is frustrating him. This concept is counterintuitive
and was presented in a summary of the etiological factors leading up to the development of splits in the inner world: "(1) that in early life they gained the conviction, whether through apparent indifference or through apparent possessiveness
on the part of their mother, that their mother did not really love and value them
as persons in their own right; (2) that, influenced by a resultant sense of deprivation and inferiority, they remained profoundly fixated upon their mother" (23).
This concept was based on Fairbairn's observations of abused and abandoned

children in the orphanage where he worked, and eventually it evolved over time into his clinically supported view of the deprived patient's "stubborn attachment" to the frustrating "bad object." Emotional deprivation results in fixation on the mother in an analogous manner that a starving person is fixated on food, despite how unpalatable it may be. Fairbairn's last addition to his original position was to add the concept that the mother's rejection of the child also involves her rejection of the child's love that he expresses toward her: "In a presence of a marked fixation in the early oral phase, the traumatic situation is particularly liable to be reactivated if the child later comes to feel that he is not really loved and valued as a person by his mother, and that she does not really appreciate and accept his love as good" (24).

This point was demonstrated by a patient who described his attempt to give his parents a Christmas gift when he was eight years old. He was the second child of three, and his narcissistic father used the family as a captive audience for his self-important melodramatic rants against the world. His mother was a depressed, unhappy, and hapless woman who went through life with a pained and frightened expression on her face. This patient felt little love from either parent. His gift to them was a miniature raft carved out of wood, which he found difficult to make. He was ashamed of his efforts, and he knew that, whatever it was, it would be demeaned and criticized by his father and ignored by his mother. In other words, by the age of eight he was sure that the love he returned to his objects would not be accepted. He destroyed the gift in a fit of frustration, and, in so doing, some dissociated material emerged from his unconscious because he substituted a hostile "gift" of a stone and a penny to each parent, labeling the gift "To the Poor." He was unable to include the final word "parents" in his inscription, but his previously dissociated memories of being unloved and unappreciated emerged from his unconscious and he acted on them. Fairbairn placed the burden of loving the child on the parents, who are responsible for the infant who has reasonable and legitimate developmental needs. Contrast this view of the child to the demonized and sexualized infant from Klein's model, from which Fairbairn took much but eliminated the assumed aggressive instinctual component. In so doing, Fairbairn restored the child to a position of well-deserved innocence, as noted by Mitchell (1981):

> For Klein, the root of evil lies in the heart of man himself, in the instincts particularly the death instinct and its derivative, aggression. The great dilemma for the child in both the paranoid-schizoid position and the depressive position is the safe discharge of aggression. The earliest anxiety for the child is persecutory; he experiences the threat of his own demise as the victim of his own projected aggression. For Fairbairn, on the other hand, the root of psychopathology and human suffering is maternal deprivation. (84)

Fairbairn's model offers modern psychoanalytic thought a very different view of humanity compared with that offered by classical psychoanalysis. In Fairbairn's model, the child is not a demon seething with instinctual energy but instead is a simple unified self, seeking his mother as a whole object, and turning away only when he himself is rejected. Even when the child is rejected, he does not necessarily become a demon; rather, he contracts his focus away from others and looks within, to his internalized objects, for solace.

The consequence of repeated early rejection convinces the child that his mother is a bad object and that his own love is worthless, and therefore he withholds his love from others later in life. Thus the child faced with an intolerable family environment has to rely on his own inner world for companionship. Fairbairn saw the internalization of objects as a discreet and defensive result of frustration. He assumed that the rejected infant and child was greedily grabbing on to small interpersonal events and internalizing them as a starving person might greedily steal bits of food. Once internalized, objects are available when external objects are absent, and the internal relationships between the child's self and his internalized objects become the focus of the emotionally frustrated child.

As the following chapters will reveal, the process and dynamics of internalizing objects was a constant problem for Fairbairn, and one he never got exactly right. His error regarding the internalization of objects was his assumption that only frustrating "bad objects" were internalized because of the child's need to "control" them (i.e., to have them available) for those times when the parent was absent or abusive. He assumed that internalization was a *forceful, specific, and defensive psychic event* and that good objects and good events were not internalized (except in the special case of the "moral defense"), because they were readily available to the child in the external world. This issue is discussed in depth in the following chapters.

Another related clinical insight in this early paper of 1940 was Fairbairn's observation regarding the role frustration plays in the child's need to be loved as the source of ensuing reactive hate. Fairbairn believed, unlike the Freudians and Kleinians, that hate is not an innate drive but a response to an unloving environment. This first theoretical paper produced an explanation for this therapeutic phenomenon that seems absolutely current:

> Since he feels that his own love is bad, he is liable to interpret the love of others in similar terms. . . . Thus he may quarrel with people, be objectionable, be rude. In so doing, he not only substitutes hate for love in his relationships with objects, but also induces them to hate, instead of loving, him; and he does all this in order to keep his libidinal objects at a distance. . . . This is the second great tragedy to which individuals with a schizoid tendency are liable. The first is, as we have seen, that he feels his love to be destructive of those he loves. The

second arises when he becomes subject to a compulsion to hate and be hated, while all the time he longs deep down to love and be loved. (26)

Fairbairn's emphasis on the object's early failures position him as an environmentalist and, as indicated by the last sentence of the quote, as an early humanist. He saw that hidden beneath the rage of the provocative attacks from patients with character disorders is a wounded and defensive infant who is convinced of his own personal "badness" early in his life. Many patients manifest their hostility toward themselves and others not only by overt expressions of rage but also in a continuous inner experience of alienation and cynicism as well as by their choice of objects. They often choose objects who are contemptuous of them and, conversely, avoid or alienate "good" objects who treat them with kindness and respect.

"A REVISED PSYCHOPATHOLOGY OF THE PSYCHOSES AND PSYCHONEUROSES" (1941)

Fairbairn's second major theoretical paper, "A Revised Psychopathology of the Psychoses and Psychoneuroses" (1941), dealt directly with his views regarding the deficiencies of the Freudian model. One has to marvel at how he took on the psychoanalytic establishment from his near isolation in Scotland without feeling intimidated or overwhelmed. The first section of this paper is a critique of Freud's and Abraham's well-established concept that the libidinal stage of development of any given patient determines the type of neurosis that he or she will develop. Fairbairn substituted his notion that all disorders (i.e., paranoid, hysterical, phobic, and obsessional) were fundamentally pre-Oedipal, with either schizoid or depressive underpinnings (30). More important, he asserted that disorders originated from failed interpersonal experiences rather than from biological energies, thus solidifying his complete abandonment of a psychology based on inherited drives in favor of a psychology of the ego: "The great limitation of the present libido theory as an explanatory system resides in the fact that it confers the status of libidinal attitudes upon various manifestations which turn out to be merely *techniques for regulating the object-relationship of the ego. . . . The ultimate goal of libido is the object*" (31).

Fairbairn boldly discounted the view of instinct theory regarding the primacy of drive as the basis for all human motivation and replaced it with the primacy of the object. The specific organ through which contact was made with the object was far less important to Fairbairn than was the quality of the interaction once contact was established. Libido was reduced in importance and assigned the role of acting as a "sign-post" to the object: "The conception of fundamental erotogenic zones constitutes an unsatisfactory basis for any theory of libidinal development, because it is based on failure to recognize that the function of libidinal pleasure is essentially to provide a sign-post to the object" (33). This is a reversal of the classical model in which the object merely serves as a libidinal discharge site with the resulting (motivating) pleasure, which ultimately leads to emotional attachment. Fairbairn also demonstrated his rejection of erotic motivation in his analysis of thumb sucking. He criticizes the Freudian notion that the mouth is an erotogenic zone that provides the baby with pleasure as an explanation that misses the point. More fundamental, Fairbairn notes, is that the baby sucks his thumb because there is no breast to suck; that is, there is no object with which to relate. Thus the baby is driven to provide its own substitute object: "Autoerotism is essentially a technique whereby the individual seeks not only to provide for himself what he cannot obtain from the object, but to provide for himself an object which he cannot obtain" (34).

It is doubtful that any psychoanalytic colleagues reading this article in 1941 would have tolerated Fairbairn's challenge to Freud's model, as it entirely dismissed the foundational concepts of Freudianism. Thus his writings illustrate and justify his biographer's assessment of Fairbairn's "fearless intellect" (Sutherland 1989). This paper then examines the child's psychological development and the consequences of a depriving relationship with the object, issues he returned to repeatedly. Fairbairn sketched out a three-stage developmental sequence that begins with a state of total dependency on thse object and ends with a mature level of functioning in which the person is totally differentiated from the object. He anticipated the work of Mahler (1975) but did not fill in the stages with observational data. Instead, he provides the reader with a broad outline of human psychological development, noting that the earliest relationship with the parent is characterized by a "primary identification" with the object. His use of the concept of "primary identification" is equivalent to the current concept of "lack of differentiation," a developmental stage in which the infant experiences no sense of separation from the object. The maturational process begins with a total identification with the object at birth, moves through a critical transition period, and ends up in a stage where relationships exist between well-differentiated objects:

> The development of object relationships is essentially *a process whereby infantile dependence upon the object gradually gives place to mature dependence upon the objec*t. This process of development is characterized (a) by the gradual abandonment of an original object-relationship based upon primary identification, and (b) by the gradual adoption of an object-relationship based upon differentiation from the object. (34)

The core of all psychopathology is experienced during the "transitional stage" between dependence and interdependence, when the individual has to give up immature (undifferentiated) attachments and face the anxiety of separation. For individuals with histories of neglect or abandonment, separation from the still needed object is equivalent to annihilation. The transitional stage exposes the patient's conflict between abandoning the only security she has known and venturing out into the world of outer objects. Note in the following quote that Fairbairn links the inability to separate with his prior point from his earlier paper "Schizoid Factors in the Personality" (1940), which asserted that love and emotional support are the engines of normal development:

> The greatest need of a child is to obtain conclusive assurance (a) that he is genuinely loved as a person by his parents, and (b) that his parents genuinely accept his love. It is only in so far as such assurance is forthcoming in a form sufficiently convincing to enable him to depend safely on his real objects that he is able gradually to renounce infantile dependence without misgiving, In the absence of such assurance his relationship to his objects is fraught with too much *anxiety over separation* to enable him to renounce the attitude of infantile dependence; for such a renunciation would be equivalent in his eyes to forfeiting all hope of ever obtaining the satisfaction of his unsatisfied emotional needs.   (39)

This elegant and articulate quote expands on his prior concept of the child's "fixation" on the mother when his needs were not met. Fairbairn understood the logic of children and recognized the impossible position they were in when their objects refused to meet their legitimate developmental needs. The child whose developmental needs are frustrated cannot move forward in life and reach out to new objects or new levels of achievement; instead, he becomes enslaved by his unmet developmental needs and returns to the very object(s) that deprived him. Fairbairn also understood that this developmental obstacle remained in place regardless of the individual's age. The observation in the preceding quote developed into Fairbairn's central concept of "attachment to bad objects," which was fully articulated in his 1944 paper.

Fairbairn also took on the very core of Freudian metapsychology, the Oedipal conflict. Even in 2009, sixty-eight years after this article was published, it seems to have been an exceedingly courageous intellectual act. He begins with an example of a female patient who was raised in a cold, unloving home, where her parents occupied separate bedrooms, and her bedroom (actually an interconnected dressing room) was located in the middle. Fairbairn's young patient was struck by a "crippling infirmity" (37) that made her more dependent on her mother, a woman who wanted her daughter to become independent as soon as possible so that she (the mother) would no longer have to bother being a parent. Fairbairn reports that the child's father was even more aloof and indifferent. As it happened, the mother died when the daughter was in her teens.

The daughter tried desperately to establish an emotional contact with her father, but her efforts were in vain. Then, one day, a thought suddenly occurred to her: "Surely it would appeal to him if I offered to go to bed with him!" Her incestuous wish thus represented a desperate attempt to make emotional contact with her object and, in so doing, to elicit love and to prove that her own love was acceptable. Such a wish does not depend on any specific Oedipal context. In the case of this particular patient, the incestuous wish was renounced and, as might be expected, the reaction that followed was that of intense guilt and shame. The shame, however, was no different from that which had arisen in relation to her demands on her mother for expressions of love that were not forthcoming, and, in default of that love, seemed to prove that her own love was bad (37).

The shame his patient experienced resulted from the patient asking for something that should have been given freely in the first place, and was also the consequence of the patient's exposure, at least to herself, of being desperate and unworthy. Fairbairn repeatedly wrote powerfully about this topic, including it in his 1944 paper about children feeling shame for their legitimate needs who, because of parental deprivation, were forced openly to beg for nurturance and, when rejected, were reduced to "beggardom" (1944:113).

Fairbairn reveals a depth of understanding of children and sympathy for their plight unheard of in the psychoanalysis of his day. His desperate patient was guilty because she thought of overstepping a boundary in order to meet her needs for legitimate nurturance, not for sex. The same point has been made in our time by Kathryn Harrison in her sensational memoir, *The Kiss* (1997). In that book, she reveals her incestuous relationship with her father, which was based on her monumental unmet needs for parental love, the result of her having been abandoned by both parents and by her grandmother with whom she lived. The memoir reads like an exact illustration of Fairbairn's model.

Fairbairn's 1941 paper then introduces the concept of "substitutive satisfactions" (40), which follows logically from his premises but is, once again, absolutely antagonistic to Freud's concept of drives. Freud believed that all manifestations of sexuality are evidence of the existence of libido, and Fairbairn, in another of his reversals, sees infantile sexuality as compensations (and poor ones at that) for the breakdown of interpersonal relationships with parents:

> Frustration of his desire to be loved as a person and to have his love accepted is the greatest trauma that a child can experience; and it is this trauma above all that creates fixations in the various forms of infantile sexuality to which a child is driven to resort in an attempt to compensate by substitutive satisfactions for the failure of his emotional relationships with his outer objects. (39–40)

The types of sexuality Fairbairn mentions include masturbation, anal eroticism, exhibitionism, homosexuality, sadism, and masochism, all of which loomed large in the early years of psychoanalysis, as they "proved" the sexual substrate of all motivation to drive theorists. Fairbairn was immersed in the language and concepts of his time, even as he was trying to establish a new model of psychoanalysis, and so his language is filled with references to genitals and the symbolic searching for the father's penis or the mother's breast. Today, substitutive satisfactions might include Internet addictions that allow minor attachments without the risk of exposing the individual's damaged self while simultaneously allowing for the facsimile of a human relationship.

Fairbairn briefly returned to the child's extremely dependent position in relation to his parents in the final section of this 1941 paper. Once again, he spoke up for the legitimate needs of the child, who had no advocates at this time in the world of psychoanalysis:

> The outstanding feature of infantile dependence is its unconditional character. The infant is completely dependent upon his object not only for his existence and well-being, but also for the satisfaction of his psychological needs. . . . We also notice that, whereas in the case of the adult the object relationship has a considerable spread, in the case of the infant it tends to be focused on a single object. The loss of an object is thus very much more devastating in the case of an infant. If a mature individual loses an object, however important, he still has some objects remaining. . . . The infant on the other hand has no choice. He has no alternative but to accept or reject his object—an alternative which is liable to present itself to him as a choice between life and death. (47)

I have quoted this paper extensively because of the fundamental nature of Fairbairn's observations, which are indisputable. This observation sets the stage for the two basic defenses against loss of an object that Fairbairn saw as universal to all humans: the moral defense and the splitting defense. The child's extreme vulnerability and focused dependency *forces him to accept his object no matter how badly he is treated*, and at the same time hide from all perceptions and memories that would interfere with his attachment to his objects. Fear of abandonment and its consequent loss of the underdeveloped self motivates all defense mechanisms and is responsible for the self-destructive clinging to frustrating objects throughout the life span that characterizes so much of psychopathology. Focusing on a single depriving object, while ignoring other potentially "good" objects, is very common in adult patients who have been severely developmentally deprived. They look to their parent (or displaced parent-object) for all their needs and ignore readily available sources from other objects.

"THE REPRESSION AND THE RETURN OF BAD OBJECTS (WITH SPECIAL REFERENCE TO THE 'WAR NEUROSES')" (1943)

Fairbairn's third major theoretical paper, "The Repression and the Return of Bad Objects (with Special Reference to the 'War Neuroses')" (1943), is the one that Beattie (2003) considers his best paper:

This is surely his masterpiece—the most vivid, accessible, clinically useful and in many ways intensely personal of all his writings, couched in dramatic religious imagery (including numerous invocations of the Devil of Scottish theology and folklore) and drawing implicitly or explicitly on all the personal and professional experience that had made him who he was, from child abuse to wartime trauma. (1183)

This monumental paper marks the end of Fairbairn's use of the Kleinian influenced two-phase model of psychopathology (early and late oral). In its place, he substituted his concept of the "Moral Defense Against Bad Objects" as the first defensive step the child takes to control his intolerably bad objects. The internalization of bad objects is the fundamental source of all psychopathology in his model. Fairbairn's reliance on his own concepts moved him farther away from the already unsupportive Kleinian school, and he was truly on his own in terms of theory building

The first clinically significant aspect of the paper is Fairbairn's presentation of his definition of the human unconscious, which, in his metapsychology, has a different source as well as a significantly different motivation for dissociation compared with the classical analytic view. Once again, Fairbairn's fearless intellect follows his own vision of the functioning of the human personality, receiving absolutely no external support from others in the field: "I now venture to formulate the view that *what are primarily repressed are neither intolerably guilty impulses nor intolerably unpleasant memories, but intolerably bad internalized objects.* If memories are repressed, accordingly, this is only because the objects involved in such memories are identified with bad internalized objects" (62).

Davies (1996) has noted that disassociation is the better term to describe what Fairbairn was talking about because an external event that was intolerable to the conscious ego was taken inside and hidden from view. This contrasts with Freud's concept of repression, which was based on forcing material from the biological id (which is already assumed to exist in the inner world) back into the unconscious because of its unacceptability to the ego and superego. Throughout the book, I use the word "repression" to mean the holding of dissociated material in the unconscious, in contrast to Freud's repression of instinctual, id-based material.

Fairbairn then described his dissatisfaction with the classical formulation of repression, which assumed that libidinal memories that were inherently positive given the concept of Freud's pleasure principle had to be repressed because of superego-based guilt associated with the Oedipal situation. The Oedipal conflict was too fanciful for Fairbairn, who had direct experience with Edinburgh's least fortunate children who were desperate for attachment to *either* parent. He postulated a completely different function of the unconscious, which was to contain actual memories (though vague and distorted) of abandonment, abuse, and humiliation

that were too disruptive for the child's conscious "central ego" to tolerate in awareness. He recognized that children, because of their vulnerability and complete
identification with their objects, are swept along and forced to participate in events
over which they have no control. Fairbairn based this part of his model on his observations of children who had been victims of sexual assaults whom he treated in
his work at the University Psychological Clinic for Children in Edinburgh, where
he was employed part time from 1927 to 1935 (Sutherland 1989). He noted that
victims of sexual abuse were reluctant and often consciously unable to describe
what had happened to them. In the following quote, he absolutely rejects the classical formulation of repression, which assumed that, beneath the trauma, these
children had enjoyed the libidinal gratifications involved in the sexual assault and
were repressing the memory out of guilt. He then replaced this explanation with
his model of dissociation. In the following, Fairbairn describes the perpetrator of
the rape as a "bad object," which at this stage of his theorizing meant a rejecting or
an abusive object. Later on, in 1944, "bad object" would be defined as having both
rejecting and promising aspects.

> I remember being particularly impressed by the reluctance of children who
> were the victims of sexual assaults to give any account of the traumatic experi-
> ences to which they had been subjected. The point that puzzled me most was
> that, the more innocent the victim was, the greater was the resistance to anam-
> nesis. . . . At the time, I felt that these phenomena could only be explained on
> the assumption that, in resisting a revival of a traumatic memory, the victim of a
> sexual assault was actuated by guilt over the unexpected gratification of libidinal
> impulses which had been renounced by the ego and repressed. . . . I always
> felt rather suspicious of this explanation; but it seemed the best available at the
> time. From my present standpoint it seems inadequate. As I now see it, the posi-
> tion is that the victim of a sexual assault resists the revival of the traumatic mem-
> ory primarily because this memory represents a record of a relationship with a
> bad object. . . . It is intolerable in the main, not because it gratifies repressed
> impulses, but for the same reason that a child often flies panic-stricken from a
> stranger who enters the house. (63)

Thus Fairbairn boldly rejected the structural model of classical psychoanalysis and
replaced Freud's appropriation of Darwin's primitive man (the id) with an unconscious populated by memories of actual events originating in the external world—
events too overwhelming and terrifying for the child's nascent ego to confront. At this
point in his model making, Fairbairn's inner world does not yet include part-selves
that are attached to these repressed bad objects but only the bad objects themselves.

Fairbairn immediately moves from this discussion to observations about shame,
linking the psychological processes of children who were sexually assaulted to chil-

dren who lived in families with neglectful and indifferent parents. He notes the parallels between the sexually assaulted children who were ashamed of themselves and the neglected children who were ashamed of both themselves and their parents: "It is interesting to observe that a relationship with a bad object is felt by the child to be not only intolerable, but also shameful. It may accordingly be inferred that, if a child is ashamed of his parents (as is often the case), his parents are bad objects to him" (64).

The child's experience of shame results from having been undifferentiated from objects who themselves were behaving in shameful ways, and also because he was devalued by their neglect. Children who were ashamed of both themselves and their parents, he concluded, were caught in a relationship from which they could not flee, neither physically nor psychologically, as they were simply swept up in the interpersonal environment.

Fairbairn, who was on the cusp of formulating "The Moral Defense Against Bad Objects," also noticed that even though the behavior of abused and neglected children demonstrated that they were ashamed of themselves and their parents, they could not be induced to admit verbally that their parents had treated them badly. This paradox puzzled Fairbairn, and he concluded that the bad object had been internalized and repressed, thus keeping the threatening memories out of consciousness:

> At one time it fell to my lot to examine quite a large number of delinquent children from homes which the most casual observer could hardly fail to recognize as "bad" in the crudest sense — homes, for example, in which drunkenness, quarreling and physical violence reigned supreme. It is only in the rarest instances, however (and only those instances of utter demoralization and collapse of the ego), that I can recall such a child being induced to admit, far less volunteering, that his parents were bad objects. It is obvious, therefore, that in these cases the child's bad objects had been internalized and repressed.   (64)

Fairbairn's emphasis on the child's unconditional dependency, described in his 1941 paper, provides the motivation for this defense mechanism, which dissociates the intolerable reality that the child is completely and utterly dependent on frustrating and indifferent parents. The child's conscious acknowledgment that his objects were "bad" would overwhelm him with the intolerable truth that he was completely alone in the world. This defense mechanism allows her to continue to believe in the illusion that she is safely attached to "good" parents. It is simply too disruptive to the child's ego to be aware of the reality that she depends on a dangerous and hateful object as she goes about her daily business.

Fairbairn was surprised to discover that the very same children who had denied that their parents were bad objects were conversely quite willing to acknowledge that they themselves were "bad":

It becomes obvious, therefore, that the child would rather be bad himself than have bad objects; and accordingly we have some justification for surmising that one of his motives in becoming bad is to make his objects "good." In becoming bad he is really taking upon himself the burden of badness which appears to reside in his objects. By this means he attempts to purge them of their badness; and in proportion as he succeeds in doing so, he is rewarded by that sense of security which an environment of good objects so characteristically confers. . . . Outer security is thus purchased at the price of inner security; and the ego is henceforth left at the mercy of a band of fifth columnists, or persecutors, against which defenses have to be, first hastily erected, and later laboriously consolidated. (65)

The moral defense allows the child to solve the fundamental problem of staying attached to abusive or abandoning objects without becoming flooded by rage or anxiety, by simply internalizing the badness of his objects and thus keeping his parents "good." The child assumes that his own badness is a "moral" one, in that he experiences himself as having done something morally wrong. This simple rationalization works for the child by salvaging some sense of personal security.

Fairbairn next focused on the possible mechanisms the child uses to tolerate bad internal objects that have to be internalized to control their "badness." What he was actually observing, in terms of his not yet formulated structural model, was the effect of parental rejection on the child's awareness of himself in relation to his rejecting object. These children saw themselves from the eyes of the rejecting part of their parents, who defined their badness in terms of lack of respect, tardiness, or lack of cleanliness. These negative self-views reflect an "acceptable" version of his failings (acceptable to the child's central ego—a concept he discusses in his 1944 paper); that is, this negative assessment, though bad, is *not intolerable*, and therefore it can be accepted by and integrated into the central ego. This central ego view of self as "bad" allows the child to preserve his emotional bond to the rejecting/exciting object by locating all the "badness" in himself. The truly intolerable and horrifying aspects of the rejecting object in relation to the child's enraged, devalued, and vengeful antilibidinal ego (another structural concept from the 1944 paper) must remain tightly dissociated in the unconscious. Meanwhile (continuing to use Fairbairn's structural model from his yet unpublished 1944 paper), the child can continue to maintain a view of his objects as "exciting objects" (i.e., containing the hope of love in the future) during those times when he is dominated by his libidinal ego, which preserves his attachment to those objects.

Upon close examination, the "moral defense" is a first approximation of the splitting defense, without the benefit of the separate internal structures. The moral defense was replaced by the splitting defense in Fairbairn's next paper, "Endopsychic Structure Considered in Terms of Object Relationships" (1944), though, typically, he never formally noted that he had replaced one with the other. The splitting defense solves (in a far more complete and satisfactory way) the abandoned or abused child's dilemma of how to remain attached to the bad object while simultaneously hiding from relationship-destroying memories of the intolerable rejections he has suffered.

Fairbairn proposed a mechanism by which the toxic effects of the internalization of bad objects were neutralized in the moral defense. He realized that once the child internalized his bad objects, he would be exposed to an even greater problem since his interior world was now subject to a flood of internalized bad objects hostile to his well-being. What followed is, in my view, one of Fairbairn's greatest theoretical failures: he tried to solve the problem of hostile internal objects by borrowing concepts from both Klein and Freud. First he borrowed Klein's concept of the forceful internalization of good objects. Klein described the child deliberately internalizing good objects as a way to protect herself from bad objects. Klein assumed that the child's death instinct caused the child to become intensely jealous of her mother and that this jealously, in turn, fueled a desire to destroy the mother and possess the valuable riches that the child believed were contained within her: "The child desires to possess all the riches he imagines contained in the mother's womb, including food, valued feces, babies and the father's penis" (Greenberg and Mitchell 1983:124). The desire to destroy and possess the mother increases the child's fear of retaliation, and she counters it by amassing a stockpile of good internal objects to protect her from the feared attacks by the external maternal object.

Fairbairn borrowed Klein's concept that the solution to toxic internal objects was to forcibly and defensively internalize good objects that would serve as a "buffer" between the bad objects and the central ego; the good objects, then, would counteract the bad objects that had been defensively internalized:

> To redress this state of unconditional badness he takes what is really a very obvious step. He internalizes his good objects, which thereupon assume a super-ego role. . . . In so far as the child leans toward his internalized bad objects, he becomes conditionally (i.e. morally) bad vis-à-vis his internalized good objects (i.e. his super-ego); and, in so far as he resists the appeal of his internalized bad objects, he becomes conditionally (i.e. morally) good vis-à-vis his super-ego. (66)

Within Fairbairn's theory, this is the only time he spoke of whole good objects being internalized. Once the good objects are internalized, Fairbairn assumed, the child could reduce his sense of absolute badness as long as his central ego associates with the good objects in his interior world and avoids the appeal of his bad objects. Neither the Kleinian concept of internalization of good objects nor the Freudian concept of the superego was used in his structural theory of 1944.

Rubens (1984) has offered a solution to Fairbairn's error in assuming that there were no internalized good objects in the inner world. Rubens's concept of the *"non-structuring* internalization" comes from Fairbairn's description of the act of internalization and splitting from his paper "Observations on the Nature of Hysterical States" (1954). This is a much later paper, but it is important to this discussion because Fairbairn described, in a long footnote, his continuing opposition to the possibility that the child would internalize an object that was *"perfectly satisfying"* (107). The key words here are "perfectly satisfying," as no parent is perfectly satisfying, and, equally important, mostly rejecting parents have some satisfying aspects. Fairbairn (1954) then addressed the process of splitting and the fate of the acceptable aspects (acceptable to the child's central ego) of the objects after they are internalized, in two numbered statements (5 and 6) in a carefully worded description of the splitting process that was a central part of his paper:

> 5. The internalized object is thus split into three objects, viz. "the exciting object," "the rejecting object" and the nucleus which remains after the exciting and rejecting elements have been split from it.
> 6. This residual nucleus represents the relatively satisfying, or at any rate tolerable, aspect of the internalized object, and it is therefore not rejected by the ego, but remains actively cathected by it under conditions which render the term "ideal object" appropriate for its description. (17)

Here, Fairbairn describes a second way for a partial good object to become internalized that is not consistent with his prior assumption that good objects were internalized to buffer bad objects. The difference lies in the fact that this good object (or ideal object) is just a fragment of the original object after the exciting and rejecting aspects have been shorn off and dissociated. This "part" good object never played a part in his theorizing, but it does allow for the internalization of fragments of good objects, which I see as a key structure in the process of change. This fragment of the parent originated when he or she was acting as an ideal object in relationship to the child's central ego. It is this structure within the patient that engages the therapist, who then becomes the new ideal object in the patient's inner world. Rubens (1984) differentiates between structuring internalizations, which create unconscious self and object structures, from non-structuring internalizations, like the ideal object that is conscious and available to interact with the external world.

The whole issue of the internalization of objects has broadened since Fairbairn's time. A farther-reaching solution to the problem of internalization was proposed by Mitchell (2000), who holds that Fairbairn started off on the wrong track in his theorizing in that he still saw humans as fundamentally separate. The modern relational perspective holds that humans are inextricably enmeshed with one another from birth, and the "internalization" of external objects assumes a separateness that does not really exist in the developing infant:

> Fairbairn started off on the wrong foot with regard to this question, because he did not fully appreciate the implications of viewing the individual mind in a relational context with other minds. To pose the question, What is the motive for the first internalization? is to begin with the premise that there is a fundamental differentiation and boundary between inside and outside. This is a premise that Fairbairn inherited from Klein. If something from outside is found inside (which is what me mean by "internalization"), then we have to explain how it got there. . . . What if a sense of oneself as a separate individual and objects as differentiated others is only gradually constructed, over the course of early development, out of this undifferentiated matrix? Then the sense of oneself populated with presences of early significant objects would not have to be accounted for solely in terms of some discreet, defensive process.   (109–111)

Mitchell's solution moves Fairbairn's model past the point at which he viewed the issue and updates it with modern concepts. As Mitchell (2000) points out, internalization of external objects is an artifact of the philosophical point from which the viewer sees the problem. When current perspectives are applied, then psychological development can be seen as the child's gradual emergence from an undifferentiated matrix between self and other. Differentiation gradually allows the child to discover that he is separate from his objects—objects who are already present in his internal and external world. As the child develops over time, after the establishment of a differentiated self, the process of internalization of objects is seen to be a seamless ongoing series of events in which all objects are taken in, good, bad, and neutral. This is the current thinking within object relations theory regarding the internalization of objects, which Scharff and Scharff (2000) make clear:

> In Fairbairn's model, however, the introjection of good experience comes as a kind of afterthought: good objects are only introjected to compensate for bad (1952). Klein disagreed with Fairbairn's ideas that introjection of good experience was secondary. She thought that under the influence of the life instinct, good experience is also taken in from the beginning (1946). Current infant research demonstrates that she was right that infants, and all of us, take in good and bad experience. But we think that it happens, not because of the life and death instincts (as she thought), but simply because we are built to take in all kinds of experience as we relate in order to grow into a person. The realities of all aspects of external experience and our perceptions of them provide the building blocks for our psychic structure. . . . They take in experience to use

as material to construct an inner world, and they then actively seek to realize that inner world in the outer world, both through interaction with others and through internal modification of their selves.   (219–220)

Scharff and Scharff's position is the one to which I subscribe, and it is at odds with Fairbairn's original position that objects were defensively and forcibly internalized, and that whole good objects were internalized only to buffer the internalized bad objects.

Fairbairn concluded his discussion of the moral defense with this famous passage filled with religious language as it describes how the (forcible) internalization of good objects saves the child from annihilation:

> Framed in such terms the answer is that it is better to be a sinner in a world ruled by God than to live in a world ruled by the Devil. A sinner in a world ruled by God may be bad; but there is always a certain sense of security to be derived from the fact that the world around is good. . . . In a world ruled by the Devil the individual may escape being a sinner; but he is bad because the world around him is bad. Further, he can have no sense of security and no hope of redemption.   (66–67)

Again, this quote refers to Fairbairn's "solution" to the problem the child creates when he internalizes the badness from his parents and then compensates by forcibly internalizing good objects to reduce the resulting toxicity.

However, the same quote regarding the moral defense can be understood somewhat differently based on Fairbairn's definition of psychopathology, along with the current assumption that good objects are freely internalized as a matter of course during development. When any given child internalizes his bad objects, he becomes bad *to the extent that his parents are bad objects*, and to the extent that he has (or does not have) contact with good objects. The child gains psychologically by assuming his parents' badness, because he is protected from recognizing that they are, in reality, bad objects. His assumption of their badness offers him temporary security—he is the sinner and his parents are in the role of God. The child's need for a secure attachment remakes his bad objects into good objects, which reduces his fear of abandonment. In reality, the toxicity of the internalized bad objects is modified by the number of good objects that the child has contact with, as well as by the intensity and duration of these good-object relationships. These good objects can be aspects of the actual parents or relationships with relatives or people outside the immediate family. Good-object relationships are not suddenly forcefully internalized, as Fairbairn believed, as an antidote, but instead they are gradually taken in to the inner world in the course of daily relating. They become competitors with the bad objects, and the child may develop stronger attachments to the good objects than to the bad ones, thus making Fairbairn's quote salient today. This accounts for the wide variation in outcomes of children raised in the same family. Any given child may have had a more intense and loving relationship with the better parent, or with a grandparent or teacher, and these good-object relationships (which are internalized) reduce the toxicity of the internalized bad object. This discussion is directly related to the next topic in Fairbairn's 1943 paper, which focuses on the sources of psychopathology.

Fairbairn's definition of human psychopathology is both stunning and unique, and it is completely congruent with the previous aspects of his model. Once again, Freud's and Klein's conception of inherited evil and the self and other destructiveness of the id is nowhere in evidence. Equally important, Fairbairn's definition allows for the positive effects of good objects or, equivalently, for the possibility that the child has internalized very few bad objects, since this definition allows for both mental health as well as psychopathology:

> Whether any given individual becomes delinquent, psychoneurotic, psychotic or simply "normal" would appear to depend in the main upon the operation of three factors: 1. The extent to which bad objects have been installed in the unconscious and the degree of badness by which they are characterized. 2. The extent to which the ego is identified with internalized bad objects. 3. The nature and strength of the defenses which protect the ego from these objects.   (65)

This definition represents a theoretical advance over Fairbairn's prior concept of the simpler "internalization and repression of bad objects," which did not mention the child's nascent self. Here Fairbairn includes the child's ego in the second statement: the "extent to which the ego is identified" with the bad object can vary from a complete identification to a complete dis-identification. Often the child's gender, as well as birth order, is the deciding factor. For instance, in a hypothetical example of a family with a sociopathic father who takes pleasure in harming animals, the son might identify with the behavior and join in, whereas the daughter might identify with the victimized animal and try to protect it.

Fairbairn's definition of psychopathology is original and emerged from a wholly different view of humankind compared with the classical psychoanalytic view. Notably it has clear applicability in the consulting room because it is so "experience-near," as Scharff and Birtles (1994) noted: "The way in which Fairbairn developed objects relations theory made it a framework which is 'experience-near.' That is, the translation of the theoretical framework to clinical experience requires only a small step, for the words and ideas of theory fit readily with issues of human development and psychopathology" (xiii).

Fairbairn's model of psychopathology exemplifies the closeness of the model to clinical reality. For example, one of the first tasks of the analyst or psychotherapist using this model with a new patient is to assess the pathology of the internalized objects and determine how firmly the individual is bound to his bad objects, both internally and externally. The extent of the patient's attachment to his bad objects then serves as a guide for the analyst or therapist regarding the level and directness of interpretations and observations that can be make without threatening the patient. Patients who are tightly bound to their bad objects will simply leave treatment if the analyst implicates their objects as the source of the patient's problems too early in the relationship. For example, the patient who presents himself as entirely dysfunctional while describing his objects as "perfect people" signals the clinician that he is tightly bound to these objects and completely unaware of their "badness." The patient's self has incorporated the badness of his objects and may act out this badness while clinging to a fantasy that he was raised by "good" objects. This type of patient will not be able to tolerate the notion that his objects failed him in any way for many months if not years of work.

The richness of Fairbairn's thought continues in the next section of his 1943 paper where he explores the reasons why the child's internalized bad objects have so much power over him. Fairbairn recognized that the combination of powerlessness and dependency produces the counterintuitive reality that the rejected and abused child is more tightly bound to and "identified" with the bad object than the child who was raised by supportive and attuned parents:

> At this point it is worth considering whence bad objects derive their power over the individual. If the child's objects are bad, how does he ever come to internalize them? Why does he not simply reject them as he might reject "bad" corn flour pudding or "bad" castor oil? . . . In a word, he is "possessed" by them as if by evil spirits. This is not all however. The child not only internalizes his bad objects because they force themselves upon him and he seeks to control them, but also and above all, because he *needs* them. If a child's parents are bad objects, he cannot reject them, even if they do not force themselves upon him; for he cannot do without them. Even if they neglect him, he cannot reject them; for if they neglect him, his need for them is increased. (67)

Once again, Fairbairn, alone in the field of psychoanalysis, was aware of the frightening dilemma of the child who is pressured by legitimate developmental needs and faced with an indifferent interpersonal environment. Although internalization is no longer conceived of as a deliberate act, this quote emphasizes the intensity of the child's need and his lack of options. This desperate and intense attachment occurs both in the inner world and in external reality, and is most dramatically demonstrated by the borderline who returns again and again to the neglectful parent, despite the parent's long history of rejections.

Fairbairn followed this quote on internalization of bad objects with a dramatic example of a patient who dreamed that he was standing by his sleeping mother and feeling enormously hungry when he saw a bowl of chocolate pudding (the patient's favorite food) next to her on the night table. He knew that the pudding contained deadly poison, but if he refused to eat it he would die of starvation. Naturally, he ate the pudding in the dream and was sickened by it (68). The patient then developed a neurotic preoccupation that his heart was damaged:

> What was really wrong with his heart, however, was eloquently revealed in another dream — a dream in which he saw his heart lying on a plate and his mother lifting it with a spoon (i.e., in the act of eating it). Thus it was because he had internalized his mother as a bad object that he felt his heart to be affected by a fatal disease; and he had internalized her, bad object though she was for him, because as a child he needed her. It is above all the need of the child for his parents, however bad they may appear to him, that compels him to internalize bad objects; and because this need remains attached to them in the unconscious that he cannot bring himself to part with them. (68)

Not much more can be said about this than Fairbairn said in 1943. Perhaps the most remarkable aspect of this paper is that it is *not* celebrated as one of the most insightful papers ever written in the field of psychoanalysis. Fairbairn also touched on clinical technique in that he emphasized the importance of the good object as a catalyst for change. He places the good-object analyst in the patient's *external* world, which was consistent with his position that good objects did not need to be internalized:

> Nevertheless, I cannot help feeling that such results must be attributed, in part at least, to the fact that in the transference situation the patient is provided with an unwontedly good object, and is thereby placed in a position to risk a release of his internalized bad objects from the unconscious and so to provide conditions for the libidinal cathexis of these objects to be dissolved — albeit he is also under a temptation to exploit a "good" relationship with the analyst as a defense against taking this risk. (69)

A number of significant points are brought out in this quote. The first is that Fairbairn, ever in need of an editor, suddenly changes the topic without warning and begins to describe his model of therapy in the middle of a discussion about the repression of bad objects. He then asserts that the attachment between the analyst and the patient allows the patient to gather enough courage from the therapeutic relationship to reveal events in his history that were too disruptive to be consciously tolerated, yet simultaneously too central and "structure building" to remain repressed—all this owing to the support of the analyst, who becomes an ideal object and relates to the patient's central ego (two structures Fairbairn had not introduced until the 1944 paper). Fairbairn also assumed, somewhat naively, that the "libidinal cathexis" in the internalized bad object, which is equivalent to the relational concept of "attachment," would somehow magically dissolve when the contents of the bad object memory was derepressed. Clinical experience strongly suggests that this is not the case. The "release" of a bad object memory is simply the first step in a long process of detoxification of its impact and importance. He also did not see, because he did not believe that ordinary good objects were internalized, that the therapist was taken in to the internal world and was competing with the bad objects and simultaneously strengthening the patient's central ego.

Exactly what types of "bad objects" was Fairbairn talking about? Let me illustrate with a patient I have described previously (Celani 2005). My patient, "Angie," was a brilliant but overwrought middle-aged woman who worked in a college as a low-level chemistry instructor where she was exploited by the senior faculty by being assigned to teach a disproportionate number of classes at a low rate of pay. She was forced to come in for therapy by her husband, who threatened to leave her because he could no longer tolerate her manic, and interpersonally avoidant, lifestyle. She was very attached to her parents and visited them often, and yet, in her work with me, she described a history of their heartless exploitation of her and all her siblings, who were used as workers on their large farm and feed-supply store. All the children were required to work at tasks far beyond their developmental level, and two of her siblings were injured by machinery they were operating without supervision. Angie was often required to drive the large feed truck to neighboring farms (this was rural, hardscrabble New England in the 1950s) when she was eleven years old. She was unable to reach the pedals with her feet, so she would bring her younger sister along to press the gas pedal, but when she had to hit the brake she had to slip down off the seat, and therefore could no longer see out of the windshield. Of the six children, her mother specifically picked on her because she was designated the "problem child," the one responsible for all the family woes. She spent much of her early childhood hiding in barns and outbuildings in order to avoid her mother. Her parents often repeated the myth that they were a wonderful and close family, thus giving her perceptions no validation, and her desperate need for good objects did not permit her bad-object memories to disrupt her fierce attachment to them.

In adulthood, she found herself in one difficult job or another, where great demands were placed on her with no support from her supervisors, a perfect re-creation of the patterns of her childhood relationships. Angie avoided closeness with her husband through manic activity and a constant sense of being overwhelmed by work, another reenactment from the internalization of relationships from her family. This reenactment placed her in the rejecting parental object position, with her husband occupying the abandoned child position. Notably, both she and her husband noticed one area of her functioning completely uncharacteristic of her—a powerful and emotional attachment to her dog. Her husband often complained that she displayed more love for and attention to her dog than she did toward him, and she reported that it surprised and unsettled her to feel the power and intensity of emotion that she felt toward her pet. In our work, I noticed her strong attachment to her parents and carefully avoided increasing her defensiveness by putting only mild pressure on her attachment, commenting on the large number of parental failures (as opposed to emphasizing the insensitivity or callousness of her objects) that she had experienced. Whenever she appeared defensive, I backed away and never insisted that she accept my position. As noted in an earlier version of this text (Celani 1993), an important technique with deeply split patients is for the therapist to be willing to abandon lines of inquiry that increase defensiveness. In this case, the moment the patient objected to my views of her objects, I proceeded along a different path. My presence as a good object over a year or so, along with only mild pressure on her defenses, produced the following dream:

> On the session before Thanksgiving, she came in completely shocked by a dream she had just the night before. Her parents, like many that I have previously described, demanded homage from their adult children, even though they had failed to nurture them during their critical developmental years. Every year, the children would each prepare part of the Thanksgiving meal, and then gather at the parents' home to celebrate. Angie's dream was that she was required to kill, butcher, and cook her dog, and present him as her contribution to the family Thanksgiving dinner.   (Celani 2005:104–105)

This demonstrates precisely what Fairbairn was describing: the "release" of a frightening and disruptive perception of objects that had the potential of being destructive of the current need-laden relationship. This perception, dissociated in her unconscious, clearly saw the parents as rejecting objects: exploitive, inhumane, and callous. As Fairbairn noted, once such a perception is "released" from the unconscious, others soon follow, and the patient may be overwhelmed by the enormity of the neglect she has suffered, and the prospect of facing life in an underdeveloped state without parents.

In the case of purely internalized objects—for example, when the parents are deceased—the perception will not allow the fantasy of a good childhood to continue. This can produce the panic of abandonment in the patient if she is not sure of the stability, availability, and empathy of her analyst. Using Fairbairn's internal structures from his paper on splitting, not yet written in 1943, and violating his notion that good objects are internalized forcibly only to counter bad internalized objects, clinical observation suggests that the good-object therapist becomes a mutative factor by supporting the patient's undernourished central ego, which allows it to expand and hold onto its integrated perceptions of its objects. In this example (which is discussed again in chapter 3), the patient's central ego had enough strength from her attachment to me and her identification with my views of her objects to overcome her fear of what had already taken place and had remained, up to this moment, dissociated in her unconscious.

Fairbairn then described the resistance that opposed the release of bad objects. This resistance stemmed from the patient's fear of suddenly confronting the many repressed hurts from her childhood. This fear of confronting interpersonal traumas that have already taken place and have been dissociated and repressed functions as a major source of resistance in therapy: "There is little doubt in my mind that, in conjunction with another factor to be mentioned later, the deepest source of resistance is fear of the release of bad objects from the unconscious; for, when such bad objects are released, the world around the patient becomes peopled by devils which are too terrifying for him to face" (Fairbairn 1943:69). This was indeed the case with my patient, who was tremulous for most of the session (and for a week afterward) when confronted with the implications of her dream, which hardly needed interpretation. Fairbairn recognized that it was not self-generated id impulses that the individual was afraid of but actual memories of frightening, shame-producing, relational events with bad objects, which are almost always memories of parental failures. A common clinical phenomenon is to see patients struggle for months before they amass the courage to "remember" early terrifying events. They cannot face these memories alone, and are extremely sensitive to the therapist's capacity to remain calm in the face of these remembered traumas.

As one reads this section of Fairbairn's 1943 paper, it appears as if he just "stumbled" on his model of therapy, and once embarked on this topic, more and more issues came to mind:

> At the same time there is little doubt in my mind that the release of bad objects from the unconscious is one of the chief aims which the psychotherapist should set himself out to achieve, even at the expense of a severe "transference neurosis"; for it is only when the internalized bad objects are released from the unconscious that there is any hope of their cathexis being dissolved. The bad objects can only be safely released, however, if the analyst has become established as a good object for the patient. Otherwise the resulting insecurity may prove unsupportable. . . . It becomes evident, accordingly, that the psychotherapist is the true successor to the exorcist, and that he is concerned, not only with "the forgiveness of sins," but also with "the casting out of devils."   (69–70)

Once again, we see Fairbairn's use of religious language in the making of his model. The "forgiveness of sins" refers to softening the patient's identification with the internalized rejecting object, thus reducing the self-contempt and overall defensiveness. The real core of his therapeutic approach is to open the patient's inner world and allow the release of dissociated memories of parental failures. Fairbairn makes it clear that the "chief aims" of psychotherapy, which is the release of bad objects from the unconscious, can occur only after the therapist is perceived as a good object. As mentioned, Fairbairn never granted the good object a structural role in the inner world; instead, he saw it as remaining on the "outside" of the patient.

The importance of "derepression of bad objects" illustrates the striking difference between Fairbairn's model of human motivation and the classical Freudian model. Fairbairn's model is based on tragic associations and frustrations rather than on inner drives and the struggle with the biological equivalent of original sin. It is a humanistic model that sees humans as influenced by others, to good or bad ends, with every child beginning life with infinite promise and innocence. For those individuals with developmental failures, Fairbairn holds the theoretical possibility of improved mental health, since a new good object can ultimately replace the bad object around which the original inner world formed. His is an optimistic model that perceives patients as victims of their early object relationships and their character problems as the result of adaptations to these toxic objects. Human behavior, no matter how futile or self-destructive, can be understood as a desperate attempt to salvage attachment to frustrating but needed objects, real or internalized.

Fairbairn (1943) then makes a point that I find central to the patient–analyst relationship, particularly in my work with battered women (Celani 1994, 1999): "From the patient's point of view, accordingly, the effect of analytical treatment is to promote the very situation from which he seeks to escape" (75). This was often the case with my population of primitive patients who desperately wanted to maintain their attachments to their violent and unpredictable abusive objects. Most frequently, patients did not want to examine their failed relationship with their parents, as it seemed to be irrelevant to their current conflict. Most wanted their current (external) bad object to come back to them and to change and treat them better. Fairbairn seldom spoke of the current bad objects in the patient's interpersonal universe. Instead, Fairbairn focused on bad internalized objects from the past, partially because of his attention to war neuroses. My experience in working with battered women suggests that the internalized objects from the past are replaced with new surrogates who are pursued with all the rage and need-driven energy with which the patient, as a child, pursued her original objects.

Fairbairn ends his 1943 paper with a section on war neuroses, which he saw as a perfect demonstration of the derepression of bad object memories that are "raw," unlike memories derepressed in the therapy situation, where the released bad object is contained, observed, and interpreted by a sympathetic good object. He also notes that the internal world of every person is different, and so one cannot predict the event that will trigger a neurotic response in any given individual:

The spontaneous and psychopathological (as against the induced and therapeutic) release of repressed objects may be observed to particular advantage in
wartime in the case of military patients, among whom the phenomenon may be
studied on a massive scale. . . . The position would appear to be that an unconscious situation involving internalized bad objects is liable to be activated by
any situation in outer reality conforming to a pattern which renders it emotionally significant in the light of the unconscious situation. (76)

The specific stimuli for the release of bad object memories varied from the terror from exploding shells "to being let down by a superior officer" (76). These
breakdowns are expanded versions of severe negative transference reactions in ana-
lytically informed therapy where the patient's unconscious structures are triggered
by some minor aspect of the analyst, which results in an outpouring of patterned
responses that were originally developed in relation to the individual's objects:

It is for this reason that the psychoneurotic or psychotic soldier cannot bear
to be shouted at by the sergeant-major and cannot bear to eat army food. For
in his eyes every word of command is equivalent to an assault by a malevolent
father, and every spoonful of "greasy" stew from the cookhouse is a drop of
poison from the breast of a malevolent mother. No wonder that the "war neuroses" are so recalcitrant! (81)

Thus Fairbairn ends his 1943 article with examples of individual meanings associated with the now derepressed bad objects from these soldiers' early developmental
history. There are no universal meanings in his model but an infinite variety of
early bad-object experiences that made each soldier's breakdown a unique event.
This is a fitting end to the article that took on Freud's drive-theory and replaced it
with a metapsychology based on an unconscious populated by dissociated images
of actual traumatic events from the external world that had been internalized and
repressed. Without a good object to buffer the derepression of these early bad-
object memories, the soldiers Fairbairn observed had little chance to integrate the
derepressed material into their central egos, and the resulting confusion and fear
overwhelmed them.

CHAPTER 2

FAIRBAIRN'S STRUCTURAL MODEL AND HIS RADICAL APPROACH TO PSYCHOANALYTIC TREATMENT

THIS CHAPTER REVIEWS FAIRBAIRN'S final two great papers: "Endopsychic Structure Considered in Terms of Object Relationships" (1944) and "On the Nature and Aims of Psycho-Analytical Treatment" (1958). Both articles were published in the *International Journal of Psychoanalysis*, the mainstream journal of psychoanalytic thought, and so both were known in the field. But, as mentioned earlier, they were politely ignored because they were considered too radical. I first approach Fairbairn's 1944 paper by discussing the structures he proposed and then examine the paper in chronological order.

"ENDOPSYCHIC STRUCTURE CONSIDERED IN TERMS OF OBJECT RELATIONSHIPS" (1944)

In the groundbreaking paper "Endopsychic Structure Considered in Terms of Object Relationships" (1944), Fairbairn presented his radically different view of the human unconscious, one that challenged (in theory) the hegemony of the three-part Freudian structure, and, in so doing, he alienated many in the field of psychoanalysis. Mitchell (2000) considers Fairbairn's structural model, with its multiple selves and part-objects, to be one of the greatest contributions to the modern view of human psychological functioning. Fairbairn's original view shifted attention away from the single individual and toward a new focus on interactive two-person patterns, which he made concrete with his description of self and object structures:

First, self-formation and other-object formation are inseparable. Because libido is "object-seeking," it makes no sense psychologically to think of a self except in relation to another. And because others become psychically relevant only when invested by the self, it makes no sense to think of objects outside of relationships with versions of the self. The second principle inherent in Fairbairn's vision . . . is that we are multiplicitous, not a single self struggling with warded off impulses, but discontinuous, multiple self organizations packaged together by an illusory sense of continuity and coherence that has both conscious and unconscious features. In contemporary relational theory, the multiplicitous organizations are much more than (cognitive) representations of self; rather, they are each versions, complete functional units with a belief system, affective organization, agentic intentionality, and developmental history.   (Mitchell 2000:63)

Fairbairn's structural model offers a vision of human personality as a related series of "multiple selves" with a central self that provides a sense of continuity and purpose.

"Endopsychic Structure Considered in Terms of Object Relationships," at fifty pages, is the longest paper in his collected works, *Psychoanalytic Studies of the Personality* (1952). It is a typically "unedited" Fairbairn paper with numerous pages devoted to philosophical debate with Freud's theory, long digressions, and several pages of repeats and rehashes of material from earlier papers. My approach to this important statement of his structural theory is to first summarize the model briefly, and then describe each of the structural pairs in detail, although, as will become immediately clear, it is impossible to discuss one self-and-object pair without referring to the other two pairs. I also note the substantial differences that I have with Fairbairn's original positions.

Fairbairn saw the human personality as composed of a "central ego" or self that evolved in relation to an "ideal object," defined as the parent when he or she is responsive and attuned to the child's developmental needs. The un-split central ego is the conscious ego and relates only to the ideal or idealized object that exists in both the internal and the external world, although, again, Fairbairn assumed that it did not need to be internalized. No parent is perfect, and those interpersonal events that are frustrating and enraging have to be dissociated and held in the child's unconscious, so that they are not associated with the ideal object in order for the child's attachment to continue unimpeded. The parent's rejecting aspects that are dissociated and held in the unconscious coalesce into a complex view of a single object appropriately called the "rejecting object," along with the child's part-self that relates exclusively to this part-object, which was originally called the "internal saboteur." Fairbairn later changed its name to the "antilibidinal ego" in his paper "Observations on the Nature of Hysterical States" (1954). The antilibidinal ego, which is a split-off part of the child's original ego, is the target of the rejecting object's attacks, neglect, and indifference, and these experiences are so toxic and destructive to the child's dependent relationship to his object that the central ego cannot acknowledge them, and so this part self must be repressed.

When the rejecting object frustrates the child's legitimate developmental needs, the emotional deprivation simultaneously creates an enormous hunger and longing for an object that is loving and supportive. The very presence of the (unavailable or indifferent) object can drive the infant into a frenzy of need. The deprived and needy child attempts to satisfy her needs by seeing different aspects of the (same) parental object as filled with the potential for love. Fairbairn calls the child's part-self that sees the hope for future love the "libidinal ego," which is consumed with the fantasy that the part-object it sees (termed the "exciting object") actually contains the desperately needed support it requires. The exciting object owes its very existence to, and gets its power from, the child's deprived state. Fairbairn assumed that the intense, need-driven frenzy of excitement was intolerable to the child's central ego, so this part-object and part-self had to be dissociated and kept in the unconscious as well. Thus two of the three self-and-object pairs (the antilibidinal ego in relationship to the rejecting object, and the libidinal ego in relationship to the exciting object) are dissociated both from the central ego and from each other.

THE CENTRAL EGO AND THE IDEALIZED OBJECT

Early in the paper, Fairbairn engages in a philosophical debate with Freud on the futility of analyzing impulses separately from ego structures and then off-handedly introduces the first of his new structures, the "central ego" (85), without elaborating on the important role this structure plays in the human personality. As noted, the central ego is the conscious, non-split part of the original ego that remains in contact with reality and relates to the healthy parts of the parental objects. Fairbairn seldom spoke of the central ego, except to note that its role was to repress the two subsidiary egos, and he spoke even less about its object "partner," the "idealized object," which was *not mentioned at all* in this paper. This is a major oversight on his part, because every developing self requires an object partner with whom it relates. Not until 1951, in an addendum to this 1944 paper, did Fairbairn formally identify the "idealized object" as the relational "partner" to the central ego: "It will be noticed that, in accordance with my revised conception, the central ego's 'accepted object,' being shorn of its over exciting and over rejecting elements, assumes the form of a desexualized and idealized object which the central ego can safely love after divesting itself of the elements which give rise to the libidinal ego and the internal saboteur" (1951a:135).

Fairbairn's neglect of these two important structures was consonant with his disinterest in normal development and functioning. The variability in the strength of the central ego, which is clearly implied in this quote, is one of the most important implications embedded in his model, but Fairbairn *never* elaborated on it. The idealized object is based on the parental object, which dissociation has stripped of its overly exciting and overly rejecting aspects. This implies that parents can be more or less "bad" to varying degrees, and therefore some parents require the child to dissociate and repress more of their relational memories of childhood interactions than other children who were blessed with less rejecting parents. Involved, attuned, and supportive parents give the child little cause for dissociation, as they behave in a manner consistent with the child's needs. Their support of the child's development allows the child's central ego to expand and increase in complexity, as the central ego is elaborated by and nourished from interactions between itself and the idealized object. Incidentally, Fairbairn's use of the term "idealized object" is another one of his poorly chosen descriptive terms, because "idealization" implies a defensive compensation for parental failures. He later used the term "ideal object" both in his 1954 paper on hysteria and in his one-page article "Synopsis of an Object-Relations Theory of the Personality" (1963:224). Fairbairn's (1951a) definition clearly indicates that the idealized object is the trustworthy and supportive "remainder" of the original object, after the overly rejecting and exciting parts have been dissociated. I prefer to use "ideal" object, which carries no implication of defensiveness on the part of the child, who has already dissociated parts of reality in order to defend his central ego from knowing the truth about his objects. This remnant of the parental object, which varies according to how supportive or rejecting the parent actually has been, is the only part of the parental object that the child *does not have to defend himself against*. The is the "part" or fragment of the good object that is internalized as the object partner to the child's central ego, as described in his 1954 paper on hysteria. The central ego–ideal object pair is exactly what you would expect given Fairbairn's structural theory, despite the fact that he introduced the idealized object later, and placed no emphasis on normal functioning. A reciprocal relationship exists between consciousness and the unconscious in Fairbairn's model (described in his 1958 paper with the physical metaphor of "territory"), so that a large unconscious implies a smaller amount of consciousness, and vice versa. Thus the greater the parents' support—that is, the more they behave as ideal objects—the larger the child's conscious central ego will be, and, conversely, the same parents will have emitted a minimum of overly exciting or overly rejecting behaviors that would have been dissociated and banished into the child's unconscious.

Children raised in abusive, neglectful, overly frustrating families will experience only a fragment of their parent's behavior as coming from the ideal object, and so much of their object's behavior will be excessively rejecting and therefore overly exciting as well. In other words, the greater the deprivation of the child's legitimate needs, the greater his need for the libidinal ego's fantasy of a loving supportive object. A child living in a mostly rejecting environment will have a central ego that has not had enough interactional experiences with the ideal object to fully develop and mature. The amount of parental behavior that must be "shorn off" (i.e., dissociated and repressed) will be proportionally greater in a child raised in a neglectful environment; thus the neglected or abused child will have a relatively larger unconscious that contains more negative (and, paradoxically, more structure-producing) interactions than does his central ego. The larger the unconscious, the more the individual will suffer from repetition compulsions and extreme transferences, and, reciprocally, the stunted, immature, and underdeveloped central ego will have greater difficulty relating to and interpreting reality, as Rubens (1984) has noted:

> The more profound the splits, the more extensive and the more deeply repressed the subsidiary selves they engender, the greater will be the pathological effect on the Central Self. Just as this Central Self is what remains after the splitting of the Libidinal and Antilibidinal selves, so too will the Central Self's ongoing experience and expression be diminished by the tendency of the subsidiary selves to limit and to transform subsequent experience and expression according to the closed systems of their defining paradigms. The more extensive the portion of the self which has been repressed, the less that will be available for open, ongoing interaction with the world. (435)

A relationship with an impoverished ideal object has consequences for the developing child's central ego in that the central ego will remain immature and weak compared with the powerful split-off subegos. As Rubens (1984) noted, the power of the subsidiary egos to distort reality through transferences leaves little central ego to negotiate realistically with the outside world.

Fairbairn derived the internal structures that became the hallmark of his model from his analysis of a patient's dream that revealed the role and dynamics of the central ego in relationship to the two dissociated part egos. All three self-and-object pairs must be discussed at this point, as they are intimately interrelated. Fairbairn recognized that the two dissociated subegos had different, though complimentary, roles; whereas the libidinal subego contains the need for attachment to the object, the antilibidinal subego is suffused with aggression as a result of its exclusive relationship to the rejecting part-object. In this quote from 1944, Fairbairn uses the term "internal saboteur," which, as mentioned, he changed to "antilibidinal ego" in his 1954 paper on hysteria:

> As regards the relationship of the central ego to the other egos, our most important clue to its nature lies in the fact that, whereas the central ego must be regarded as compromising pre-conscious and conscious as well as unconscious, elements, the other egos must equally be regarded as essentially unconscious. From this we may infer that the libidinal ego and internal saboteur are both rejected by the central ego; and this inference is confirmed by the fact that, as we have seen, the considerable volume of libido and of aggression which has

ceased to be at the disposal of the central ego is now at the disposal of the subsidiary egos. Assuming then that the subsidiary egos are rejected by the central ego,
it becomes a question of the dynamic of this rejection. . . . So there is no alternative but to regard it as aggression. Aggression must, accordingly, be regarded
as the characteristic determinant of the attitude of the central ego towards the
subsidiary egos.   (104–105)

Clearly Fairbairn could see that the libidinal ego was filled with the need for
love, which had been thwarted by the parent's excessive rejecting behavior. The
child's need for love does not go away, and this painfully needy structure has to be
repressed (rejected by the central ego) because the longing for the exciting aspect
of the parental object is so intense in deprived children that it cannot be consciously tolerated. Effectively, the child is forced to hide from the daily reality that
he or she is starving for love and affection. From the same analysis of that patient's
dream, Fairbairn recognized that the antilibidinal ego is suffused with aggression.
In my view, a significant point that Fairbairn failed to grasp is that this aggression is
not subtracted ("at the disposal of the subegos") from the central ego, as he implies,
but is a consequence of the punishing and hostile relationship between the antilibidinal ego and the rejecting object. The notion that the antilibidinal ego "has"
aggression that once "belonged" to the central ego echoes the Freudian notion that
a limited amount of psychic energy is divided between the structures, an implication of which Fairbairn was probably unaware.

Fairbairn's assertion that the central ego held the two subsidiary egos in the
unconscious (i.e., rejected) via aggression is also unlikely to be true. This is
because the child of rejecting parents has two subegos (libidinal and antilibidinal)
that have had far more intense interactions (albeit negative ones) with the rejecting
and exciting parts of the parental objects than the child's central ego has experienced with the ideal object. In effect, more "personality," or structure, exists in the
subegos than in the central ego. The numerous and intense interactions between
the child's antilibidinal ego and the rejecting object builds a rich series of memories that becomes a complex (albeit enraged) antilibidinal ego that is hostile to the
rejecting object structure. The internalized rejecting object is an "ego" structure
as well, in that it is a part of the child's ego that is identified with the behavior and
attitudes of the actual rejecting object. The child's antilibidinal ego develops a
canny and "counterpunching" strategy to fight back against the rejecting object.
In children raised in rejecting families, these subego and part-object structures are
much more developed and powerful than the central ego. The central ego has had
very few interactions that contribute to the child's development, simply because the
parental objects are so rejecting that they only infrequently behave as ideal objects
and meet the child's developmental needs. We can assume, therefore, that Fairbairn's assertion that the central ego keeps the subegos repressed with aggression

is probably incorrect. Because the central ego lacks *substance* and developmental experience that would allow it to develop and dominate the personality, it cannot remain in the dominant position when one or the other of the subegos is active. But more important, clinical experience with borderline patients demonstrates that *neither of the two subegos, nor the part-objects to whom they relate, remain exclusively in the unconscious,* as Fairbairn also claimed. This significantly contradicts Fairbairn's position that the subegos are aggressively pressured by the central ego to remain in the unconscious. Borderline patients demonstrate that *either* the libidinal *or* the antilibidinal ego can become the dominant, conscious ego; the emergence of either appears linked not to the central ego's lack of aggression but to its lack of substance and development (Celani 1993:1994). Although Fairbairn acknowledged that a reciprocal relationship existed between the subegos and the central ego (129–130), his writing suggests that he *never* suspected that the subegos could become the dominant ego.

As I have noted, in healthy families the child's central ego is very large, robust, and filled with memories of appropriate support from the ideal objects. Simultaneously, the antilibidinal ego is very small, as the child has experienced few untoward interactions with the rejecting aspects of the objects that had to be dissociated, and so few relational events have been split off and repressed in the unconscious, with the result that little antilibidinal subego is striving for awareness. In extremely supportive environments, the child develops enough central ego to voice his or her complaints *without* needing to split them off. Similarly, the child has no need to develop a hope- and fantasy-filled libidinal ego to remain attached to the parents if they are readily available and emotionally supportive. The central ego thus becomes dominant not because it aggressively represses the subegos but because it is large and filled with both conscious and unconscious memories of gratifying interactions with the objects (despite Fairbairn's assertion that good objects are not internalized). Just as important, the robust central ego is not pressured by split-off memories of bad objects simply because there is so little material in the subegos that had been dissociated. This type of childhood scenario allows the integration of frustrating aspects of the objects into the conscious central ego, because the good aspects of the object easily overwhelm the meager amount of frustration, which allows the child's central ego to integrate the negative experiences into a single, ambivalent view of his or her objects. This analysis demonstrates that Fairbairn's model does account for healthy as well as pathological development.

This revised view of the dynamics of the inner world differs from the view that Fairbairn originally presented. The central ego can be overrun by either of the subegos or taken over by either the internalized rejecting object or the internalized exciting object, not just temporarily but nearly permanently (Celani 2001, 2007). Fairbairn's theory did introduce, inadvertently and obliquely, the concept of an empty, impoverished, and deprived central ego, though, as mentioned, he never spoke of it directly. This same point, that the central ego can be taken over by one of the other subegos, has been made by Sutherland (1989), Fairbairn's colleague and biographer, who equates the concept of "observing self" to that of "central ego":

> The power of the whole self to manage behavior with optimal adaptiveness is thus the result of the integrity of the whole self against the pressure from sub-selves, and these two sets of forces vary according to the past history of the person and the nature of the external environment to which behavior is being directed. . . . With a sub-self becoming dominant, it is difficult to specify where the "autonomy" of the self is then located. Even under strong compulsions, there is usually an awareness of the situation of being "possessed," as though the observing self remains intact though powerless to exert enough control over it. (170–171)

Thus there is a reciprocal relationship between the subegos, and the shifting strength of one versus the others determines which sub-self the clinician will face in the consulting room.

THE LIBIDINAL AND ANTILIBIDINAL SUBEGOS AND THEIR ASSOCIATED OBJECTS

Fairbairn's writing was always chaotic and challenging to follow, and, in this style, he introduced (almost inadvertently) the concept of two separate facets of the bad object (exciting and rejecting). His writing gives readers the impression that he wrote before he outlined his ideas, and new concepts tumbled into his mind while he was writing about unrelated topics:

> Thus, in my opinion, beneath the level at which the central ego finds itself confronted with the super-ego as an internal object of moral significance lies a level at which parts of the ego find themselves confronted with internal objects which are, not simply devoid of moral significance, but unconditionally bad from the libidinal standpoint of the central ego whether in the role of an exciting or that of a rejecting object (internal persecutors of one kind or the other). (93)

Here Fairbairn has given the two facets of the bad object names, without either defining them or describing the parts of the ego that are related to them. He followed this by filling out his model with another reference to the previously mentioned analysis of a dream of a female patient:

> The (manifest) dream to which I refer consisted in a brief scene in which the dreamer saw the figure of herself being viciously attacked by a well-known actress

in a venerable building which had belonged to her family for generations. Her husband was looking on; but he seemed quite helpless and quite incapable of protecting her. After delivering the attack, the actress turned away and resumed playing a stage part, which, as seemed to be implied, she had momentarily set aside in order to deliver the attack by way of interlude. (95)

Fairbairn's analysis of this dream supplied all the material for the formulation of his structural model. He noted that he had discarded Freud's notion that dreams are based on wish fulfillment but contended, instead, that they represent inner relational dynamics between parts of the self and internalized objects: "I have now modified my view to the effect that such figures represent either parts of the 'ego' or internalized objects" (99). He concluded from his analysis of this patient's dream that three pairs of ego-and-object structures exist: the conscious central ego and its (as yet unspecified) ideal object, plus two pairs of repressed part-selves and associated part-objects. Fairbairn used the preexisting language of classical psychoanalysis when he labeled one of the subegos the "libidinal ego," but, like many radical thinkers, he changed the meaning of "libidinal"; his definition did not imply Freud's concept of diffuse sexuality but signaled an attachment to and need for love from the object. He purposely called the other "part-ego," a structure that seemed to be charged with aggression, the "internal saboteur," because the dream suggested that this part-self attacked the other two structures in the interior world: the libidinal ego and its associated "exciting object." This part of the dynamic relationships between the interior structures appears to be incorrect, as I will presently explain. He concludes this section with this comment:

> I was accordingly led to set aside the traditional classification of mental structure in terms of ego, id and super-ego in favour of a classification couched in terms of an ego-structure split into three separate egos — (1) a central ego (the "I"), (2) a libidinal ego, and (3) an aggressive, persecutory ego which I designate the internal saboteur. Subsequent experience has led me to regard this classification as having universal application. (101)

This model of internalized object relations, which is the culmination of Fairbairn's thought, is almost correct, but it contains, in my view, a *critical* error (Celani 2001). The error involves the dynamic relationship between the internal saboteur (now called the "antilibidinal ego") and the rejecting object. Fairbairn concluded from the patient's dream that the antilibidinal ego was an *ally* of the internalized rejecting object, which is the split-off part of the rejecting and punitive parent that has been dissociated and repressed: "But meanwhile my justification will be that the dreamer's mother, who provided the original model of this internalized object, was essentially a rejecting figure, and that it is, so to speak in the name of this object that the aggression of the internal saboteur is directed against the libidinal ego" (104).

My view is based on the argument that the part of the parental object to which the antilibidinal ego relates is the rejecting part-object, and this is the part of the parent that attacks, neglects, humiliates, and demeans the child. In Fairbairn's view, the internal saboteur attacks other structures "in the name of this object" and thus is *cooperating* with the rejecting object. The antilibidinal ego is repressed by the central ego because it has been a *victim* of assaults by the rejecting object, and so *it is in no way an ally of the rejecting object*, which is out to destroy its very being. The rejecting object is intolerable for the child's central ego to accept, because conscious awareness of the hateful and rejecting aspects of the object would destroy the needed attachment to the (same) object. Each subego relates exclusively to, and is *defined by*, the part-object to which it relates. The two part-selves, or egos (libidinal and antilibidinal), were originally parts of the child's central ego, but the antilibidinal ego has been exposed to intolerable aggression, neglect, or abuse while the libidinal ego has experienced unendurable longing, both intolerable to the central ego. Each repressed subego is a small functional self whose "character" is formed in response to the behavior of the rejecting or exciting part-object. The antilibidinal ego (or self) is filled with fear, self-contempt, a desire for revenge, and the yearning to reform both the internal rejecting object and the actual external object. Patients with histories of abuse often have a self- and object-hating, cynical, and challenging antilibidinal ego whose major complaint is that the parental object(s), or new displaced surrogates, have failed them in their parenting and leadership roles.

The antilibidinal ego attempts to fight back against the rejecting object as best it can from its diminished, dependent position. In my interpretation of Fairbairn's model, the antilibidinal ego never attacks the libidinal ego, simply because *it does not know that the libidinal ego even exists*, as it has been spit off and is unavailable. Fairbairn (concluded, however, that the antilibidinal ego does attack the libidinal ego and its exciting object (108), as if it were able to cross the repression barrier. This assumes that the libidinal and antilibidinal egos know about each other and are both contained in an "open" unconscious. Were this true, then the whole purpose of splitting would be defeated, as the libidinal ego would know about the experiences of the antilibidinal ego and this would destroy any hope of love from the object. In practice, my borderline patients acted as if the antilibidinal ego had no awareness whatsoever of either the exciting object or the libidinal ego. The whole purpose of splitting is to keep these two separate views of the object apart so that the deprived child's libidinal ego can continue loving and longing for the exciting object while the antilibidinal ego can fight back against the rejecting aspects of the very same object with all its energy, without the libidinal ego (or the central ego) ever knowing.

In many families, the rejecting aspects of the object(s) are so powerful, and the resulting frustration of legitimate developmental needs so severe, that the antilibidinal ego and its hostile relationship to the rejecting object become the largest part of the personality. Rubens (1984) has noted the importance of these negative and intense part-self and part-object relationships: "There exists, at the very structural foundation of these subsidiary selves, an attachment to some negative aspect of experience which is felt as vital to the definition of the self. . . . The raison d'être of these endopsychic structures is to continue living out these 'bad' relationships" (434).

Thus the bulk of the rejected child's personality is created by these "bad" relationships, which are far more intense and frequent than are the less common (if not completely absent) "normal" developmentally supportive daily experiences between the child's central ego and the ideal aspects of the parent. The mostly unconscious relationship between the antilibidinal ego and the rejecting object, as well as the relationship between the libidinal ego and the exciting object, distort new relationships in the external word so that the same relational configurations are endlessly reenacted.

Fairbairn assumed that the libidinal ego had to be repressed, because the "alluring-teasing" aspect of the out-of-reach object was intolerable for the child (and later the adult) to bear. This assumption is also contradicted by work with borderline patients and battered women (Celani 1993, 1994), who frequently split into their libidinal egos, which they experience *consciously*, when they are in despair and fear the loss of their object. In other words, under these conditions of extreme need, the libidinal ego becomes the dominant ego structure and represses the central ego, and its dominance gives the individual hope for the future. These patients verbalize and treasure clearly expressed hopes that the exciting object (the only object the libidinal ego can see) will love them at some future date. It is not unusual, for example, for a battered woman who has split into her libidinal ego to declare that she is embarking on a romantic weekend with her boyfriend (her exciting object), while still covered with bruises from a recent beating. Her alternative perception of her partner as a violent, ruthless criminal is now repressed in her antilibidinal ego, which relates to him only as a rejecting object, and both the part-self and the part-object are completely unavailable to her consciousness. If the therapist insists on mentioning the now dissociated antilibidinal view of the object to the patient, while the patient is dominated by her libidinal ego, the patient will likely react with hostility and resistance, and may even terminate her treatment. It is this illusory libidinal ego hope that draws the battered woman back to her bad object (exciting and rejecting) again and again (Celani 1994).

There are also times when patients identify with the rejecting internal object, which is a complete self that now inhabits their inner world, and this structure seeks to reenact an abusive relationship with new, external objects. The individual reared in an abusive and depriving family has over-learned two roles: that of the victim (antilibidinal ego) and that of the ruthless, unassailable abuser (rejecting object). Identifying with the rejecting object and finding a victim to reject in the external world (such as a child or another dependent) provides many patients an enormous relief, for it allows them to discharge their frustration and experience the same sense of ruthless power that had been used against them in their childhood. Children who torture animals and elder abuse by family members both appear to be enactments of this dynamic.

Fairbairn saw the splitting defense as the ideal answer to the dilemma of rejected children: it allows them to hide from the loss of their ideal object if they express hostility, and also to hide from the loss of themselves if they express the need for love and are rejected. In effect, rejected children create a good object for themselves by stripping their mother (or father) of their hostility and by focusing their love toward an illusory exciting object. Fairbairn made it clear that the libidinal ego has an "excess" of libido (115) and that the antilibidinal ego also has aggression to spare. The excesses of libidinal need for the exciting object comes from a history of frustration of the child's need for love and support, and translates internally to the intensely libidinal relationship between the libidinal ego and its exciting part-object. One of the more dramatic observations that I observed of the libidinal ego's attachment and, conversely, the antilibidinal ego's rage at disappointment came in a group-home setting for incorrigible teenagers. On a number of occasions, I saw the explosive consequences when a social worker in the group home had to tell one of her teenage patients, who had been longing for and talking incessantly about a promised weekend visit from her mother, that the mother would probably not arrive. The resulting violence, rage, and self-destructiveness of the aroused antilibidinal ego spoke of unending despair. The individual's libidinal ego, which was eagerly anticipating the visit just moments before the news of this latest abandonment, was instantly dissociated, and the previously longed for (exciting) object instantly became a rejecting object, thus bringing up the antilibidinal response. Despite these upheavals, the patient's libidinal ego would return within a few days and dominate the patient's consciousness, thus repairing the attachment and continuing the hope for love in the future. The patient's insistence that her object will love her, despite all the evidence to the contrary, is an enormous source of resistance: "In terms of my present standpoint, there can be no room for doubt that the obstinate attachment of the libidinal ego to the exciting object and its reluctance to renounce this object constitute a particularly formidable source of resistance-and one which plays no small part in determining what is known as the negative therapeutic reaction" (Fairbairn 1944:117).

The libidinal ego repeatedly returns to the exciting (part) object because it promises the patient future satisfaction. This promise is both an internally generated fantasy as well as an internalization of small bits of reality of the parent, as even the most dysfunctional parents occasionally indulge their children. The libidinal ego, unaware of the hurt and despair in the antilibidinal ego, remains attached to the promise of future love from the exciting object. Thus the libidinal ego is ferociously loyal to and focused on the exciting object, and any attempt to interfere with this attachment directly produces enormous resistance. Patients who act out the extreme needs of the libidinal ego include those who are obsessed with and stalk a particular object or others who throw themselves at one object after another. These behaviors represent the extreme end of the continuum of the libidinal ego's quest for satisfaction. Fairbairn recognized that the child's unmet developmental needs leave him no choice but to hope that future gratification will be forthcoming from his needed objects. The very presence of the parental object, even if she (or he) is fast asleep, sets up desire and longing in the frustrated child. Fairbairn was realistic in his view that the power of the attachment between the libidinal ego and the exciting object would preclude an easy solution to the necessary separation from that part-object.

Interestingly, there is resistance from *both* subegos against letting go of their respective part-objects in the internal world, even though they are endlessly frustrating to the split-off selves. If the patient's libidinal ego gives up hope on the exciting object, it will never be nourished, and yet, if the antilibidinal ego gives up its fight with the rejecting object, it will never have the satisfaction of turning a bad object into a good one or, alternatively, of destroying an enemy. The lack of alternatives is also based on the reality that the individual is fixated at an earlier stage of development by the deprivation he experienced, and therefore he is not developmentally ready to give up on his parental objects. This is another of Fairbairn's profound clinical insights about the emotional lives of children: that the desperately needy, abused, and neglected child is more *deeply attached* to its bad objects than the normal child is to his good objects. Any attempt to separate the child (or later the adult patient) from his illusions, including fantasies of revenge and of the possibility of defeating the rejecting object, can be counterproductive, if not outright disastrous. Fairbairn truly understood the power of "attachment" (both of love and hate) as a source of resistance. If the therapeutic relationship is mismanaged, and the therapist is too eager to separate the patient from his bad objects, the patient may perceive that he is in a life-and-death struggle with the therapist who may appear to be taking away or undermining the most meaningful aspects of the patient's life.

THE INTENSITY OF THE ATTACHMENT BETWEEN SUBEGOS AND THEIR OBJECTS

The intense hate contained in the antilibidinal ego serves as the "attaching" emotion between the antilibidinal ego and the rejecting object, just as "need for love" is the attaching emotion between the libidinal ego and the exciting object. As Fairbairn noted, "The truth is that, however well the fact may be disguised, the individual is extremely reluctant to abandon his original hate, no less than his original need, of his original objects in childhood" (117). The antilibidinal ego directs its cynical, passive hostility toward the internal rejecting object and also projects it on innocent bystanders in the external world, as it sees them as new versions of the internal rejecting object. The dominant antilibidinal ego will often interact with others with various passive aggressive behaviors including thwarting, or aggressive cynicism. Extremely angry patients dominated by their antilibidinal egos will take it upon themselves to mount a "crusade" against their rejecting objects, and these individuals are often the most difficult to separate from their bad objects. Their goal of hurting the powerful, rejecting object and thus re-creating themselves as a potent force cannot be given up, for, if they do, they lose the possibility of achieving personal significance.

The intensity of the emotions contained in both the libidinal and antilibidinal egos are of a different intensity compared with the relaxed and self-enhancing relationship between the central ego and the ideal object. The supportive parent who is mostly an ideal object allows the child's central ego to grow and elaborate, because it "follows" the child and reacts to the child's needs. The child's central ego is not overwhelmed by fear or need, and so it can internalize aspects of the object at its own pace. Conversely, the relationship between both subegos and their respective part-objects is fraught with tension, and the subego is locked into a rigid relationship with the respective part-object, as Scharff and Birtles (1994) demonstrate using a metaphor from chemistry:

> The model becomes more sophisticated, beyond the range of Fairbairn's insights, when we see that the repressed relationships—both libidinal and antilibidinal object relations sets—are ones which are excessive, characterized by painful affective tones because the valence of attraction is too great. Consequently, these are both relationships which pull the central ego too far toward the object. That is to say the "compound" or object relationship which is formed is held too tightly to allow the self or ego an independent existence. The relationship between the Central Ego and Ideal Object, on the other hand, is one that is not characterized by an excessive attraction and allows for the survival of an experiencing self. (xviii)

This explanation of the source of the ferocious attachment between the subegos and their part-objects adds to our understanding of the extreme difficulty an analyst encounters when attempting to separate the emotionally saturated subegos from their loved or hated objects. The intensity and purposefulness built into this attachment is not encountered in "normal' object relationships. Thus it can be puzzling to the clinician who confronts a patient who describes an exceedingly toxic relationship between his objects and himself. "Normal" logic would suggest that patients would flee from their objects at all costs, and yet they return, ever eager for another confrontation.

Still another reason for the attachment between a patient and her frustrating objects (whether internal or external) comes from the patient's fear of losing important parts of her personality that are, in fact, limited though functional sub-personalities that have been central to the individual's functioning (Celani 1998). During the development of many children, the antilibidinal ego plays a critical role in psychologically fighting off the attacks of the rejecting object, thus preserving a fragment of the child's self. This structure contains rich and dense memories of itself in interactions with the most vital and emotionally intense (though hateful and destructive) aspects of the objects. Over time in treatment, the relationship between the patient's central ego and the ideal-object therapist will gradually build up the patient's central ego to where the patient will gradually pay more attention to his new internalized good object than to his internalized bad object. As the central ego grows and elaborates with increasing interactions with the ideal-object therapist, the power of the rejecting object to challenge and reactivate the antilibidinal ego will be reduced, and an internal crisis will result as *neither structure can exist without the other.* Ogden (1994) addresses this issue in the following quote, in which the "object component" he refers to is the internal rejecting object and the "self-component" is the antilibidinal ego:

> The suborganization of ego identified with the object experiences as much need for object relatedness as the self component in the internal relationship. . . . The object component may taunt, shame, threaten, lord over, or induce guilt in its object (the self component of the internal relationship) in order to maintain connectedness with the self component. These efforts at control over the self component become greatly intensified when there is a danger of the bond being threatened, e.g., by a more mature form of relatedness to the therapist. (106)

This clinical scenario can develop after a long-term therapeutic relationship, and it manifests itself as a sudden upwelling of resistance, even attacks, on the therapist after these issues have apparently been resolved, often in the last months of multi-year treatments. These often puzzling upwellings are the last efforts of one of the structures, usually the internalized rejecting object, to remain alive in the patient's inner world.

THE DYNAMICS OF SPLITTING

The richest section of Fairbairn's paper on endopsychic structure follows his description of the inner structures and focuses on the dynamics of the splitting defense. Once again, Fairbairn writes with casual disregard for the logical sequence with which he presents the material. At this point in the paper, he has already introduced the subegos but has not addressed why they needed to be split off. He begins by questioning Freud's assumption of biologically inherited aggression: "Thus, I do not consider that the infant directs aggression spontaneously towards his libidinal object in the absence of some kind of frustration" (109). Fairbairn dismissed Freud's id as the source of human destructiveness, and restored the innocence to childhood, as he saw aggression as a product of frustration and not as an innate biological imperative. He then suggested that infants in primitive societies, who have continuous access to their mothers, have less frustration and thus more readily move from dependency to independence. The child frustrated by an absent or uncaring mother becomes overwhelmed by the possibility of experiencing hostile ambivalence toward his needed object. An integrated, but mostly hostile, vision of the object is absolutely intolerable, as it would allow the child to see just how badly he was being treated. This reality would threaten his attachment to his needed object and produce an abandonment panic, thus requiring the splitting defense: "Since it proves intolerable to him to have a good object which is also bad, he seeks to alleviate the situation by splitting the figure of his mother into two objects. Then, in so far as she satisfies him libidinally, she is a 'good' object, and in so far as she fails to satisfy him libidinally, she is a 'bad' object" (110).

Fairbairn then goes on to say that the child internalizes and represses the "bad" aspect of the object because external reality is "unyielding" (110) and because he has more control in the inner world. He then reiterates his opposition to the concept of internalizing good objects, because he sees internalization as a deliberate and defensive act—again, a position that, in my view, is *completely* incorrect. Once the "unsatisfying object" (111) is internalized, the child is confronted with a second problem:

> Unlike the satisfying object, the unsatisfying object has, so to speak, two facets. On the one hand it frustrates; and, on the other hand, it tempts and allures. Indeed its essential "badness" consists precisely in the fact that it combines allurement with frustration. . . . In his attempts to control the unsatisfying object, he has introduced into the inner economy of his mind an object which not only continues to frustrate his need, but continues to whet it. (111)

This is the same problem that Fairbairn (1943) struggled with when he created the dynamic explanation for the moral defense. Previously he assumed that the child detoxified bad internal objects by forcibly internalizing good objects to act as buffers. Splitting is his improved solution to the very same problem. This time, he uses the concept of dissociation of the two "specialized" subegos, the libidinal and antilibidinal, along with their part-object representations: "As repression of the objects proceeds, the incipient division of the ego becomes an accomplished fact. The two pseudopodia are rejected by the part of the ego which remains central on account of their connection with the rejected objects; and with their associated objects they share the fate of repression" (112). Again, I point out that "dissociation" would be a better term than "repression" because these objects originated in the external world, and the events that were unendurable were traumatic scenarios of rejection and indifference.

Fairbairn then speaks of the dilemma faced by children with deprived histories, and his empathy most likely emerged as a result of his personal experiences and from his work in the University Psychological Clinic for Children. Again, this was unusual in 1944, as the dominant view in psychoanalysis was that the child was a "demon" (Grotstein and Rinsley 1994), filled with sexual and aggressive drives. Fairbairn recognized that the rejected child is exceedingly insecure, as he is unconditionally dependent on an object or objects that are indifferent to his well-being. Fairbairn then produced a section of brilliant writing supporting his position that the child is able to discharge his hostility toward his mother only internally and unconsciously, through the antilibidinal ego's (alleged) attacks on the exciting object, because outright rejection of the mother in the external world is too dangerous. It is very possible that this position is an autobiographical artifact; Fairbairn, as a child, may have felt it was impossible to attack his mother even obliquely. As I will demonstrate, however, children and young adults with engorged antilibidinal egos *are able* to attack their external rejecting objects in disguised ways. However debatable his starting point, Fairbairn produced a profoundly sympathetic view of the deprived child in relation to an impossible reality:

> From the latter standpoint, what he experiences is a sense of lack of love, and indeed emotional *rejection* on his mother's part. This being so, the expression of hate towards her as a rejecting object becomes a very dangerous procedure. On the one hand, it is calculated to make her reject him all the more and thus to increase her "badness" and make her seem *more real* in her capacity of a bad object. On the other hand, it is calculated to make her love him less, and thus to decrease her "goodness" and make her seem *less real* (i.e., destroy her) in her capacity of good object. (112–113)

This is consistent with Fairbairn's unmodified structural theory, where the child was assumed to be trapped by his needs, with no possible outlet for his hostility other than internal attacks by the antilibidinal ego on the exciting object and associated libidinal ego. Clinical experience, particularly with borderline patients, suggests that the deprived adult *solves* the dilemma of hostility toward the objects, not by internal antilibidinal attacks on the libidinal ego and the exciting object but by oblique attacks on the rejecting object, and, second, by the *splitting defense itself.*

These oblique attacks by the antilibidinal ego occur when the child's s frustration-based hatred, encapsulated in the antilibidinal ego, is so intense that it is acted out, albeit indirectly, in the external world against original or displaced rejecting objects. In the following example, the splitting defense itself was not able to contain the revenge-based hate in the patient's antilibidinal ego. This, too, conflicts Fairbairn's assertion that the antilibidinal ego acts only in the interior world (and, worse, is an ally of the rejecting object). This example comes from my experience with a patient whose family was characterized by abuse, and, even more important, abuse directed toward one child while others were spared, thus further infuriating my patient's antilibidinal ego. This patient, whom I wrote about previously (Celani 1994), began therapy in his thirties and reported that as a teenager he had a history of poorly disguised "accidents" that were small episodes of antilibidinal revenge directed against his rejecting object father. His early childhood consisted of an endless series of cruel humiliations directed against him by his father, who simultaneously favored his two siblings. His mother was as much a hapless victim of her husband as the children were, and she offered no support. As a teen, he was barred from using the heirloom rowing shell that his brother was allowed to use. His repeated begging finally forced his father to set a date when he would instruct his son on its use. When that day came, my patient was just stepping into the delicate shell from the dock for the first time when he "accidentally" slipped and plunged a foot through its thin hull. Similarly, he was not allowed to drive his father's English sports car (although his brother was), but he somehow managed to back the old family station wagon (which was the only car he was allowed to drive) into the sports car in the country club parking lot, crushing its front end. Later he was allowed to take his friends out on his father's sailboat as a high school graduation present, and he "forgot" to replace the bailing plugs when they returned to the mooring, and the boat slowly sank. Finally, several years later, after he was allowed to drive the sports car, he "accidentally" left the handbrake on as he drove down the interstate at top speed, and the resulting heat in the rear axle caught the lubricant on fire and ravaged the back half of the car. All these events occurred in his teenage and young adult years, as earlier in childhood he needed his objects too desperately to retaliate in any way. Second, all his attempts at revenge were disguised under the cloak of "accidents," so he was not consciously aware of their source. Not surprisingly, this patient reported that when his father was dying he stayed home to take care of him, a familiar pattern I have noted previously (Celani 2005). This is often seen in patients who are attempting to finally secure the love that was not developmentally available during their childhoods. The sadism of this patient's father created his enormous antilibidinal ego, but the deprivation of his developmental needs (by both parents) simultaneously created an equally powerful hope-filled libidinal ego. When his father died, my patient took his father's clothing and had it retailored to fit himself, a last desperate effort to stay attached to the depriving but alluring object (Celani 1993). This is the clinical translation of Fairbairn's (1940:23) concept of fixation on the parental object, who is seen, even into adulthood, as the most significant object in the universe and the only one who can release the child into higher levels of functioning.

Second, the child takes refuge from his hostility toward his objects by means of the splitting defense itself, which prevents the patient from detecting that his exciting objects are in any way related to his tightly repressed rejecting objects. Splitting "packages" memories of the most painful rejections and then represses them, allowing the developing child to hide from the massive failures of her object. When there is a preponderance of emotional abandonment compared to appropriate central ego support, the child cannot metabolize the much larger-size package of remembered failures within a very small-size package of gratifying memories. Thus integration of the two views of the object into one single, ambivalent object perception can never take place.

Today, with the increased knowledge of early childhood development, and especially that based on the work of Mahler (1975) and Hamilton (1988), it is apparent that infants split objects naturally, as they are not capable of associating two opposite affective experiences with a single object. Therefore, it is not the initial splitting that is important, but the child's inability to integrate positive and negative object images later on in development. This inability to *stop splitting* is a consequence of the preponderance of frustrating early experiences. If the deprived child were able to fully integrate both good and bad memories of his childhood, then he would become aware of the overwhelming number of abusive or frustrating events he had suffered (as well as the pitifully small number of loving supportive events), and this awareness would destroy his attachment by provoking appropriate resentment and eliminating unrealistic hope for the future. Thus splitting begins as a normal process and then becomes a defense in children with excessive frustration.

Fairbairn continues the theme of the child's impossible dilemma, and it becomes quite clear that this issue was on his mind, regardless of the topic of his writing. His first theoretical paper in 1940 emphasized not only the child's need for the parents' love but also his need for the parents to accept the love he returned to them. In his 1944 paper, Fairbairn continues that theme and illustrates his awareness of and empathy for the child who has parents who cannot accept the love he returns to them:

> At the same time, it also becomes a dangerous procedure for the child to express his libidinal need, i.e., his nascent love, of his mother in face of rejection at her hands; for it is equivalent to discharging his libido into an emotional vacuum. Such a discharge is accompanied by an affective experience which is singularly devastating. In an older child this experience is one of intense humiliation over the depreciation of his love, which seems to be involved. At a somewhat deeper level (or at an

earlier stage) the experience is one of shame over the display of needs which are disregarded or belittled. In virtue of these experiences of humiliation and shame he feels reduced to a state of worthlessness, destitution or beggardom. His sense of his own value is threatened; and he feels bad in the sense of "inferior." . . . At a still deeper level (or at a still earlier age) the child's experience is one of, so to speak, exploding ineffectively and being completely emptied of libido. Thus it is an experience of disintegration and of imminent psychical death.   (113)

This rich passage concisely summarizes Fairbairn's view of the child's experience of being rejected, an event he saw as equivalent to "psychical death." He sees rejected children as facing, at the very least, the experience of humiliation and, at worst, a reduction of the sense of self to "worthlessness, destitution or beggardom." This, in my view, is Fairbairn at his very best, in that he conveys the emotional reaction of children so vividly to his readers. In addition to feeling impotent rage at the rejecting object, who should be loving and supportive toward him, the child's antilibidinal ego experiences humiliation, because he is forced to beg for gratification of his legitimate needs that are being disregarded and demeaned. Here one feels that Fairbairn's deft and sensitive awareness of the child's dilemma stems from his own direct experience. Certainly his relationship with his father was characterized by an almost complete rejection of Fairbairn's needs (Beattie 2003), and his attachment to his mother was based on her terms, not his needs (Sutherland 1989). Undoubtedly, this personal history made him more sensitive to the bleak future of children under his care at the child guidance clinic.

Toward the end of this long and fruitful paper, Fairbairn's writing becomes less focused, but he touches on a number of issues relating to his structural theory, perhaps most important, the Oedipal situation. He reformulates this important psychoanalytic concept in a surprisingly powerful and clinically significant manner, as his reinterpretation of the Oedipal situation fits his model and also offers a completely new vision compared with classical psychoanalysis:

The child finds it intolerable enough to be called upon to deal with a single ambivalent object; but when he is called upon to deal with two, he finds it still more intolerable. He therefore seeks to simplify a complex situation, in which he finds himself confronted with two exciting objects and two rejecting objects, by converting it into one in which he will only be confronted with a single exciting object and a single rejecting object; and he achieves this aim, with, of course, a varying measure of success, by concentrating upon the exciting aspect of one parent and the rejecting aspect of the other. He thus, for all practical purposes, comes to equate one parental object with the exciting object, and the other with the rejecting object; and by so doing *the child constitutes the Oedipus situation for himself.*   (124–125)

Clinically, the "simplification" Fairbairn describes—of seeing one parent in the exciting object role and the other in the rejecting object role—is one of the most obvious and frequently seen phenomena in patients with character disorders. Fairbairn's model of this complex interpersonal situation crosses gender lines; both male and female patients can deify or demonize either their maternal or their paternal object. This universal human tendency emerges directly from Fairbairn's position that the child cannot survive childhood without a "good" object, even if it has to exist only in fantasy. Once again, one can speculate on the possible autobiographical origins of this insight, since, as mentioned, Fairbairn had two bad-object parents, one less rejecting than the other. The patient's "simplified" view of his objects—one as "all" exciting and the other as "all" rejecting—will, under clinical scrutiny, reveal exciting, rejecting, and ideal aspects in both objects. I have had many patients who, after a number of years of work, have realistically reversed their initial view of both objects.

Fairbairn's 1944 paper finally gave voice to his structural model, parts of which he was clearly formulating during his earlier papers. His model of the "endopsychic situation" is a template for all human motivation and has far-reaching clinical implications. The structural model gives therapists an outline of the human personality that has real clinical application, as it organizes various possible projections during the transference into a readily understandable framework

"ON THE NATURE AND AIMS OF PSYCHO-ANALYTICAL TREATMENT" (1958)

The last of Fairbairn's papers to be reviewed, "On the Nature and Aims of Psycho-Analytical Treatment" (1958) is devoted to the process by which psychoanalysis leads to psychological change and growth. Several of Fairbairn's ideas in this paper, including his challenge to the belief of therapist neutrality and the recognition that mutual influence is at the heart of change, are active concerns of relational psychoanalysis today, more than fifty years after this paper was written. As with all of Fairbairn's papers, it was intended as a rebuttal, initially to a paper by Thomas Szasz, "On the Theory of Psycho-Analytic Treatment" (1957). It is also a "classical" Fairbairnian paper in that it is poorly organized, filled with philosophical debates with other models, and in need of editing.

Fairbairn outlines his position regarding the mutative factors in the treatment process that affect patients, leaving no doubt that his model of psychoanalysis has taken a completely separate path, which in many ways is nearly the philosophical opposite of classical Freudian thought. His second paragraph reflects how completely different his model is from Freud's:

In brief, my theoretical position may be said to be characterized by four main conceptual formulations: viz. (a) a theory of dynamic psychical structure, (b) a theory to the effect that libidinal activity is inherently and primarily object seeking, (c) a resulting theory of libidinal development couched, not in terms of presumptive zonal dominance, but in terms of the quality of dependence, and (d) a theory of the personality couched exclusively in terms of internal object-relationships. The first two of these formulations taken in combination may be said to represent a substitute for two of Freud's basic theories—his classic libido theory and his final theory of instincts. The third formulation is offered as a revision of Abraham's version of Freud's theory of libidinal development. And finally, my object-relations theory of the personality is intended to replace Freud's description of the mental constitution in terms of the id, the ego and the superego. (374)

Fairbairn intended to dismantle Freud's model completely and replace it with his own view of human psychological functioning. I have noted that Fairbairn was isolated geographically and had little ability to promote his model, which, consequently, was ignored within the psychoanalytic world. His clear, wholesale replacement of Freud's theory with his own theory generated resistance within the tight confines of the analytic world because his model gave his classically trained analytic colleagues no choice but to accept one theory or the other, as the fundamental assumptions underlying the models are mutually exclusive, as Mitchell (2000) notes:

In a review of Fairbairn's book, *Psychoanalytic Studies of the Personality*, Winnicott and Kahn (1953) put the central issue bluntly. Fairbairn they suggest, asks us to choose between his theory and Freud's. They chose Freud's. Placing relationality at the center of motivation, development and psychodynamics, in the way Fairbairn did, was regarded as obliterating what was most central to Freudian psychoanalysis—its foundation in drive theory. (79–80)

Despite the existing background of rejection, this article was published in the *International Journal of Psychoanalysis*, which seems quite remarkable today given the hardening of the lines between different psychoanalytic schools of thought. Looking back, this paper is filled with modern concerns, not only about the therapist's neutrality but also about the patient's need for re-parenting, the hidden influence of the analytic situation on the creation of patient material, as well as the thoroughly modern concept of psychotherapy as a struggle between the patient and the therapist to create new meanings in each other.

Fairbairn also comments directly on the most striking gap in his writings, which was his lack of direct examples of how to apply his model in the clinical setting:

It may seem strange that hitherto I have made only the scantiest reference in print to the implications of my theoretical formulations for the practice of psycho-analytical treatment. From this fact it may be inferred that, even in my own opinion, my views are of merely theoretical interest and their implementation in practice would leave the technique of psycho-analysis unaffected. Such an inference would be quite unwarranted—the fact being that the practical implications of my views have seemed so far-reaching that they could only be put to the test gradually and with the greatest circumspection if premature or rash psychotherapeutic conclusions were to be avoided.   (374)

Fairbairn's intention to reveal these "practical implications" of his model is only partially (at best) fulfilled in this paper. His model implies fundamental changes to the process and technique of psychoanalysis based on his description of the unconscious, which had a completely different source and purpose compared with the unconscious Freud proposed, a different and more complex set of inner ego and object structures, and a fundamentally different motivation for all human behavior. Clearly, looking back at Fairbairn's model fifty years later, the field of psychoanalysis *could not begin to imagine* the full implications of his model.

Fairbairn outlined a two-step procedure inherent in the treatment process in which the analyst must first break through the "closed system" of the patient's inner world of transference projections and, when that is accomplished, must use the "real relationship" with the patient to restart the patient's thwarted emotional development. My view of psychotherapy using Fairbairn's model includes a "third step," which is to *foster and maximize the internalization of the ideal object therapist into the patient's inner world* as an alternative "new" attachment that will serve to reduce the attachments to the bad objects to which the patient has been clinging. This position violates Fairbairn's position that good objects are not internalized. However, he was ambivalent and wavering about the role of the good object, as illustrated by this comment from his 1943 paper: "The moral would seem to be that the appeal of a good object is an indispensable factor in promoting a dissolution of the cathexis of internalized bad objects, and that the significance of the transference situation is partly derived from this fact" (74).

Fairbairn never explained the process by which the cathexis (attachment) to the bad object is dissolved, but my view is that this comes about when the patient internalizes the therapist as a good object, allowing the patient to abandon his attachment to the bad objects. (I discuss this position in detail in chapter 4.)

The promise of Fairbairn's model was not fulfilled in this paper, despite his clear statement that his model offers a fundamentally new approach to psychoanalysis. In reality, Fairbairn apparently could not bring himself to deviate far enough from what he had already accepted as correct analytic practice to actualize his ideas in the clinical setting. Like all true pioneers, Fairbairn was limited by the theories of his time, and he himself could not imagine all the therapeutic changes that were initiated by his bold theory, as Mitchell (2000) noted:

> A second lesson is that it is probably a mistake to expect any great innovator to really grasp the revolution in which he or she is participating. Because they are standing in one worldview and struggling to give birth to another, they cannot possibly envision the full fruition of their efforts. . . . Fairbairn is a case in point. He too was a man of his time, operating with the conceptual and linguistic conventions that were the intellectual coin of his day. (103)

Fairbairn did alter the traditional framework of analysis by abandoning the couch and by fundamentally changing the rules regarding the interpersonal relationship between analyst and patient. However, he did not specify the mechanisms by which the "good-object" therapist helps the patient mature, nor did he specify how the process of breaking through the patient's "closed system" is to be accomplished. Despite his occasional citation in his past writing of the role of the good object, and his faulty assumption that good objects are never internalized, he now gave the patients' relationship with their *external* good object the primary mutative role in the treatment of psychological disorders:

> It becomes obvious, therefore, that from a therapeutic standpoint, interpretation is not enough; and it would appear to follow that the relationship existing between the patient and the analyst in the psychoanalytical situation serves purposes additional to that of providing a setting for the interpretation of transference phenomena. In terms of the object-relations theory of the personality, the disabilities from which the patient suffers represents the effects of unsatisfactory and unsatisfying object relationships experienced in early life and perpetuated in an exaggerated form in inner reality; and, if this view is correct, the actual relationship existing between the patient and the analyst as persons must be regarded as in itself constituting a therapeutic factor of prime importance. The existence of such a personal relationship in outer reality not only serves the function of providing a means of correcting the distorted relationships which prevail in inner reality and influence the reactions of the patient to outer objects but provides the patient an opportunity, denied to him in childhood, to undergo a process of emotional development in the setting of an actual relationship with a reliable and beneficent parental figure. (377)

We can only assume that Fairbairn felt sufficiently secure and indifferent to criticism from the larger world of psychoanalysis to read this paper in front of colleagues in the British Psycho-Analytical Society on June 18, 1958. There he proposed that the relationship with the (external) good object acts as a required catalyst to internal (structural) change as well as an object around which the patient can resume his stalled emotional development. The process by which the good external object impacts the inner world of bad objects remains a flaw in his theory, as he continued to insist that good objects were not internalized. He simply cites an unnamed transformative power that the good object has on the inner world. But his position on the process of change is entirely consistent with his earlier position that rejection of the child's needs leads to fixation (1940), and he sees the external good object as acting as a catalyst that allows the patient to restart and continue on his once thwarted path of development, a process now referred to as either re-parenting or the corrective emotional experience. None of this was acceptable to the world of classical psychoanalysis (then or now), and Fairbairn knew that these new concepts would not be well received.

Fairbairn was also one of the first to note the interactive context in which development takes place, a concept that classical analysts had long rejected, as noted by Mitchell (1997):

> The central, largely unacknowledged feature of psychoanalysis is its fundamentally *interactive* nature. Over and over across the history of psychoanalytic ideas, theorists and clinicians who have pointed out the importance of the analyst's participation in the analytic process, to the intersubjective nature of the analytic situation, have been isolated, as if with garlic cloves or fingers forming the sign of the cross. The debased form through which interaction is externalized and then detected in "fallen" analytic approaches is established through incantation of the dreaded words: "suggestion," "reassurance," "interpersonal," "environmentalist," and "corrective emotional experience." (3)

Fairbairn knew that he would be condemned, but this did not dissuade him from offering more new and equally unacceptable ideas, including his startling statement that he had abandoned the use of the couch in his analytic work. This change also implies that he had modified the rule of free association, the cornerstone of psychoanalysis. Free association requires that the patient remain visually isolated from the analyst so that his unconscious is free of interpersonal constraints, enabling him to report "deeper" material. This technique is completely unnecessary in Fairbairn's model, as his model assumes that the entire unconscious is "visible" to the analyst by observing the repeated interpersonal patterns that the patient reenacts both within the transference and in relationships in the outside world (the external transference). Fairbairn led up to this revision of the analytic method by noting what is now a contemporary issue in psychoanalysis—the exploration of the unique impact that the analyst and psychoanalytic procedures have on the patient's productions: "However, it must be remembered that, even within the field of pure science, the results obtained are partly conditioned by the method employed to obtain them; and therapeutic results are even more dependent upon the method used and may be limited by the limitation of the method" (378).

Fairbairn continues this line of thought: that the treatment situation influences the patient in ways that were not understood. He recognized that he could not remain an out-of-sight analyst because that would only increase the patient's feelings of abandonment, which he saw as the fundamental source of psychopathology. He assumed that the visual isolation from the therapist, advocated in classical analytic technique, would place the patient—who was there because of unsatisfactory and distorted object relationships in the first place—in a mildly traumatic situation and one that is therefore not "neutral" as classical theory maintained:

> But it seems to me beyond question that the couch technique has the effect of imposing quite arbitrarily upon the patient a positively traumatic situation calculated inevitably to reproduce such traumatic situations of childhood as that imposed by the infant who is left to cry in his pram alone, or that imposed upon the child who finds himself isolated in his cot during the primal scene. If this view is correct, then it follows that the couch technique is very far from being as "neutral" as it is supposed to be, and that the analyst, in employing this technique, is equally far from being "neutral." It also follows that the data provided by the patient who finds himself isolated upon the couch must be significantly influenced by the trauma thus arbitrarily imposed; and it is difficult to believe that the therapeutic result is not similarly influenced. (379)

Originally analytic neutrality was supposed to protect the patient's autonomy, based on the assumption that every individual is "full" of id-based psychic energy. Classical analytic theory did not accept the concept of the "needy," "empty," or "impoverished" self, a concept that Fairbairn had (inadvertently) introduced in 1944 with his concept of the central ego. Fairbairn boldly rejected the assumption that isolating the patient visually was increasing analytic "neutrality" in the light of his understandings of the trauma associated with early abandonment which actually made the use of the couch a form of interpersonal deprivation. Fairbairn also looked at the larger issue regarding the method employed by psychoanalysis, which he saw as producing unintended and unrecognized results. This was the beginning of his astute questioning of the actual process of analysis: specifically, that by isolating the patient, the analyst is unwittingly skewing the type of material the patient is producing. Today a key tenant of relationality is that the patient and analyst are in a relational matrix and each influences the other.

Also notable in Fairbairn's view of the couch tradition is how he reconceptualized the Freudian "primal scene" and gave it a new meaning in accordance with his model. The Fairbairnian infant is not consumed with rage at his father for the father's sexual possession of the mother, but, rather, he is discomforted because he is isolated from *both needed objects* and is distressed because his legitimate dependency needs are not being met. It is the isolation from needed objects that creates the trauma, not the inherited sexual drive toward the mother and resulting conflict with the castrating father. This is yet another example of Fairbairn's intellectual courage, which was to follow the path of his thought regardless of the consequences.

Fairbairn then criticizes the analytic community for its insularity and self-fulfilling view of change, which was that a change would be neither "deep" nor lasting if it occurred when the strict drive-based interpretative framework was violated:

> It is certainly in complete conformity with these instances when the attitude is adopted that if an analysed patient does not "get better" it is necessarily because he is unsuitable for psycho-analytical treatment, and that, if a patient "gets better" by means of some non-analytical form of psychotherapy, it is all very well, but it is not psycho-analysis. Such purism resolves itself into an apotheosis of the method at the expense of the aims which the method is intended to serve. (379)

Fairbairn's challenge of the concept of "deep" analysis, so valued by classical analysts of his day, came from his secure belief that he had offered a new and mutually exclusive view of the unconscious. Fairbairn's unconscious, which is created by dissociated memories of the child interacting with the intolerably rejecting or intolerably teasing bad object, is seen in all interpersonal relationships. Mitchell (1997), paraphrasing Greenberg (1991), notes the problems that have been created by different and competing notions of the unconscious, all living under the umbrella of the now expanded field of psychoanalysis:

> In Freud's day, it made sense to define psychoanalysis in connection with a particular set of beliefs about "deep" unconscious motivation, because there was consensus, more or less, about what was *in* the depths, what was *in* the unconscious. Today there is not. The Kleinian unconscious is quite different from the self-psychological unconscious, which is quite different from the unconscious of interpersonal psychoanalysis, which is quite different from various forms of object relational unconscious. (23)

Fairbairn goes on to define the reparative effects of psychotherapy in terms of his structural model. Given that trauma based on early rejection caused the initially intact ego to split into subegos and part-object, Fairbairn saw that the most important task of psychoanalysis was to reunite the two split-off egos and objects back into the realm of the central ego. He used the word "synthesis" to describe the reparative nature of his treatment model:

I consider that the term "analysis" as a description of psycho-analytical treatment is really a misnomer, and that *the chief aim of psycho-analytical treatment is to promote a maximum "synthesis" of the structures into which the original ego has been split, in the setting of a therapeutic relationship with the analyst.* The resistance on the part of the patient to the achievement of theses aims is, of course, colossal; for he has a vested interest in maintaining the early split of his internalized object, upon which, according to my theory, the split of his ego depends, and which represents a defense against the dilemma of ambivalence. (380)

The psychological function of the splitting defense is to avoid ambivalence, because the enormous disparity between the thousands of frustrating developmental events compared with the fewer loving and supportive events is intolerable to the individual. Thus splitting can continue into middle age, for the fantasies of the libidinal ego that the original objects were supportive are needed until the individual can rebuild her central ego with a good-object relationship. Conversely, splitting has to keep the antilibidinal ego's hatred- and fear-filled relationship to the rejecting object securely frozen in the unconscious so that it will not endanger the dependency relationship on the parental objects or with the ongoing fantasy of a good childhood. I believe that Fairbairn was excessively optimistic about the possibility of psychic repair in that he underestimated the possibility that the patient's antilibidinal ego's hostile transference toward the therapist as a rejecting object would be a major source of resistance. Instead, he assumed that resistance was largely based on fear of the release of bad objects. For example, he seldom ever mentioned in his (admittedly few) clinical examples that any of his patients accused him of being a rejecting object, but clinical experience suggests that the most common pattern of resistance is when the deeply split patient repeatedly attacks and rejects well-meaning good objects (including the analyst) and discards them the moment they disappoint him.

Fairbairn then proposed that the ultimate source of resistance was the individual's attempt to keep his inner world a closed system. His metaphor for amelioration of this situation was a physical one, like the breaching of a citadel by an external force:

Implied in these various manifestations of resistance on the part of the patient is a further defensive aim which I have now come to regard as *the greatest of all sources of resistance—viz. the maintenance of the patient's internal world as a closed system.* . . . The maintenance of such a closed system involves the perpetuation of the relationships prevailing between the various ego structures and their respective internal objects, as well as between one another; and since the nature of these relationships is the ultimate source of both symptoms and deviations of character, *it becomes still another aim of psycho-analytical treatment to effect breaches of the closed system, which constitutes the patient's inner world, and thus to make this world accessible to the influence of outer reality.* (380)

Fairbairn saw that attachment to internal objects was the only reality that the individual trusts and knows, regardless of the difficulty it caused her in the external world. Fairbairn's general position, that the internal world opposes external interference, has been noted by Mitchell (1997):

> The analyst arrives at a way of understanding the pattern through which the patient organizes her subjective world and perpetuates her central dynamic conflicts. The analyst delivers this understanding in the form of an interpretation. But the patient can hear the interpretation only as something else — it is slotted into the very categories the analyst is trying to get the patient to think about and understand. (45)

Specifically, the patient might "slot" the analyst's interpretation as a hostile comment coming from a rejecting object or, conversely, as an alluring promise coming from an exciting object. Fairbairn recognized that transference interpretations are frequently futile because transferences themselves are a result of closed system relating on the part of the patient. This is precisely Mitchell's point: that interpretations from the analyst are misunderstood as coming from objects similar to those in the inner world and are misinterpreted in a rigid and predictable manner. Interpretations, according to Fairbairn's structural theory, can work only when the patient is interacting with the analyst from his central ego and seeing the analyst as an ideal object. As we will see in chapter 4, the analyst's task is to fight his way out of the patient's powerful transferences and make himself known to the patient as the person he really is, a process that gradually erodes the patient's restructuring of reality. Interpretations made by the therapist when the patient is dominated by either his antilibidinal or his libidinal subego are often futile, because, according to Fairbairn, they are co-opted by the inner world:

> For such a change to accrue, it is necessary for the patient's relationship with the analyst to undergo a process of development in terms of which a relationship based on transference becomes replaced by a realistic relationship between two persons in the outside world. Such a process of development represents the disruption of the closed system within which the patient's symptoms have developed and are maintained, and which compromises his relationships with external objects. (381)

This passage is a precursor of the current concept of subjectivity, in which two individuals regard each other as separate, independent subjects. Fairbairn continued

his line of thought with his next example of the power of the internal world to distort the efforts and intentions of the therapist, the only example in which he reports
a patient viewing him as a rejecting object. An unnerving characteristic of this
clinical example is that the patient speaks as if she were reciting parts of Fairbairn's
model. One reason for this is that Fairbairn's patients were educated, upper-class
individuals who knew a great deal about his theory; Guntrip, for example, was both
his patient and an analytic theorist in his own right. In the following monologue,
Fairbairn was illustrating the contrast between his model's interpretation of a self-
destructive patient and Freud's death instinct by using a patient he called "Ivy." It
is a small extract from an extraordinary and lengthy passage revolving around this
patient's self-destructiveness based on an attachment to frustrating and overpower-
ing objects. Fairbairn's patients were from an era with far greater social controls
than exist today, which is probably why they seem more constrained from expressing even indirect hostility toward their objects. This is very unlike our current cul-
tural scene where even slavishly dependent young adults can, and do, strike out
indirectly at their bad objects:

> I can't wait to get my hands on myself to destroy myself. That is my life—a
> drawn out ecstasy of slowly killing myself. That is wicked; and it's the only wick-
> edness I can do. . . . The greater the frustration outside, the greater the ecstasies
> inside. I want to have no inhibition in bringing about my own destruction. . . .
> My aim is to sail as near to the wind as I can to killing myself. My aim is to carry
> out Mother's and Father's wishes. . . . I do it partly to please them, and partly
> to annoy them. . . . I feel my unconscious life is my true life; and it is a life
> of frustrated excitement, which I seem to regard as bliss. I feel I have a strong
> urge to destroy myself. . . . I want to see how near I can get to the edge of the
> cliff. There is a bit of me that keeps me alive; but my real purpose is directed
> at killing myself and frustration. I have trouble over you; for I don't want to tell
> you things. *If I have a relationship with you, it interferes with my death circuit.*
> You interfere with my neurosis and my desire to destroy myself. You are just
> a nuisance. . . . The worse I get the better I'm pleased, because that is what I
> want—which is a negation of all that is right. . . . I want to devote myself to
> working myself up to a state of need and not having it satisfied. This is involved
> in my desire for self-destruction. I must accept that I frustrate myself. I expect
> that originally I was frustrated from the outside: but now I impose frustration on
> myself; and that is to be my satisfaction. It is a terrible perversion.   (384)

This case perfectly illustrates Fairbairn's objections to Freud's death instinct, and
it also makes the point that the inner world is a closed system that resents intruders
from the outside. Note that this patient did perceive Fairbairn as a rejecting object,
because he was frustrating her desire to operate entirely in her inner world.

The experience of seeing extreme internal self-destructiveness was common in my practice and included a young woman whom I saw briefly when she was twenty years old. She informed me that she "was attracted to sleaze" and described how she acted out with indiscriminate sexuality and drug use, and was a target for aggression in her role as a "groupie" for a rock-and-roll band that treated her with absolute contempt. This attraction was a repetition of her antilibidinal ego's relationship to her crass and dysfunctional parents, who violated boundaries, behaved in antisocial ways, and were contemptuous of her. One of her antilibidinal "tests" of me as a therapist was to come into the session under the influence of drugs and see if I could detect her impaired status. When I failed to do so, I was seen as an expert who was unworthy of his position and therefore a rejecting object who failed just as her parents had failed. Some twenty-four years after she left my practice, I learned that she had committed suicide. She had continued to see, and reject, one therapist after another, as her inner structures turned good objects into bad ones via her transferences. As I thought about the intensity of her antilibidinal ego's relationship to her rejecting objects, my first uncensored response was to wonder why it had taken her so long to destroy herself.

Similarly Fairbairn's self-destructive patient, "Ivy," described her inner world as a closed system that constantly re-created the need, and the frustration, from her childhood. Her inner world also illustrates just how intense and meaningful the relationship between the rejecting object and the antilibidinal ego can be, with the rejecting object demanding destruction and the antilibidinal ego responding by almost destroying her, thus perpetuating the relationship between these two powerful structures. Here frustration allied with aggression provides the core of this attachment between the structures and becomes the source of all meaning in this patient's life.

Fairbairn concludes his paper with his view that the therapeutic relationship is a contest or struggle between the patient, who is trying to force the analyst into a preexisting pattern, and the analyst, who is resisting the patient's distortion of him and, simultaneously, trying to be seen as a real person in the external world. The following passage also demonstrates that Fairbairn realized that every interpretation was an attempt on the part of the analyst to break into the patients closed system:

However neutral a role the psycho-analyst may assign to himself therapeutically, he cannot escape from the necessity of becoming an interventionist if he is to be therapeutically effective and it must be recognized that every interpretation is really an intervention Thus in a sense, *psycho-analytical treatment resolves itself into a struggle on the part of the patient to press-gang his relationship with the analyst into the closed system of the inner world through the agency of transference, and a determination on the part of the analyst to effect a breach in this closed system and to provide conditions under which, in the setting of a therapeutic relationship, the patient may be induced to accept the* *open system of outer reality.* (385)

This struggle between the different worldviews of the patient and therapist is one of the ways that relational psychoanalysis now sees the therapeutic endeavor. The complex entanglement of two individuals who are both engaged in an interpersonal struggle to effect change in each other was completely foreign to psychoanalysis in 1958, when it was assumed that the analyst was a neutral force completely aloof and separate from the patient. The analyst was assumed to be a cool observer, not an emotionally enmeshed individual fighting to impress his view of reality on a patient who was distorting every word and seeing the analyst as identical to the ancient internalized objects in his inner world.

The following observation by Mitchell (1997) illustrates a modern view of Fairbairn's position regarding the patient's struggle to experience the analyst as part of his inner world and, conversely, the analyst's struggle to penetrate the inner world and be seen as a real object:

> It is often very difficult for patients to let their analysts know that they are beginning to feel that the analyst, even in offering interpretations, is only the latest in a long line of those from whom they have suffered seduction, betrayal, abandonment, torture, pathetic disappointment. It is also very difficult for the analyst to pick up and hear the patient's hints in these directions, because the analyst wants so much to feel that the analysis is going well and that interpretations are truly analytic events rather than reenactments of chronic disasters. . . . Generally speaking, the analyst, despite his best intentions, is likely to become entangled in the same web he is trying to explore. . . . The analyst making an interpretation of the patient's tendency to transform all encounters into battles is likely to be feeling embattled himself and trying to use interpretation as a potent weapon in his arsenal. . . . Thus, the analyst's experience is likely to be infused with the very same affects, dynamics and conflicts he is trying to help the patient understand. (47)

Writing thirty-nine years after Fairbairn's "press-gang" passage was written, Mitchell illustrates exactly what Fairbairn was talking about long ago. In structural terms, the patient's antilibidinal ego misinterprets the analyst's best efforts and forces him into the reciprocal relational position: that of the rejecting object. Fairbairn recognized that analyst and patient were in a relationship based on mutual influence, and that the outcome of this struggle would determine the success or failure of the therapeutic enterprise.

A footnote in the paper notes that the paper was read by Fairbairn on June 18, 1958, to the British Psycho-Analytical Society. This strikes me as a supreme act of intellectual courage, as Fairbairn knew just how far outside the acceptable "enve-lope" his model was compared with the positions of everyone else in the room. Sutherland (1989), Fairbairn's biographer and an analyst himself, was present when Fairbairn read his paper to his colleagues, and he described the reaction of the audience:

> This paper had a mixed reception. Discussion brought out the difficulties of defining what Fairbairn meant by the analyst making a good personal relation-ship. He had described in the paper that his main modification to the treatment situation was to do away with the couch and sit so the patient could see him if he chose to look. Fairbairn had come to believe that the couch isolated the patient in the way a crying child is left alone or is isolated in his cot during the primal scene. . . . There was an impression gained that he was changing the method to present himself as a good object, and Mrs. Klein was heard to remark that he was no longer doing analysis, or words to that effect.   (156)

These objections are not surprising and, in fact, were to be expected. His audience immediately saw a problem with Fairbairn's abandonment of the couch, as it changed the relationship between analyst and patient by reducing the analyst's assumed neu-trality. His reformulation of his role of "good object" was noted as well.

This paper illustrates just how prescient Fairbairn's thinking was and how he anticipated many of the trends that are currently issues in psychoanalysis, includ-ing the role of the treatment parameters that covertly influence the patient's mate-rial, the hidden impact of the analyst's behavior on the patient, the investigation into the fundamental process of psychoanalysis, and the concept of the psycho-analytic process as one that involves a struggle between patient and analyst as each tries to influence the other. All these issues are now seen by many as the very heart of the analytic enterprise.

CHAPTER 3

THE DYNAMIC RELATIONSHIPS BETWEEN
THE PATHOLOGICAL EGO STRUCTURES

THIS CHAPTER FOCUSES ON Fairbairn's four pathological self and object structures, with an emphasis on understanding patient productions during the clinical interview. When working with patients suffering from severe splits in their ego structures, it is critical to know which subego or internalized object is dominant. The discussion begins with a description of each ego structure and then the relationship of each to its object partner. This is followed by an examination of the four fundamental relational patterns of transference that can emerge between patient and therapist, along with techniques that can be used to soften the patient's rigid adherence to her inner structures. The chapter continues with a lengthy discussion of the reemergence of dissociated material from the antilibidinal ego, and with therapeutic strategies that foster its integration into the central ego. Finally, the negative therapeutic reaction is examined in terms of Fairbairn's inner structures.

The four internal ego structures are not composed of hundreds of separate actual interpersonal events that are sequentially dissociated and held in the unconscious. Rather, they are complex views of the object over time that are melded together and modified by the child's fantasies and fears that were appropriate to the age at which the dissociation took place:

> It is important however to keep in mind that these constellations do not represent a simple internalization of an actual experience with an external person. They are multilayered representations built up at different levels of development over the years as the growing person takes in the experience of relationships as modified by his own fantasies and by the limited ability to understand that which was present during the particular stage of development at the time of each experience. (Scharff 1989:401)

Thus each of the four structures is complex; each is a limited sub-personality with a distinct view of the world as well as the ability to plan and make decisions, and each can become the dominant ego directing the patient's life.

THE ANTILIBIDINAL EGO

Although my effort here is to focus on the antilibidinal ego, it is impossible to speak of one structure without referring to the others, as seen in chapter 2. It may seem difficult at first for the clinician to differentiate the antilibidinal ego from the rejecting object. However, they are vastly different and play distinct roles in the interior world, as well as in the transference relationship. The fundamental difference between these two structures is that the rejecting object attacks, demeans, and humiliates the antilibidinal ego from a position of power, and its rejection can be absolute. The antilibidinal ego is the self of the developing child that relates exclusively to the rejecting object, and its response to these attacks are self-hate, shame, and sarcasm toward those in power, which often manifests later in life as a self-righteous condemnation of those who have failed in their assigned role (as parent, leader, or authority). In some cases, this amounts to "whining" and chronic complaining about the failures of their objects, whereas in other patients it can take the form of an interpersonal revenge-based "crusade" against the specific objects or a displaced group of objects, one that takes on the emotionality of a religious war. I turn now to an example from Fairbairn's 1954 paper on hysteria, cited previously (Celani 2001), that clearly demonstrates that Fairbairn saw patients with exactly the same type of relationship between the antilibidinal ego and the rejecting object as we see in our patients today. The exceptional aspect about this passage is that the patient is actually thought to be the analyst Harry Guntrip, whom, as noted, Fairbairn treated in analysis:

> In his inner world he was constantly engaged in an argument with his mother over his right to possess a penis and to use it as he wished—a right which, in the light of his mother's reactions (to which reference has already been made), he felt that she denied to him. This imagined argument with his mother assumed the essential form of an attempt on his part to convert her to a "belief in penises," in place of the hatred of penises which he attributed to her (not without reason). More specifically, he sought to persuade her to accept his own penis, and to give him permission to use it: for, in his bondage to her, he felt that he did not dare to use his penis without her permission—except in secret masturbation, about which he felt extremely guilty. (Fairbairn 1954:34)

This is a classic example of a relationship characterized by "whining" and complaining between the child's antilibidinal ego and the rejecting aspect of the maternal object. Here the antilibidinal ego is engaged in a lobbying effort to reform the position taken by the all-powerful and implacable rejecting object. Once the relationship between the antilibidinal ego and the rejecting object is internalized, neither structure is able to assimilate information from the external world that might modify its position. I have noted earlier that Fairbairn *did not see* the hostile and antagonistic relationship between the antilibidinal ego and the rejecting object. He mistook the relationship between the antilibidinal ego and the rejecting object as a cooperative one, in which the antilibidinal ego does the bidding of the rejecting object, yet this example from his own work illustrates just the opposite. Here the patient's antilibidinal ego is pleading and lobbying for permission and understanding of his legitimate needs from his insensitive parental object. The flaws in Fairbairn's original understanding of the dynamics between the internal structures blinded him to the therapeutic possibilities of working to counteract the self-defeating and rigid relationship between these structures.

Odgen (1990) has also written of the antagonism between the antilibidinal ego and the rejecting object. He noted that the struggle between theses structures is never won, as they fight each other to an eternal "draw":

> The suborganization identified with the object is under constant pressure from the self component of the relationship to be transformed into a good object. Such a transformation is strenuously resisted by the object component, because this type of massive shift in identity would be experienced as an annihilation of an aspect of the ego. The internal object relationship is vigorously defended from two directions: The self-component is unwilling to risk annihilation resulting from absence of object relatedness and instead strives to change the bad object into a good one; at the same time, the object component fends off annihilation that would result from being transformed into a new entity (the good object). (157–158)

Ironically, Odgen is a Kleinian and Winicottian, and yet he is one of the few writers in the field who has described the struggle between these antagonistic components in Fairbairn's structural model. The powerful, yet often pathetic and neglectful, parental object, who has been internalized as the rejecting object, maintains its enormous status in the inner world because the child's infantile antilibidinal ego needs the rejecting object to become a good object and act as the catalyst for its development. This is a task in which the rejecting object steadfastly refuses to participate. The child's antilibidinal ego's total dependence on the rejecting object keeps it forever responding to this antagonistic inner structure, which never loses its potency. In some patients, the antilibidinal ego gives up trying to reform the bad object and switches to a strategy of exposing the bad object parent to the public. Like the snake and the mongoose, these two structures simply cannot leave each other alone.

One of the most striking characteristics of the antilibidinal ego is its self-righteous desire for revenge and its demand for reparation for the hurts it has suffered. I am not exaggerating when I say that some borderline individuals have spent most of their lives demanding, in various impotent and self-defeating ways, that their original parental objects are somehow "charged" with violations of the parent–child contract. Ogden (1990), who colorfully describes the antilibidinal ego as the "wronged and spoiling self," emphasizes the actions of the antilibidinal ego in the inner world; however, when this subego becomes the dominant ego, it often attempts to expose the parental object's badness in the external world as well: "The second category of bond to a bad internal object is the tie of the wronged and spoiling self to the unloving, rejecting object. This often takes the form of a crusade to expose the unfairness of, coldness of, or other forms of wrongdoing on the part of the internal object" (156).

The antilibidinal ego has a sense of purpose and direction, and consequently its antagonistic relationship to the internalized rejecting object is easily projected onto objects in external reality. As we will see, the intensity of the relationship between the part-self and part-object structure causes the antilibidinal ego to feel that it is engaged in a self-righteous mission, which forecloses the intrusion of external objects into this meaningful and intensely emotional internal world. Kopp (1978), an existential psychologist whom I have previously quoted (Celani 2005), illustrates this aspect of the antilibidinal ego:

> Imagining themselves to be the heroes or heroines of as yet uncompleted fairy tales, such people simply cannot (will not) believe that the villains who have disappointed them will go unpunished, or that they themselves will remain blameless yet uncompensated victims. Surely there must be someone who will avenge them, and take good care of them, someone who will right the family wrongs and reward the good children. (38)

Perfectly captured here is the tone of one of the most common attitudes of the antilibidinal ego. It waits for an opportunity for revenge and validation at the hands of a higher authority—a demand that is never answered. Mainstream psychoanalysis has also looked at the issue of revenge, as Beattie (2005) notes:

> Revenge and vengeful fantasies may occur in many forms and on many levels, both conscious and unconscious, and may be expressed as readily through masochistic reaction formation as through overtly sadistic behavior. They have deep roots in early conflicts, traumas and humiliations at the hands of parents, siblings and others. They need not, however, imply a primitive mode of object relatedness, for the vengeful person may demonstrate both a capacity for delay and self-control, an empathic attunement to the victim's feelings and motivations. (513)

The desire for revenge is one of the most common aspects of the antilibidinal ego, and, as mentioned, it gives purpose and meaning to this functional part-self. Indeed, the antilibidinal ego can overpower the central ego precisely because it has a strongly held mission and well-developed strategies, whereas, in comparison, the lost and depleted central ego has had too few interactions with the idealized aspect of the parent to give it direction or purpose.

I have dealt with borderline individuals whose antilibidinal ego structures became so powerful that the patient left treatment in favor of a hoped-for victory over the displaced rejecting object. Case 3.1 demonstrates the power of external objects to provoke transference reactions that externalize the patient's internal relational patterns. I was not able to stop this particular patient from terminating treatment because his antilibidinal ego had an attachment to, and fascination with, a new version of his original rejecting object. This attachment, operating through the emotions of hate and revenge, became a greater force than the attachment between his central ego and me as an ideal object. In this example, the upsurge in antilibidinal acting out occurred because of a change in management in the assembly plant where the patient, Mr. Hayes, was employed.

CASE 3.1

Mr. Hayes was raised by a stern and critical father who often commented to visitors and relatives that his son would never amount to anything. As a young man, Mr. Hayes's insecurity prevented him from obtaining appropriate employment, and he drifted from one menial job to another. Ultimately, he found a job at an electronics assembly plant that was more appropriate than prior jobs. He became exceedingly dependent on his supervisor and was hypersensitive to criticism of his work. If he was criticized, he would go into an antilibidinal-ego state dominated by feelings of being deeply wounded and would retaliate by passively resisting instructions. After one year of therapy, he had made good progress in terms of starting his own part-time business and reducing his passive-aggressive behaviors at the job. It appeared that his dependent hostility toward the displaced bad objects was in good control. At this juncture, the plant was sold and a new management team took over and began an aggressive program of enforcing trivial work rules. His new supervisor repeatedly cited him for minor infractions, and Mr. Hayes called on the union to defend his positions, which they did. His antilibidinal ego rejoiced at the support from the union, and all his historical relational grievances were projected onto the "all-bad" management. He began plotting endless revenge scenarios and filed complaint after complaint with the union regarding management's abuse of him. He spent hours dissecting the established work manual and began calling various supervisors in the middle of the night regarding details of the work rules. I attempted to reduce this spiral of acting out via interpretations regarding the similarities between his original bad object and the unfair management, but these were ignored. As Mr. Hayes became increasingly caught up in this clash with his new bad objects, treatment became less and less important to him and he eventually left.

Mr. Hayes's antilibidinal ego was motivated by hate and the desire to vanquish his frustrating objects. His investment in doing so was amplified by the support from the union to which he belonged, and it appeared that he was willing to destroy himself, if necessary, in order to inflict injury on the hated objects. I noted earlier that Fairbairn (1944:117) recognized that the dependent, abused child was reluctant to give up his hate toward the bad objects. The rage stored in the antilibidinal ego toward the bad objects, and the individuals absolute dedication to destroying them at any cost, makes dealing with this form of acting out very difficult.

Occasionally, an antilibidinal-dominated patient will try to induce the therapist to take up his cause and actively participate in the effort to defeat the external rejecting objects. The therapist will feel the intense hostility (and the possibility that the patient will split him into a rejecting object) if he or she does not actively participate in the patient's revenge scenario (more on this in chapter 4). The only answer at these tense junctures is to reiterate the methodology and parameters of therapy and face the consequences of the patient's anger.

The material contained in the antilibidinal ego is generally the therapist's major ally in the interior world, as it holds the dissociated memories (though symbolized and exaggerated) of actual events in the individual's developmental history. Material from the patient's antilibidinal ego is on display during the initial sessions, although, paradoxically, the patient is actually engaged in a libidinal-ego–exciting-object relationship with the therapist. In other words, the *material* that the patient relates to the therapist about his maltreatment by others is from the antilibidinal ego, but *it is relayed through the patient's libidinal ego* because the patient is hoping for support, sympathy, love, and compensation from the exciting object, the therapist. The real antilibidinal pain, rage, and humiliating memories are still dissociated because they remain too intolerable to accept, although, with luck, small bits will emerge as the narrative develops. The patient's recounting of antilibidinal-based material acts as the entrée into the patient's interior world, and it is best for the therapist to give the patient as much time as necessary to delineate all the various aspects of the relationship of his antilibidinal self with the frustrating/exciting object. By simply listening attentively, the patient will experience the therapist's attention as supportive of the patient's personal reality and worldview. This will further stimulate the libidinal ego's hope that love and compensation are just around the corner. Keep in mind, however, that the libidinal ego is infantile, naïve, and unrealistic, and seeks compensation for all the hurts it has experienced from a higher power, which appears to be embodied in the "savior" therapist. Conversely, other patients may start out dominated by pure libidinal ego material and present an unrealistic — often near-delusional — view of the goodness of their objects, which also requires patience on the part of the therapist.

Remarkable is that the antilibidinal ego is known to writers outside the closed world of psychoanalytic theory, as evidenced by Katherine Ann Porter in her essay "The Necessary Enemy" (1948), which I cite in a previous volume (Celani 2005).

Even though she knew nothing about psychoanalysis and suffered from many characterological problems herself, Porter (1948) was able to identify most of the important facets of this structure: that it contains hostility toward ostensibly loved objects, that it remains in the unconscious most of the time, and, when it does become conscious, it causes the individual great distress:

> She is a frank, charming, fresh-hearted young woman who married for love. She and her husband are one of those gay, good looking young pairs who orna- ment the modern scene rather more in profusion perhaps than ever before in our history. They intend in all good faith to spend their lives together, to have children and to do well by them and each other — to be happy, in fact, which for them is the whole point of their marriage. . . . But after three years of marriage this very contemporary young woman finds herself facing the old- est and ugliest dilemma of marriage. She is dismayed, horrified, full of guilt and foreboding because she is finding out little by little that she is capable of hating her husband, whom she loves faithfully. She can hate him at times as fiercely and mysteriously, indeed in terribly much the same way, as often she hated her parents, her brothers and sisters, whom she loves, when she was a child. Even then it had seemed to her a kind of black treacherousness in her, her private wickedness that, just the same, gave her her own private life. That was one thing her parents never knew about her, never seemed to suspect. For it was never given a name. (182–183)

Porter recognized that the origin of this structure is in childhood and that the experience of hating an object can be transferred from one intimate relationship to the next. She also understood that most individuals try to hide from or otherwise deny the existence of this structure and that it paradoxically contains a self-affirm- ing kernel of truth. The antilibidinal ego, in other words, knows the truth about past angry and rejecting relational events within the family, and these mostly hid- den perceptions provide the individual with an authentic perspective. Unfortu- nately, these truths are encountered in frightening, highly symbolized, and disrup- tive ways that tend to make them less credible to the individual. The task of the therapist is to help the patient accept the perceptions of this structure and not allow them to slip the memory back into the unconscious. In short, it must be integrated into the central ego, thus reducing the potency of the hateful attachment between the antilibidinal ego and the rejecting object.

THE INTERNALIZED REJECTING OBJECT

The internalized rejecting object is a dynamic structure that is a condensation of the actual rejecting aspects of the parental object along with the child's fantasies and fears. The patient's internalized rejecting object poses a more difficult prob-lem for the therapist, and this structure is generally not an ally. As noted earlier, a very strong hostile attachment exists between the antilibidinal ego and its associ-ated rejecting object. This attachment comes from the characterological patient's desperate need for objects of any type in the inner world to counteract inner empti-ness. This hate-filled, acrimonious attachment is also a consequence of the lack of good-object alternatives in the child's developmental history. There simply were no other objects to which the child could become attached. The patient's identifi-cation with attitudes and behaviors identical to those of the rejecting object—that is, when they enact the role of the rejecting object with an "other" in the external world—is the source of the often heard observation that the patient has become a clone of the once vilified parental objects.

When relating to the therapist from the position of the rejecting object, the patient can, and will, demean, ignore, and attack the therapist with furious inten-sity. Patients can do this because their identification with this part of the object allows them to assume (as their parental objects once did) that there are no conse-quences attached to their behavior. The prototype for this relational configuration is the child in relationship to a parent who is uninhibited about being aggressive toward, or neglecting, his or her child. The rejecting object can attack in an abso-lute, apodictic style, defining the child as bad, deficient, or unworthy. The patient, who identifies with the internalized rejecting object, will act the same way toward the therapist.

To simplify a great deal, the opinion of the rejecting object regarding the "quali-ties" of his child is the single greatest source of psychopathology. The "opinion" of the parent is conveyed to the child not only verbally, but through neglect, indiffer-ence, labeling, and, in extreme cases, through actual physical or sexual assaults. To reverse the sequence, the child would not have a hurt, rejected, angry antilibidinal ego if he was originally able to block out, ignore, or somehow rebuff the rejecting object, a task that is simply impossible. It is the emotional intensity and overwhelm-ing importance of early relational events that create the antilibidinal ego's powerful defensive responses, which coalesce into an emotionally reactive and hypersensi-tive part of the personality. The relationship between the humiliated and enraged antilibidinal ego and the attacking accusations of the rejecting object is the very relational "meat" of the inner world. Once this relationship is internalized, the patient can (and will on those occasions when the opportunity arises) play out the role of the rejecting object in the therapy dyad. When the patient adopts the role of the rejecting object, the therapist will be pressured into the role once occupied by the patient's antilibidinal ego.

The internalized rejecting object does present the therapist with a small oppor-tunity to lessen its negative influence via the simple expedient of personifying the structure as an alien and ego-distonic artifact from the patient's history. The effect of this technique is small, simply because the patient cannot expel a bad object from the inner world without replacing it with a strong central ego attachment to the ideal object therapist. Nonetheless, this technique does help to foster the patient's differentiation from his internal objects. The therapist must first openly acknowledge the individual's destructiveness toward himself and others, and the patient must be able to tolerate this assessment, which is a therapeutic achievement in itself. Next the therapist must connect the patient's identification with the rejecting object to the patient's developmental history. For example, the patient, cited previously, who covertly attacked many of his father's prized possessions was publicly disowned by his father repeatedly. As noted, he was forced to do excessively difficult or demeaning tasks while the other children in the family were indulged. This patient's father also played sadistic tricks on him while he was struggling to do these tasks. Not surprisingly, this patient was unmerciful in his self-criticism and projected much hostility onto others, as when he identified with his rejecting object and found a vulnerable target. Every time the patient identified with the rejecting object and discharged hostility toward external objects, I would exclaim, "It's wonderful to have old George [the patient's deceased father] around." This technique does not deny the patient's hostility, but it connects the immediate events with the patient's internal objects and past history. One result of this technique is to teach the individual to have compassion for himself. It demonstrates to the patient that he has a reason for his anger and hostility, that it is not his personal "badness" but rather an unconscious identification with the internalized rejecting object from which he could not flee. Over time, this technique of personifying the rejecting object can allow a more complex and compassionate view of the patient's self to emerge. This technique also allows the therapist to talk about an internal object that is being singled out, not as an inherent part of the patient's self but rather as a toxic and unwelcome part of the self.

THE LIBIDINAL EGO

The libidinal ego, in contrast to the antilibidinal ego, is the part-self that creates the most obvious havoc in the lives of many patients, particularly borderlines. The libidinal ego develops in relation to one of Fairbairn's most potent concepts, the "exciting object," which consists of memories (and fantasies) of the parent based on the few times when she actually indulged the child or extravagantly promised to love the child if only the child would behave in some prescribed manner. This subego believes that it will be the recipient of unlimited love and appreciation from the exciting object, and this compensatory fantasy keeps it stubbornly attached to the object. The libidinal ego is an important defensive structure because it contains the hope and promise of love that keeps borderline individuals and others with severe character disorders from collapsing into abandonment depressions. Almost any disappointment (stored in the split-off antilibidinal ego) can be forgotten and instantaneously replaced by a maddeningly naïve hope that the disastrous parent will finally come through with the love he seems to promise. When caught in the thrall of this ego state, the borderline individual will behave as if the parent had always been a benevolent, loving object. The unrealistic hope and trust in the exciting part of the bad object then leads the person to make decisions that have absolutely no relation to reality and invariably are detrimental to the individual's own best interests. These include wanting to visit the parents while ignoring all the pain of the past or purchasing expensive gifts for the parental objects who have abandoned or abused the patient in the past. The characterological patient's expectations of love appear absolutely absurd to the therapist, who has all the information from the patient's (mostly dissociated) antilibidinal ego at his disposal. As an example of how far from reality the libidinal ego can lead a patient, here I describe my work with a middle-aged client raised in England by a rejecting tyrannical father and a depressed, servile mother. The patient began to receive frequent harassing and bizarre phone calls in the middle of the night. During these calls, the caller would not speak but would breathe audibly into the phone, and then hang up after the patient asked who was calling. Her father (who continued to live in England) had always favored her brothers, and now that he was in his late seventies he never bothered to call or write her at all. My patient's libidinal ego was derepressed by these phone calls, and she reported that she thought the calls were from her father. Her deprived libidinal ego transformed the reality of middle-of-the-night phone harassment into "check-up" calls from her exciting-object father, who her libidinal ego assumed was displaying a distorted sense of concern for her. This desperate, central ego deficient patient behaved irrationally because the storehouse of information lodged in her antilibidinal ego, which would protect a normal integrated individual from unrealistic hopes, was split off and unavailable while she was dominated by her libidinal ego.

It is almost impossible to describe the potency of the libidinal ego when it takes over the borderline patient's functioning. There is almost nothing the therapist can do to dissuade borderline or other characterological patients from carrying out their naïve and self-destructive plans during the first months, or even years, of therapy. The more the therapist reminds the patient of past (now split-off) disappointments that came from the very same parent (or new displaced object), the more rigid and defensive the patient becomes. When the libidinal ego takes over the personality, the therapist is faced with the raw power of unmet childhood needs that demand gratification, and the desperate dependency on the illusory exciting object that has been created out of sheer necessity. When any given patient is dominated by the libidinal ego and is actively in the process of acting out the fantasy that the exciting object will actually be gratifying, the therapist is placed in one of the most taxing and frustrating positions in all of psychotherapy. The therapist, who has an investment in the patient's differentiation from the bad objects, must sit quietly while the patient goes on a self-destructive binge, in pursuit of the exciting object that is sure to abuse or disappoint the patient once again. The allure of the exciting object is so powerful, especially with the truly deprived, that the therapist cannot even *begin* to warn the patient from acting out her fantasies. It is futile and unproductive to confront the patient with information that will be forcibly dissociated, as the patient can be in a nearly delusional state during the pursuit of the chimera of the exciting object. The therapist's only tactic is to contain his own mounting frustration and wait for the inevitable shift to the antilibidinal ego when the frustrating side of the bad object once again fails the patient. This power of the libidinal ego is well illustrated by the case of Janet, whom I have described previously (Celani 1993).

CASE 3.2

Janet was in the custody of the state and came for therapy at eighteen years of age. She reported a life of severe abandonment and abuse. She had been expelled from her home by her mother, who had reported her to the police for drug use, and was consequently living in a "supervised" apartment. In truth, social services provided little supervision, and Janet, along with three other youths from similar backgrounds who lived in the same building, acted out in terms of random sexuality, drug and alcohol abuse, and shoplifting. Exploration of her history revealed physical abuse and extreme forms of control exercised by her mother. For instance, after Janet was expelled from her home, her mother required that she return on holidays so that the family's relatives would not know that she had been forced out. In order to ensure that her daughter would appear at these gatherings, her mother would hold her valued possessions as hostages. At different times, Janet returned home only to find her prized dress cut into thin strips and hung on the shrubbery or the destroyed remnants of the furniture from her room displayed on the front lawn. The therapist was astonished at the treatment she had received at the hands of her sadistic mother and unknowingly overly supported her antilibidinal ego's position before her central ego had developed enough strength to separate from her needed object. The therapist's validation and overt support of Janet's struggle against her bad object resulted in an abandonment panic, a consequence of premature awareness by her central ego of her mother's extreme hostility. This awareness challenged her continuing attachment to her mother and triggered an unwelcome split from her antilibidinal ego into her libidinal-ego view of her mother as a way of rescuing the relationship with her still needed object. Janet came for her sixth session, dressed uncharacteristically in conservative clothing, and announced that she was moving back home. The therapist reminded her of her past (antilibidinal) views of her mother as an abusive, paranoid near-demon, but Janet dismissed these memories off-hand. She reported that she was angry at her mother last week and now felt that "blood was thicker than water." The inexperienced therapist became increasingly agitated and insisted on reminding her of her past statements about her mother and strongly suggested that she remain separate from her mother, to the point of getting into a heated debate. Janet left the session early, enraged at the therapist for contradicting her libidinal-ego view of her mother.

Case 3.2 demonstrates the power of the libidinal ego to motivate the patient, and the inability of an incompletely internalized therapist to have an impact on libidinally motivated behavior. An experienced therapist would not have overly supported antilibidinal perceptions so early in the treatment process, which inadvertently promised Janet that the therapist would immediately and completely fill the enormous emotional gap left by the abandoning object. At some point, outside the consulting room, her central ego caught a glimpse of the "badness" of her object, which was still intolerable to her consciousness. The therapist had not been internalized as an alternative object, so the patient faced an abandonment panic that caused her to defensively split back into her libidinal ego's view of her mother. I have learned to tolerate, and actually embrace, my patients' libidinal ego's fantasies of the exciting object because this structure acts as an "emergency net" that keeps the borderline patient from emotional collapse, particularly during the first months, or even years, of therapy.

THE EXCITING OBJECT

Much has already been said about the exciting object, an internal structure that originally derived its power from the deprived child's long-term lack of emotional support by the object. The developing child is informed by a thousand events that his or her mother is the one object in the world that is supposed to love and cherish her child. The deprived child experiences the object as an exciting object because of the pressure from its pressing developmental needs that have been unmet and ignored. As time passes for the child of a rejecting object mother, the necessity for the hope of love in the future grows exponentially larger. It is this self-generated promise of future support and love that ultimately sustains many emotionally abandoned children, since the ratio of emotional support to frustration is overwhelmingly skewed toward rejection in their developmental histories. In the past, some readers of Fairbairn have assumed that "exciting objects" were parents who over-stimulated their children, a completely errant understanding of the model. The "excitement" inherent in the exciting object comes from the hope that the enormous reservoir of extreme need in the child (and later in the adult) will be met by love and support from the object. In adulthood, it is not rejection that is devastating to the borderline individual but *the loss of hope*—the loss of the exciting aspect of the bad object, as described powerfully by Armstrong-Perlman (1991), who observed patients who had suffered psychological collapse and required in-patient treatment: "The loss of the relationship, or rather the hope of a relationship, cannot be borne. . . . The need is compulsive and the fantasy of loss is experienced as potentially catastrophic, either leading to the disintegration of the self, or a fear of a reclusive emptiness to which any state of connectedness, no matter how infused with suffering is preferable" (345).

Thus the exciting aspect of the bad object is the most difficult of all the inner structures for the therapist to come to terms with. It is obviously counterproductive to insist that the patient give up hope in her exciting object, as this will only plunge the patient into an abandonment crisis. I often begin a discussion of this subject with patients by pointing out their history of rejection followed by occasional gratification from their parents and linking this to their relationship with new, displaced objects. However, as mentioned, the only way patients can finally let go of the fantasy that their exciting object contains love is for them to develop a powerful central ego–ideal object relationship with the therapist or analyst that allows for a gradual integration of the exciting/rejecting object back into the realm of the central ego, a process discussed in chapter 4.

The therapist must understand and respect the power of, and need for, fantasy regarding the exciting object and use a delicate touch when dealing with this sensitive and essential inner structure. Knowledge of the structures and how they operate is the therapist's greatest ally when working with characterological patients. Most borderline patients, for instance, are extremely predictable and easier to work with once the therapist knows the content and strength of these structures. However, a blunt and uninformed approach, as illustrated in Janet's case, can turn any one of the structures into a potent enemy.

TRANSFERENCE PARADIGMS

Fairbairn's structural theory offers four possible pathological transference patterns that emerge directly from his theory. In this discussion, I exclude the relationship between the patient's central ego and the ideal-object therapist, as this is discussed in chapter 4. Bollas (1998) cites Heimann regarding the importance of knowing who is speaking to whom in the therapeutic dyad: "When we think of the figure of authority in these analyses, we may turn around Paula Heimann's (1956) question about the patient's transference—who is speaking to whom and why now—and ask of the analyst, 'Who is the speaker, and to whom is he speaking, and why?' This is not an easy question to answer, and one must avoid the temptation to oversimplify" (12).

Fairbairn's model provides the analyst or therapist a structural theory that helps answer this question in a way that is not a simplification and, more important, reveals the contents and relational patterns within the structural components that make up the patient's personality. When I say "contents" of the structures, I mean the patient's unique relational patterns within his transference that indicates the types of rejection he was exposed to in his development. These individualized patterns are encoded in the patient's antilibidinal ego's relationship with the rejecting object. This can include, among a host of other behaviors, mockery, silence, contempt, criticism, indifference, unresponsiveness, and dismissiveness. The unfolding of the patient's transferences offers the analyst a good facsimile of the behaviors that caused the patient to use the splitting defense in the first place.

Negative transference, within Fairbairn's metapsychology, is the consequence of the patient seeing the therapist through the prism of her antilibidinal ego, which pressures the therapist into the rejecting object role, or, conversely, the patient identifying with the rejecting object role and seeing the therapist as weak and hapless. The patient "press-gangs" (Fairbairn 1958) the therapist into becoming the "relational partner" to the structure that is dominant in the patient's inner world. Conversely, unrealistically positive transferences, which are fragile and can be dissociated the moment frustration arises, emerge out of the two positive structures. When the patient views the therapist from the perspective of the libidinal ego, she will expect to experience the joy of a reunion with the exciting object. The reciprocal relationship is also possible when the patient identifies with the role of the exciting object and tempts the therapist with the promise of success if he is able to cure so important and complex a patient as she claims to be, thus inviting the therapist into the role of the libidinal ego.

TRANSFERENCE: PROJECTION OF THE PATIENT'S FRAGILE EGO ONTO THE THERAPIST

The first transference pattern I discuss is the most global and is not a projection of one of the internal structures (libidinal or antilibidinal subegos or the parts of the patient's ego that are identified with objects) onto the therapist but the projection of the patient's *entire* damaged ego structure onto the therapist. Technically, this projection lies outside Fairbairn's structural theory, but it is consonant with the structural model in that internal states are projected onto external objects. When this type of global transference grips the patient, he believes that he is faced with a therapist who has the identical ego structure as he has—a frightening proposition indeed! During these critical moments, the therapist must quickly assess the transference projection and then move against the projection as soon as possible, in order to maintain the focus on the actual bad object(s). It is essential, when working with ego-impaired patients, to reject and correct negative projections as much as possible, because they are experienced concretely and can cause the patient to panic. If they are not understood and left unexamined, they can disrupt, even terminate, the therapeutic relationship. This is illustrated in case 3.3, where a negative projection by the patient, Mr. Williams, caught me unaware and disrupted the ongoing work (Celani 1993).

This example clearly demonstrates how concrete and literal the borderline patient can be. Mr. Williams could not continue the session thinking that he was in the hands of a therapist as chaotic and poorly structured as he himself

---

CASE 3.3

Mr. Williams came early for all his appointments and usually ate a sandwich in the wait-ing room. He had a tenuously integrated ego and needed time before his appointment to compose himself. I had difficulty ending the session with the prior patient and entered the waiting room to use the upstairs bathroom. Mr. Williams mentioned that I appeared har-ried. When I came back down the stairs, Mr. Williams, as he entered the consulting room, again said that I seemed rushed. The session started exactly on time. As I sat down, Mr. Williams noticed that I had missed one of my belt loops when dressing that morning and pointed this out to me. All three of his comments were derivatives based on his fear that I was rushed and the pressure would disorganize my ego as it did his. However, I did not understand the significance of these three derivatives but instead saw that Mr. Williams had suddenly become very hostile. He complained that all the good magazines were in the consulting room, that therapists were labeling people, making a big deal out of everyone's pathology and not allowing the patients to be themselves. All these were past themes, but they suddenly arose all packaged together with greater force than ever before. Mr. Williams displayed a clear sense of fear, refused to produce any new material, and threatened to leave the session. I asked that he not leave and continue the session, assuring him that I would be able to understand what was going on. He continued to accuse me for my pry-ing speculations and finally said that he felt like the next client in a lawyer's office after the attorney had returned from a murder trial. I understood this derivative and told him that I was accustomed to seeing one patient after another, did not need time between patients to organize my thoughts, and was ready to hear whatever he had to say. My response cleared the air, as his final derivative had alerted me to the fact that he had transformed me into a preoccupied, harried therapist who had an ego as poorly organized as his own. This clear differentiation of my ego structure from his allowed my patient to produce new material.

---

was. A clear, simple, and secure response to projections of this type is essential to challenge and disperse this type of transference before it causes the patient to terminate treatment.

THE LIBIDINAL-EGO PATIENT/EXCITING-OBJECT THERAPIST: THE FIRST SPLIT

The most common projection at the start of treatment with the borderline patient is the patient's projection of her exciting object onto the therapist. In general, this is a fragile and unstable transference that can shift suddenly. When characterological patients, particularly borderline individuals, are dominated by their libidinal egos (even though they are relating antilibidinal pain), they will demand that the therapist *completely* confirm every statement they make. If they are disappointed by the ther-apist's response, they will suddenly split and see the therapist as a rejecting object. I have spent hundreds of hours "pinned" in my chair by wounded, self-righteous borderline patients who almost "dared" me to disagree with their perception (and thus become a rejecting object) of the world as a corrupt and evil place that was in dire need of their corrective influence. It is hard to view the outpouring of antilibidinal hurts to the therapist as creating a libidinal ego–exciting object relationship with the patient. However, when patients recount their painful histories, they are seeking confirmation, praise, and support for their *heroic* struggles with their bad objects. The simple act of paying attention to the patient's story turns the therapist into an exciting object, whom the patient's libidinal ego sees as an object who will compensate them for all the pain that they have suffered. The patient's demand for perfect agreement allows no hint of an interpretation (which the patient would experience as a total act of disloyalty) or even *a comment of any type* that does not perfectly confirm the patient's extreme positions. Should the therapist simply look out the window for a moment, there may occur a lightning-fast split of the patient into the antilibidinal ego, an uncomfortable situation for the therapist who will find it impossible to offer an interpretation at this early stage of work.

Not all transformations of the therapist as an exciting object are so fragile, however. In general, the libidinal-ego patient–exciting-object therapist transference scenario is provoked by the therapist's position as a source of interpersonal gratification that is precious to the patient. Very often mild versions of this transference pattern in which the patient looks eagerly for confirmation and approval are unconsciously welcomed by the therapist as a refreshing change from patient projections from the hostile side of the split. In some cases, a therapist's unrecognized narcissism allows him or her to accept adoration as a savior long after it should have been confronted and corrected. The projection of the exciting object onto the therapist results in an unrealistic and excessively positive transference that is fragile and likely to break down when the patient experiences the slightest frustration within the relationship. The patient may assume that a passing comment from the therapist was a promise of gratification if the patient agrees to engage in one behavior or another. This requires that the therapist forcefully confront the patient's unrealistic hopes. Frequently, this type of transference will manifest itself in terms of boundary or framework violations, including inappropriate demands for closeness. For example, a patient once wrote me a letter that was a critique of our first session. It contained praise of my "technique" and a promise that she would be my "best patient ever." The patient was projecting the fulfillment of all her unmet dependencies onto me, implying that we had made a pact to gratify each other's needs. In this case, I countered her projection of the exciting object onto me by describing the limits of the therapeutic relationship, noting the lack of reality in the patient's assessment of my technique. In practice, it is a relatively easy task to confront a patient's unrealistic libidinal-ego fantasy about oneself as a therapist, which may or may not impact the patient's libidinal ego and limit (actually prohibit) out-of-bounds demands by the patient. The therapist must maintain existing boundaries and deny any extra-therapeutic relationship with the patient in all situations, except when the patient has the potential to commit suicide if the therapist fails to comply.

Excessive idealization of the therapist is a clear signal that the patient perceives the therapist from her libidinal ego as an exciting object. This also indicates that the opposite subego, the antilibidinal ego, must be present as well, though temporarily out of view. A method of preparing the patient for the inevitable split and reversal is for the therapist to note (in concepts appropriate to the particular patient) how idealization always turns into disappointment at some future date. The therapist should ask about past idealized objects and chart the history of their downfall. Once this is done, the therapist can predict the patient's shift of perception of the therapist, using the general formula that has been revealed by the patient's specific history. Then this event can be reframed as an important landmark in treatment, for example, the therapist might say: "I will be very interested in the moment that you suddenly see me in exactly the same way as you saw your favorite uncle Paul. When you suddenly discover that I am the same type of corrupt character that he turned out to be; then we will really be getting somewhere." This is an attempt to preempt that very perception, a form of immunization to the projection before it is even made. This may be seen as spoiling the therapist's analysis of the transference, but the real goal is to engage the central ego and simultaneously weaken the subegos. No one technique is powerful enough to defeat the patient's transferences, but this one often has the effect of softening the patient's response to the shift from libidinal ego to antilibidinal ego when it does occur. It moves the literal and rigid borderline patients into a position where they act more like a neurotic—that is, to a point where they do not take their transference projections quite as seriously as they once did. This technique also engages the patient's central ego and strongly suggests that it is the patient's perception, rather than the object, that is shifting.

THE ANTILIBIDINAL PATIENT/REJECTING-OBJECT THERAPIST

Although most patients initially perceive the therapist from the perspective of their libidinal egos, the opposite ego structure lurks just below the surface. Severely deprive or abused patients know no other reality. Keep in mind that the libidinal ego is a structure designed to rescue children from despair, and it would not be present at all if patients had experienced love and support in their history. The moment any hint of frustration emerges, the patient will assume that the therapist is identical to the internalized rejecting object, and the nascent therapeutic alliance may be ruptured. As noted, early refusals by the therapist to agree with all the patient's positions will trigger a split from the libidinal ego into the antilibidinal ego, and the patient will act as if the therapist had destroyed all trust, having demonstrated that he or she is insufficiently on the patient's "side." Luckily for the therapist, the intense emotionality, threats, and histrionics that emerge from the patient's antilibidinal ego are often quickly forgotten. The following exchange took place between Ms. Kimber, a borderline woman engaged in a legal battle with the Social Security Administration, and her therapist, who tried to make a single observation and was met with an antilibidinal barrage:

PT: I can't believe what those lying bureaucrats are up to—they are trying to cut my monthly payment because of my part-time job. I called a lawyer but he is only interested in my money. Why won't anyone do their job? I can't believe how corrupt the world is, where have all the honest people gone?

TH: I see you have had a difficult week. I remember that you have had trouble with them before.

PT: Trouble—I guess so! It sounds like you don't believe me—they are a bunch of lazy, stupid, clock-punchers, waiting to go home. Are you saying I have trouble all the time with everybody? I am beginning to think that you are as bad as the rest of them.

TH: I guess you don't remember that we have been working together continuously for two years, including those times when you could not pay me for several months. [Here the therapist is making a clear distinction between himself and the patient's attempt to transform him into a rejecting object.]

This example demonstrates how forceful the therapist must be at times to block the patient's projections of the rejecting object onto him. There is no time for a subtle, detailed analysis of the projection. If the projection from the patient's antilibidinal ego is not opposed, then the patient will embrace a complete antilibidinal view of the therapist as a rejecting object. The therapist's task is to confront the projection as fast as possible and as forcefully as necessary. If the therapist fails to do so, then the patient will begin to act in a manner commensurate with his or her vision of the therapist as a rejecting object. This will cause progress to halt, as demonstrated in the prior example of Mr. Williams. The patient will conclude that his perception is entirely justified, based on past experience with the original rejecting objects. This aggression from the patient can provoke counter-transference retaliation if the therapist is forced out of his or her ideal object role by the patient's hostility. An immediate and tactful confrontation of the patient's negative projections can reduce the therapist's counter-aggression by not allowing the patient to perceive the therapist as a rejecting object. Therapists must point out the contrast between their efforts and intentions compared with those of the original bad objects. Needless to say, the therapist must act consistently as the good object to lend credence to this strategy.

THE REJECTING-OBJECT PATIENT/ANTILIBIDINAL THERAPIST

The other transference scenario from the negative side of the borderline's split structure occurs when the patient identifies with her internal rejecting object and takes that role to maneuver the therapist into the position of the frustrated, impotent, and discredited child. This occurred in the treatment of Mrs. Dowd, who was raised by an alcoholic, punitive, and controlling father who kept her in constant suspense as to why she was being punished. As a child, she attempted to guess what she was doing wrong, but no matter how hard she tried, she was never able to discern the key to the puzzle. The following vignette illustrates how the therapist became trapped in the same position, that of a dependent, frustrated child trying desperately to guess what he had done wrong:

PT: I am so frustrated! I have tried everything but nothing sticks inside. I go to A.A. meetings, I went to meditation, studied philosophy and now I am on my fifth psychiatrist (*her voice increases into a high scream*) and nothing works. I feel worse than ever. You tell me something different every week, but I can't remember it anyway. Why can't (*another high pitched scream*) YOU help me!

TH: Well, we have some clues, but everything I seem to say gets you angry or doesn't seem to fit.

PT: I am alone! I will always be alone! Nobody likes me, nobody visits me, everyone hates me!

TH: I have told you a number of times that you are substituting your childhood experience of the world for today's reality. You have two daughters who visit you, an ex-husband who calls you every couple of days, a job with many colleagues, and you attend Alanon meetings every week. I just don't see how you can claim you are alone.

PT: You don't get it, do you? You never can understand me! Nothing I tell you makes sense to you. I want to quit right now!

TH: (*agitated and desperate*): Now look here, I am doing the best I can. What about that idea that we talked about last week about your mother.

PT: Wrong, wrong, wrong! It's my father not my mother! She left us when I was five and she never said anything anyway.

TH: But didn't we conclude—

PT: Look, if you can't figure this thing out I am going to quit and find someone who knows what they are doing.

This exchange is typical with a patient experiencing a negative therapeutic reaction and also illustrates a strong identification with the rejecting object of her childhood, which forced the therapist into his antilibidinal ego. The inner experience of the therapist is likely to be identical to the historical experiences stored in the patient's antilibidinal ego: rage, powerlessness, confusion, and a desire to terminate the relationship with the patient. This particular therapist sought supervision and was able to tell the patient that he was experiencing emotions identical to those that she had felt as a child. The interpretation was made during the next session, when the patient was not emotionally enraged and was operating out of her central ego. The startling truth of the therapist's similar emotional reaction connected him to the patient's remembered experiences from her childhood and put the patient and the therapist on the same "side," as two people who have experienced a unique trauma that others could not readily understand. This transference interpretation opened new avenues of understanding for both patient and therapist. It also exposed the patient to the reality that the parent toward whom she had conscious antipathy was alive in the form of the rejecting object, which was deeply lodged in her inner world. Naturally, this type of interpretation can only be used when there is some access to the patient's central ego.

THE EXCITING-OBJECT PATIENT/LIBIDINAL-EGO THERAPIST

This last patient–therapist transference position appears least frequently, but the creative borderline patient can, on occasion, maneuver the therapist into this interpersonal stance. This transference scenario is the province of a mixed group of hysteroid and psychosomatic borderline individuals who turn themselves into exciting objects and attempt to arouse the therapist's libidinal ego, based on the therapist's hopes of curing a (self-proclaimed) complex, important, and interesting patient. Experience suggests that patients who attempt to provoke the therapist's libidinal ego in this manner have a relatively poor prognosis. They appear to be more interested in manipulating and defeating the therapist's efforts than in getting better. The patient sets himself up as the exciting object, often by presenting himself as mysterious, interesting, and potentially brilliant, if only the "right" therapist would release his potential. This type of patient may use the covert promise of improved functioning as interpersonal "bait" to arouse the therapist's hopes. Consider case 3.4.

The therapist's desire to be accepted by this special patient, Mr. Macy, resulted from the successful activation of his libidinal ego by the talented patient. The resident had placed himself at risk of rousing the patient's sudden disapproval and being shifted to a position of resentment and impotent anger when the patient suddenly split into his rejecting object position—the position from which he viewed all his previous physicians. This indeed occurred, as the patient predictably became critical of the treatment he was receiving and dissociated his identification with the exciting object while simultaneously derepressing his identification with his internal rejecting object. The resident then joined the long list of failed "helpers" that

CASE 3.4

Mr. Macy came for a consultation and carried a large package of papers with him. He presented himself as a victim of the medical profession and referred to his medical records to emphasize just how difficult and complex a "case" he had become. He noted that his artistic and musical talents, which he claimed were considerable, were lying unused because of his complex psychopathology. He then described the various disciplines he had contacted for treatment, all of which seemed to hold out promise but ultimately failed him. At one time, he had been diagnosed as a multiple personality, whereas another clinic diagnosed him as having an attention deficit disorder. He was currently undergoing treatment for his latest diagnosis, sub-clinical temporal lobe epilepsy, but he felt that these treatments were not working either. He presented himself as eager to hear what the resident psychiatrist had to say, and reassured the young physician that he held no grudges toward his previous doctors. The resident recognized the aspects of a severe borderline disorder and assured Mr. Macy that psychotherapy was the treatment of choice. Later the resident reported feeling competitive with the other phantom physicians and also felt a powerful pull toward the patient. His counter-transference toward the patient consisted of feelings of gratitude that the patient came to him and a desire to be accepted by this special and very complex patient.

would be used as bait to stimulate the hopes of the next mental health professional who would be sought out to rescue this creative, and revenge-driven, patient.

THE DEREPRESSION OF ANTILIBIDINAL MEMORIES

The most important aspect of the repressed antilibidinal ego is its "contents"—that is, the internalized memories of relational events between the child and his objects that were too overwhelming to be integrated into his central ego. Fairbairn (1958) described the fundamental essence of change as the synthesis of previously split-off and repressed material from the unconscious structures into the realm of the central ego, where it can contribute to a painful, ambivalent, and integrated view of the once split objects. I referred to the following passage earlier in discussing Fairbairn's 1944 paper, but it is worthwhile noting it again to emphasize the fundamental goal of psychoanalytic or psychotherapeutic treatment within this particular metapsychology:

Thus I conceive it as among the most important functions of psychoanalytical therapy (a) to reduce the split of the original ego by restoring to the central ego a maximum of the territories ceded to the libidinal ego and the internal saboteur, and (b) to bring the exciting object and the rejecting object so far as possible together within the sphere of influence of the central ego. (129–130)

Fairbairn never presented a clear example of this process, a serious oversight that I will attempt to correct. He also assumed that derepression ("the release of bad objects"), when it did occur, would *automatically* reduce the attachment of the antilibidinal ego (or the libidinal ego) to its respective rejecting and exciting part-objects, and that the previously repressed material would be integrated into the central ego without resistance. This is simply not the case. Occasionally during the inquiry into the patient's relational history, a patient will help the process along by suddenly derepressing powerful material that had been repressed in one of the internal structures. To illustrate this process, I return to the example of Angie from chapter 1, my patient who was reared in rural Vermont in an unloving family and was forced to work far beyond her capacity (Celani 2005). Her adult life was a near perfect repetition and re-creation of the relationships that were all-encompassing in her childhood and now resided in her inner world. Her husband demanded that she see a therapist as a condition of continuing their marriage, as she now occupied the role that her parents once occupied as the excessively busy, aloof, and work-pre-occupied rejecting object, while her husband was in the position of the rejected, worthless, and ignored child. Conversely, at her job, she was in the overworked, easily dismissed, and resentful antilibidinal position and her employers were the new rejecting objects. Her libidinal attachment to her parents remained intact, despite years of their disregarding her, as her desperate need for good objects did not allow the repressed bad object memories to disrupt her attachment to them.

Once her dream of butchering and cooking her dog as her contribution to the Thanksgiving dinner was derepressed, her central ego had a brief moment to view the material that had been dissociated in her inner world. This is what Fairbairn (1943) meant by the term "release of bad objects," which are symbolized memories that are too frightening and disruptive to remain available to the central ego: "For, when such bad objects are released, the world around the patient becomes peopled with devils which are too terrifying for him to face" (69). The therapeutic goal at this critical moment is to support the patient's vision without emphasizing how bad the parents really were, so as not to inadvertently provoke an abandonment crisis. I attempted to support the validity of Angie's suddenly derepressed perception of her objects and did not allow her to dismiss it as a random and inappropriately hostile unconscious fantasy about her parents. I linked her symbolized perception of her parents as people who were willing to sacrifice their children for their own needs to the many parental failures she had blandly described and defended as "nor-mal" behavior. My support of her symbolized view of her objects as valid, plus the attachment she had to me as an ideal object, served as an alternative attachment she could rely on. This support allowed her central ego to tolerate this powerful and exceedingly negative vision of her parental objects. Once a perception like this is "released" from the unconscious, the attachment between the patient's central ego and the therapist as a supportive ideal object is critical to keeping the material in the patient's consciousness. If the patient's central ego is horrified by the dere-pressed material, and there is insufficient emotional support from the therapist, then the danger looms that the patient may once again dissociate the material. This indicates that the patient's central ego cannot tolerate knowing the enormity of the neglect she suffered and cannot face the prospect of facing life in an under-developed state without the comforting illusion of loving parents.

Fairbairn saw the role of the analyst or therapist as a new idealized object who offers the patient a new and secure attachment, allowing the patient to tolerate what previously had been intolerable, though, again, Fairbairn never gave his readers a detailed example. He was fully aware of the therapist's role in helping the patient understand confusing psychic material, as well as a new, secure (external) attach-ment. Fairbairn (1943) noted the extremely different consequences of derepression within the confines of psychoanalysis compared with the sudden derepression of bad objects experienced by soldiers in the field. Most frequently, soldiers who expe-rienced sudden derepressions collapsed emotionally, often into psychosis, because their central egos were not supported by a sympathetic ideal object.

Angie's release of her bad-object perception provoked massive anxiety in her, but the support and interpretation of the meaning of the dream allowed a gradual integration and synthesis of material from her antilibidinal ego into her central ego. In effect, the supportive validation of this perception (along with her attachment to me as an ideal object) allowed Angie to tolerate this disruptive and ambivalent perception of her objects, which slowly became part of her central ego where it was conscious and thus always available. The extremeness of her derepressed view of her objects had to be tempered by interpretations that modified her antilibidinal rage against her parents, from seeing them as monsters into a more balanced cen-tral ego view of them as ordinary, selfish, and disinterested people. The central-ego acceptance of this vision of her parents deprived her antilibidinal-ego structure of its hate-based attachment to them as rejecting objects. This central-ego view also challenged and modified her libidinal-ego fantasy that the very same parents had the potential to love her in the future. Typically, the synthesis of parts of the antili-bidinal ego's view of the parental objects into the central ego also reduces (or out-right destroys) the libidinal ego's hopes, as the failed objects are seen more realisti-cally. The central ego's realistic vision of the parental objects, particularly of their emotional limitations, destroys unrealistic libidinal-ego fantasies. This accounts for the greater probability of success when working to validate the perceptions of the antilibidinal ego as opposed to challenging the touchy, unrealistic, and defensive libidinal ego. Once the material from the antilibidinal ego is integrated into the central ego, then the unrealistic hopes of the libidinal ego soon dissolves, and the libidinal ego similarly dissolves as it merges into the central ego as well.

Another similar example of a sudden derepression of dissociated antilibidinal mate-rial came from my patient Roberta, a recently married graduate student who came for motivational help with her studies. She was well along in her graduate program, but she had lost interest in pursuing her degree. She was still receiving financial support from her parents and often accepted lavish vacations with them, even though their aggressive behavior toward each other, and their indifference to her, annoyed her. Exploration of her history revealed that she blamed much of her parents' indifference toward her in childhood on the fact that she used drugs (thus exonerating her parents' empathic failures). Her use of drugs started at an early age and went almost completely unnoticed by her wealthy and preoccupied parents. They lived in Boston and ate dinner out almost every night, leaving Roberta and her brother home with domestic help. When she was sixteen, she attempted suicide by running headlong into one of the windows in their high-rise apartment, and the impact with the fixed window knocked her out for a time. She did not tell her parents when they eventually returned that evening. Like Angie, Roberta held onto a mostly libidinal-ego view of her objects, with occasional antilibidinal statements about her intrusive mother, that were immediately retracted or minimized. The therapist was helped by Roberta's recounting of a dream, described in case 3.5, that contained a rich vein of dissociated material.

This type of dream is extremely helpful to the process of therapy as it produces the patient's repressed antilibidinal vision of what had happened to her in childhood—once again symbolically. The therapist's job is to support the vision without using it as a "victory" in his quest to unearth the extent of the neglect or abuse the patient suffered. The therapist must quietly support the antilibidinal vision and keep it in mutual awareness without criticizing the patient for her continued attachment to the bad objects.

Sometimes the antilibidinal ego bursts out of the unconscious for an instant and the event is too brief and too disruptive to hold onto. Consider cases 3.6 and 3.7, from my practice, which demonstrate what occurs when dissociated material emerges from the antilibidinal ego during the therapy process.

These cases pale in comparison with an example described by Mitchell (2000). This particular dream came from a thirty-year-old female patient raised by a depressed mother who was an underachieving college professor and was threat-

CASE 3.5

Roberta dreamed that she was attending the rehearsal dinner for her wedding. Typically, her mother had taken over all the arrangements as well as the guest list, and consequently all her mother's friends were in attendance while none of Roberta's friends were there. Roberta was sitting at the end of the table with her future husband like a statue of the good child she was demanded to be. Her mother was tipsy and began playing a "camp" game that consisted of placing a knife at right angles over a fork and then hitting the handle end of the knife, sending it arcing into the air. The flying knife pierced her skull, killing her.

CASE 3.6

The wife of a physician came in for treatment and described her relationship with her mother, who lived three hundred miles away. Her mother would call her every morning and "organize" her day for her, checking up on what she had accomplished the day before and laying out the plan for the day. My patient was bereft of a central ego and was so dependent that she was unable to either hang up or in any way separate from her needed object. During our general discussion, she broke out into what can only be described as "savage" tears and wailed, "She ruined me!" This event was over so quickly and repressed so thoroughly by the patient that I was not able to keep it in the patient's consciousness. She fiercely resisted discussing the event and within a few sessions forgot it entirely.

CASE 3.7

A second patient described being left night after night by his (divorced) mother, who worked for a major media company. He had a key to his apartment so he could let himself in after school, and, like clockwork, a hired cook would arrive at six o'clock and fix him dinner. The hired women were from Central or South America and invariably fixed him a variation of rice and beans. Not surprisingly, he never learned to care for himself. Many years later, he was preparing a prepackaged frozen dinner for himself; when he peeled off the foil and saw the rice and beans. He was suddenly overcome with antilibidinal rage at his suddenly derepressed abandonment and threw the meal against the wall.

ened by her daughter's successes. The patient's father was flirtatious and violated boundaries with his daughter. Both parents valued appearances over the unhappy realities of their mutual relationships. Mitchell (2000) describes his work with this patient in detail (70–75) and concludes by relating a powerful dream that emerged from the depths of his patient's antilibidinal ego:

> In an early dream there had been a group of mothers holding damaged babies who all looked like generic, vapid "Barbie" dolls. The mothers were expressing outrage about the harm that had come to their babies and were trying to bury them; but the babies kept rising out of their common grave, only to be brutally clubbed by the mothers over and over again. Becky and I both found this image a powerful representation of the interpersonal world of her childhood, as well as the continual self-brutalization she inflicted upon herself in her inner world.   (74)

Like my patients, Mitchell's patient had symbolized her childhood experiences in a dream that clearly conveyed the experience of having a parent who attempted to crush her individuality. Thus derepression of material from the antilibidinal ego is a powerful way to uncover the extent of developmental trauma suffered by the patient. Frequently, however, there are no dramatic dreams, and the therapist must rely on the development of a narrative history of the patient's childhood that slowly uncovers the extent of parental failures that had to be dissociated.

THE NEGATIVE THERAPEUTIC REACTION

The discussion of Fairbairn's structures has not taken into consideration the activity of the antilibidinal ego when it is at its worst. When the antilibidinal ego is deeply attached to the battle with the rejecting object, then all external objects that present themselves are misperceived as rejecting, and this rigid distortion from the internal world sours every relationship. Occasionally, the whole therapeutic process will be stymied by the presence of an antilibidinal ego that actively destroys all the therapist's efforts. All heartfelt attempts to understand the patient, even when applied by a seasoned clinician, can fail to produce measurable results in some borderline patients. Many patients report that they are worse off as a result of the treatment and that therapy is nearly "killing" them. This lack of progress, plus clear signs of active sabotage of the therapist's efforts, is evidence of resistance, most likely originating in the antilibidinal ego. One experienced clinician described his resistant characterological patients as "immunized" against his influence by their attachments to bad objects.

Seinfeld (1990) noted that a second reason for the negative therapeutic reaction is the "structural deficit" (11). The structural deficit is found in patients who have had too little central-ego interactions with the ideal object. In Fairbairn's model, this is represented by the internalization of a very small fragment of the ideal object because so much of the original object was rejecting and exciting and had to be dissociated. Because the patient has had so little prior experience with good objects, he does not know what to make of the good-object therapist, as Seinfeld (1990) notes:

> From the perspective of the structural deficit, the therapist as a potential good object is perceived as alien, strange and unfamiliar. If the patient is so impoverished in positive object experience that he is hardly receptive to accepting the therapist as a good object, then the internal bad object does not need to be strongly activated to defend against the potential good object because there is so little threat involved. (12)

The good-object therapist enters the patient's awareness as an interloper, without the protection afforded to the existing internalized objects. As Seinfeld (1990) notes, those patients with little experience with good-object parents do not know what to make of, or how to relate to, the well-meaning therapist. Conversely, the patient holds onto his bad objects desperately, like a mountain climber holds onto a thin, frayed rope. Fairbairn (1940) noted that bad internal objects are "infinitely precious (even as precious as life itself), and the internalization . . . of which is a measure of their importance and the extent of dependence on them" (22). Thus the therapist is faced with internal opponents that fight against his best efforts with determined aggression. Consequently, the negative therapeutic reaction is to be expected, particularly with borderline patients on the extreme end of the spectrum. The relational configuration that gives rise to the negative therapeutic reaction is when the patient rigidly holds onto an antilibidinal ego position and perceives the therapist to be a rejecting object regardless of his or her supportive efforts. The antilibidinal ego is revenge-driven but simultaneously passive and undermining, and frequently the patient will try to do everything in her power to ruin the therapeutic enterprise:

> Revenge can also be enacted in the consulting room, as a way to slow down or sabotage treatment, sometimes in an effort to prevent the analyst from experiencing any pleasure or accomplishment in the work. A patient may be passively resistant out of resentment at the analyst's having all the power in the analytic situation, while another may be taking revenge against parents who want the treatment to succeed. (Beattie 2005:518)

This is a constant issue in the psychotherapeutic and psychoanalytic process. The therapeutic relationship replicates early relational configurations in which the patient was damaged by her parental objects, who had all the emotional power and misused it against the best interests of their child. Now the patient is expected to embrace the "helpful" parent-like object and forget all that had happened to her in the past, often an impossible task that leads to all manner of relational configurations projected into the transference.

The more experience the patient has had in her development with a rejecting-object parent, the greater the power and creativity of her antilibidinal-ego structure. The goodwill of the therapist will be subverted in ways not immediately evident. The well-developed and muscular antilibidinal ego sees all objects, including the well-meaning therapist, as a rejecting object, because it has absolutely no faith in the possibility of goodness in others. For instance, I once worked with a number of members of the insular local law enforcement community, all of whom knew one another. Over the years, I had a number of patients, both single and married, who consulted me. Two of my single patients, who had little emotional connection with each other, secretly decided to thwart and undermine my efforts by having an emotionless affair with each other. I often took the position that engaging in meaningless affairs was self-destructive and against their best interests. This covert and hostile act came from both their passive-aggressive and defiant antilibidinal egos, which were focused on undermining my efforts because I was perceived as a rejecting object. Had these patients identified with their internal rejecting-object structures and viewed me in the antilibidinal position, a very different scenario would have ensued. Their rejecting-object structures might have angrily confronted me for offering them behavioral guidelines or for judging their behavior in any way, and they may even have terminated treatment. Notably, both individuals told me of the affair in the ensuing years when I was more firmly established as an ideal object in relationship to their central egos.

One of the most resistance-producing attitudes of the rejecting object is the active rejection of the need of the patient's central ego for a good object. These hostile and self- denying attitudes are similar to the original rejecting object's attitudes toward the patient; that is, the parental object convinced the child that he or she was not worthy of any support. It appears counterintuitive that the antilibidinal ego should be so attached to the relationship with the rejecting object, since so much pain was involved. Fairbairn went to great lengths to point out that the alternative to rejecting the rejecting object is death, so the child *has to accept* the assessment of the parent despite its negativity. The two following examples illustrate active forms of the negative therapeutic reaction. The first vignette displays the intense cynicism of the patient's antilibidinal ego in relationship to the therapist's whom the patient had transformed into a rejecting, though still needed, object. The second case, in contrast, concerns a patient who identified with his internal rejecting object and frustrated the therapist's efforts to help in the same patrician way that he was frustrated by his paternal object as a child. The second example is, paradoxically, less problematic to the therapist, as patients who repeatedly identify with the rejecting object and see the therapist as an antilibidinal object tend to leave therapy because of their indifference to the loss of the devalued therapist.

Mr. Landis was a forty-year-old architect who had lived a nomadic life, moving from one urban center to another, supporting himself by teaching in small colleges and consulting at various architectural firms. He was being treated by a psychology intern at a general hospital for a reduced fee. As a child, Mr. Landis was dealt with by the domestic help, but his parents indoctrinated him on the importance of believing in the goodness of the family as well as keeping up good appearances:

PT: I was talking to one of my friends who also comes here and he was saying that he was going nowhere with this so-called therapy. How do you explain my lack of progress? You are the one with all the college degrees. I still have this problem with women. Cindy left me yesterday, and just twenty-four hours later I want her back. I know that the moment I get back with her I am going to feel obligated and trapped. When is this nonsense going to stop?

TH: We seem to go over the same material again and again. You are caught in the dependency-engulfment cycle, both with Cindy and with me. One session you want to quit, and the next day you call me at home. Once you truly get the message that I am trying to help, you should feel less ambivalent about me. This attachment to me will generalize to your relationship with Cindy. [The student therapist was relying on his theory to cope with his aggressive patient.]

PT: I am sick of that "love your therapist" crap. Why should I trust you? This therapy could be a big lie, just like Hitler and his big lies.

TH (*his anger rising*): Are you comparing our work to Hitler? I hope you are kidding. I have listened to nine months of your hostility, but this is really too much.

PT (*apparently unfazed by the therapist's comments*): Well it seems that way to me. I don't see why you are planning another vacation just when Cindy dumped me. You make enough money to live in style. I'm surprised that you are willing to leave this gold mine for one second.

TH (*angrily*): One minute you compare therapy to one of Hitler's big lies, and the next you complain that I am abandoning you and now you claim that I am ripping you off. I guess you forgot that you are paying half the normal fee, and that I am on a fixed salary. You also seem to forget that it was your father who preached to you and tricked you into believing that he loved you, not me.

Mr. Landis was, in fact, not improving outwardly, as he could not believe in the goodness of his therapist (Seinfeld 1990). He projected his early experience of being indoctrinated by his parents onto the therapist, and at this early point in therapy no amount of direct confrontation seemed to reduce this conviction. He also projected greed onto the intern therapist despite the strong reality to the contrary, to the point that his complaints sound as if they originated from his internalized rejecting object. However, his attacks are clearly antilibidinal, as his continuing need for, and dependency on, the therapist underlay his hostile barrage of accusations. The therapist could feel the patient's desperate dependency and, though angered, remained in his central ego and pointed out the flaws in Mr. Landis's complaints and attacks. There is no essential difference between the negative therapeutic reaction and an antilibidinal patient–rejecting-object therapist transference, except for the duration and stubbornness of this form of "extended" transference. Experience suggests that in some instances the negative therapeutic reaction prevents any progress from ever occurring, and at other times the progress made is slow and painful, and comes at great cost to the therapist.

All negative therapeutic reactions are not as overtly hostile as in the case of Mr. Landis. Another less common form that frequently ends in premature termination is when the patient acts out the role of the rejecting parental object while the therapist is pushed into the reciprocal role, that of the patient's antilibidinal ego. The emotions that the therapist experiences in this scenario are likely to be identical to the emotions experienced by the patient as a child, when he or she was at the mercy of the original rejecting objects. In this scenario, patients unconsciously turn the style of their original rejecting objects against the therapist and undermine the therapist's efforts to be helpful.

Turning to our second example, Mr. Shields was raised by two argumentative parents who had such a distorted view of reality that all his (legitimate) complaints were reduced to absurdity by their apparently logical counterarguments. He lived in a world of upside-down logic and had the repeated experience of having all his needs and perceptions dismissed by his parents, who treated him as if he were completely unimportant:

PT (*smiling broadly and brushing himself off*): Sorry I'm late but I was working on my car and just lost track of time. (*Holds up a book for the therapist to see*) I just wonder what you thought of this fellow.

TH (*warily*): What is that, Dale Carnegie?

PT: Yeah, a really great book for motivation. I remember what you said about that theory of yours, and I thought that you ought to read this and see what you think. I figured that it would help you out (*smiles broadly*).

TH: I don't think you are getting the point about therapy being a cooperative venture.

PT (*ignores the therapist's comment*): I used this book when I was selling encyclopedias in New York City, it really worked miracles. You really have to get motivated to sell door to door, while smiling broadly.

TH (*angrily*): You come in twenty minutes late and bring in some superficial pop psychology and grin like the cat that ate the canary! I cannot ignore your hostility toward me and the whole therapy process.

PT (*still smiling broadly*): Hey, I didn't want to hurt your feelings Doc, I just thought it was a great book.

This patient's lateness and challenge to the therapist's authority appears to be antilibidinal, because it seems to be passive-aggressive. However, Mr. Shields was unattached to the therapist and in a position of power, in that he was able to dismiss the therapist without misgivings. The rejecting object's indifferent stance is absolutely impossible for the hypersensitive, dependent, and reactive antilibidinal ego–dominated patient to assume. The antilibidinal ego wants to reform, change, and influence the rejecting object, whereas, in contrast, the rejecting object is indifferent to the fate of the antilibidinal ego. Mr. Shields's behavior was more of a gesture from a "patrician" rejecting object, who has the option of ignoring and writing off the relationship with the therapist with no consequences to himself. When he terminated, Mr. Shields did so not in an angry or a defiant manner but with indifference. This is in stark contrast to Mr. Landis, who alternated between antilibidinal attacks and dependent demands for support. Mr. Shields's rejection of the therapist placed the latter in the position of being ignored, and dismissed, with no recourse left open to him, precisely the position that the patient had been in as a child.

CHAPTER 4

A FAIRBAIRNIAN APPROACH
TO THE THERAPEUTIC RELATIONSHIP

THIS CHAPTER FOCUSES ON the relationship between the patient's central ego and the therapist as the ideal object. It also looks at transference and transference interpretation from a strategic/clinical perspective rather than a structural one. In my clinical practice, I repeatedly worked with more than a dozen borderline patients simultaneously, including battered women (Celani 1994), patients with eating disorders, and numerous marginal, middle-age adults still living with their elderly parents (Celani 2005). My metaphor for this style of practice was that it was similar to a harried flight instructor who had a group of novice pilots all flying at the same time, none of them having bothered to take ground-school instruction. My only contact with each student pilot was via a weak radio through which I was trying to instruct the student on the fundamentals of flying, while they were doing loops, barrel rolls, and crashing. In fact, borderline patients, whom I use throughout this chapter as the focal group for treatment, are involved in high-risk interpersonal environments with too little knowledge of themselves and are burdened with primitive emotions that are easily triggered by frustration or the threat of abandonment. Their extreme needs, intense emotions, and use of the splitting defense results in endless dramatic twists and turns in their relational worlds. Perhaps the most descriptive and powerful statement of the reality of working with borderline patients can be seen in this poetic passage written by Youngerman (1995):

> As clinicians we recognize unmistakably that all too common jarring sense of finding ourselves unexpectedly quite alone, suddenly out of touch, having lost the affective thread to the patient, or more likely, of having been thrown without warning into an emotional realm entirely different from the one shared a moment before. . . . Not limited to a simple swing of mood or shift in verbalized associations, these sea changes are severe interpersonal disruptions, tragic operas of aloneness full of sound and fury, passionate betrayal and dramatic

misalliance, signifying emptiness. Instant loves and hates, intimacy at first sight, at second thought, repudiation, the endless crises of the borderline world create a sadly steady instability: identity and alliance are maddeningly idealized or damned, all perfect or all evil in dazzling reversals. The threat of abortive termination or bleakly unproductive continuation clouds our customary ways of working, challenging our conventional clinical wisdom and upsetting our self regard as therapists. How can such a needy patient never quite connect to our finest interpretations and even flee our most dedicated caring?   (419)

The simple answer to Youngerman's question (Why do they flee?) is that patients who use the splitting defense frequently transform their therapists into one of the negative internal structures that they project onto him. Once the therapist is either transformed into a rejecting object or seen as a whining incompetent antilibidinal object, the patients respond accordingly. Flight from therapy *is* the patient's logical response after he or she transforms the therapist into a rejecting object or an incompetent, weak antilibidinal self, *as the patient can see no other reality*. The borderline patient uses her internalized structures as the template for her understanding of external objects, including her relationship with the therapist. All the expectations of hope, hate, rejection, love, and the desire for compensation for past wrongs are played out within the analytic dyad. Thus the therapist's most caring and sensitive interpretations may feel like the lash of a whip to the patient who was dealt with maliciously by his parents, who (for instance) used pseudo-psychological jargon to demean her as a child. It takes a special willingness to tolerate rejection and abuse as well as a sense of humor and the enjoyment of play on the part of the therapist to repeatedly "lend" himself to the patient in the hopes that it will foster the patient's development. Despite the goodwill on the part of the therapist, he or she will be misinterpreted in ways that have little basis in reality while simultaneously receiving endless abuse.

INITIATING THE DEVELOPMENT OF A NARRATIVE HISTORY OF THE PATIENT'S CHILDHOOD

Schafer (1998) has written persuasively about the "narrativity of knowledge," which, within the field of psychoanalysis, refers to the development of an agreed-on reappraisal of the patient's developmental history within the parameters of the specific metapsychology used by the analyst or therapist. Schafer acknowledges the reality that there are many competing "brands" of psychoanalysis, each with its own metapsychology or "master narrative." Thus interpretations from competing models lead to different sets of conclusions for each patient, illustrating that there is no ultimate truth in any given analytic model. The master narrative in Fairbairn's model is the story of a deprived child who is forced, by the necessity of retaining his attachment to his rejecting objects, to split his inner world in order to hide from the intolerable reality that he was not loved:

> We are left finally with some large, basically epistemological questions concerning knowledge, authority, and evidence. These questions are brought out forcefully by the introduction into psychoanalysis of the narrational point of view—specifically, the narrativity of knowledge. . . . According to this point of view, the clinical psychoanalytic dialogue is best understood as a series of tellings and retellings by both parties to the dialogue. In addition, the interpretive lines followed by the analyst in his or her interventions and increasingly accepted, assimilated and used by the analysand may be understood as derived from master narratives. These master narratives make up the so-called general theory and major concepts of the analyst's school of psychoanalytic thought. The analyst's detailed interpretive efforts may then be regarded as story lines that are manifestations of these master narratives.   (Schafer 1998:239)

Fairbairn's explanatory model provides the therapist with one of several possible roadmaps of human psychological functioning that he or she then applies to the patient's issues and shares explicitly with the patient. Within Fairbairn's metapsychology, the therapist is charged with the task of unearthing the "reality" (as best as can be attained) regarding the patient's abuse and neglect in childhood as well as his consequent attachment to bad objects in both his inner and his outer world. The development of this narrative of the patient's childhood experiences will never follow a linear path because of the distorted and perilously shifting perspective the patient takes as one of the subegos dominates his consciousness. Every individual's interior world is unique, and in the development of the narrative the therapist must discover the personal meanings within the repressed self and object pairs, as Davies (1996) notes:

> Indeed, constructivism, one of the cornerstones of a relational perspective, insists that there is no unique reality, only interpretations of it, and that each individual's interpretation must be created out of his own particular system of internalized self- and object-representations, as those representations come to be constructed out of an admixture of real events and elaborate systems of unconscious, fantasized elaborations.   (555)

Here Davies presents a modern update of Fairbairn's original concept of the internal world, with its three part-selves in relationship with three part-objects. Davies notes that there is no fixed amount of trauma that creates a fixed quantity of psychopathology, so each individual's internal attachments must be understood as a unique configuration. The relationship between, say, the antilibidinal ego and the rejecting object varies from person to person and may involve, for example, not only specific types of deprivation and abuse but also, perhaps, a sudden shift in behavior of the rejecting object from attacks on the child self (the antilibidinal ego) to self-hate and guilt. This shift in the rejecting object would call on the child's demeaned antilibidinal ego to suddenly feel empathy for the erstwhile rejecting object and force the child to split back into his libidinal ego in the hopes that, by comforting the very object that just abused him, he could repair the now pathetic exciting object so that love remains a possibility in the future. A central part of the therapist's task is to understand the patient's emotional pattern and unique meanings in terms of the master narrative and make sense of the patient's confusion and chaos.

Fairbairn (1958) noted that the word "analysis" should more accurately be changed to "synthesis," because the fundamental task of therapy is to reintegrate the split-off selves into the patient's central ego, while simultaneously integrating the split-off intolerable aspects of the object into a single integrated view. The prior discussion on the derepression of bad-object memories in dreams is one significant way that the central ego can be strengthened as split-off parts of the repressed ego structures are assimilated into it. As noted previously, the most fundamental requirement of the Fairbairnian therapist is for her to know to whom she is speaking (to the subegos, internalized objects, or central ego) as she tries to bring the partially repressed (and, similarly, partially conscious) fragmented selves into the awareness of the central ego. Davies (1996) describes the inner world as composed of "averagable" and "irreconcilable" self and object representations. In Fairbairn's original language, "averagable" means views of the self and object that are acceptable to the central ego, whereas "irreconcilable" refers to the child's split-off memories regarding a hostile or an uncaring object that are intolerable to the central ego. Although Davies (1996) does not specifically cite Fairbairn's model, her view appears to be based on Fairbairn's (1944) structural theory as well as on his model of psychotherapy (1958):

> This view of the "relational unconscious" suggests, then, a dissociatively based system of averagable and irreconcilable mental representations of self in ongoing relationship with a complementary system of averagable and irreconcilable representations of significant others. Those experiences that can be averaged, generalized, affectively modulated, and ultimately encoded linguistically within memory systems and subsystems will essentially come to form the "glue" of psychic integrity. They will give a sense of identity and continuity over time, an experience of self-awareness predictability. But what about those representations of self and other that elude codification, those that are unencoded, irretrievable, yet ever present? Those experiences of self with other that feel irreconcilably different, strangely incompatible, linguistically inexplicable,

or affectively uncontainable fall away into the nascent underpinnings of the relational unconscious. (563)

This thoroughly modern view of Fairbairn's unconscious is the deep sea that the therapist must troll across, again and again. The integration of unintegrated parts of the patient's self that appear in the narrative (or in dream material) that are unrelated to the therapist, such as derepressed memories of parental objects, are relatively easy to deal with when they are not suffused with strong transferences that are projected onto the therapist during the process. Thus understanding dream material, or sudden uncharacteristic perceptions about the parental object (or displaced bad objects), is relatively straightforward when uncomplicated by transferences.

THE TRANSFORMATION OF THE THERAPIST INTO ONE OF THE INTERNAL EGO STRUCTURES

The greatest difficulties and, indeed, the greatest opportunities during the development of a narrative of the patient's history are the times when the patient projects onto the therapist one of the four repressed structures: the badness of the rejecting object; the cynicism, argumentation, and passive undermining of the antilibidinal ego; the promise of love from the exciting object; or the glow of naïve anticipation of the libidinal ego. Each of Fairbairn's internal structures is a specific class of projections that involve a self in relation to an object. Patient projections onto the therapist have been called "isomorphic transformations" by Levenson (1991), a concept equivalent to transference but one that carries more of the sense of what actually happens to the "target" of the transformation. In other words, the therapist finds herself feeling and acting like the internal object that was projected onto her, a concept equivalent to "projective identification" in Kleinian theory. The therapist, effectively, is "transformed," or "press-ganged" to use Fairbairn's (1958) term, into an internalized object from the patient's inner world. Thus the patient behaves as if the therapist were indeed hateful or promising or worthless or offering love, and at the same time the therapist feels pulled along by the interpersonal current. The therapist's training and expertise can vanish in an instant as she begins to become ensnared in the intensely emotional projection pouring out of the patient. Fairbairn's structural theory helps to organize this process by giving the therapist the possible positions into which he will be "transformed":

> This tendency to isomorphism is so powerful that it will engage the therapist in some way, pull him in, make him a part of the system he is observing; either as countertransference, participant-observation, authentic encounter,

whatever. . . . Moreover, it is very curious that in therapy the patient may be telling about what goes on in his life with his mother or father. The therapist is engaged in trying to make sense of what is being told or at least of expanding the amount of information he has. At some point, he will suddenly become aware that the interaction that the patient is discussing has now been shifted to the transference; that is to say, it is now being played out with *him* in some dimension. (Levenson 1991:20)

These "transformations" feel uncanny, unfair, and confusing to the therapist, especially if she is working at a cognitive level. Fairbairn's model has the advantage over other models of psychoanalysis, as his metapsychology offers the therapist four fundamental categories (six if the conscious central ego–ideal object relationship is included) that allows him to explore just who is talking to whom. The patient simply cannot relate to the therapist (or any other external object) without projecting these internal structures, and it is the therapist's task to sort out what is going on—often a difficult job when the therapist is being treated, for example, like the reincarnation of the rejecting object. Transferences are powerful because they are driven by unrequited love and hope on one side of the split, and by unretaliated rage and humiliation on the other. The patient may literally tremble with rage when accusing the therapist of some heinous deed that the therapist has no idea he committed. The intensity of any given projection can cause the therapist to loose his footing if the transformation is both convincing and overwhelming, as Levenson, (1991) notes:

Let's not minimize the fact that the therapist risks himself and his own integrity of self in every real therapeutic engagement. . . . The major anxiety for the therapist is that he will be "transformed" by the patient; that is, that in his experience with the patient he will be converted into an object in the patient's world. This transformation is not mere fantasy of the patient, it is a genuine threat to the therapist and his reality. . . . Therapy proceeds not so much by virtue of the therapist's capacity to provide the patient with a de novo experience as by his capacity to resist being converted into an old and familiar experience. (63–64)

Thus Levenson sees the therapist's ability to resist transformation into a familiar object in the patient's inner world as one of the mutative factors in psychotherapy. This is very close to Fairbairn's conception of the internal world as a closed system that distorts external objects until they seem familiar to the internal world. Hostile and aggressive transferences must be interpreted in such a manner that they add understanding to the narrative, without disrupting the progress of the historical inquiry into the patient's childhood. This point has been made by Davies and Frawley (1991), who see the therapist's willingness to be "transformed" and his or her understanding of the projective/introjective nature of the analytic process as central to the patient's recovery. Here the patient population that Davies and Frawley (1991) are describing is composed of adult survivors of sexual abuse who had, by necessity, split off large parts of their traumatic experience:

> As with all analytic work, it is ultimately the analyst's ability to both participate in and interpret the unfolding historical drama and to relate this history to current interpersonal difficulties that encourages the progression of insight, integration and change. Parts assigned in the dramatic productions of patients for whom dissociative trends predominate are fluid and ever changing. They are assigned, reassigned, and assigned again. . . . Our belief is that the interpretive process within the analytic experience is the only way to end the dissociation, projection, projective identification, and reintrojection that makes the history of abuse not only a painful memory, but an ongoing reality. . . . Included in our conceptualization of the transformational aspects of treatment are the patient's experience of the analyst's availability and constancy, the analyst's willingness to participate in the shifting transference-countertransference reenactments, and, finally, his or her capacity to maintain appropriate boundaries and set necessary limits. Though verbal interpretation provides the patient with a highly significant, cognitive conceptualization of the analytic experience, we believe the experience itself to be equally mutative. (30–31)

Davies and Frawley's statement regarding the mutative factors of treatment corresponds closely to Fairbairn's model of the unconscious. Unlike these authors, however, I do *not* view the resolution of the transference projections from the patient's inner world as the single most important factor in treating this population. Rather, I see it as the necessary *first step* that allows the patient to see the therapist for who he or she is, which then allows the second step of the process to take place: the internalization of the therapist as an ideal object into the patient's internal world, which promotes the restarting of the developmental process. If transference distortions persist, the therapist will not be internalized as an ideal object because he or she is being misperceived as excessively rejecting or excessively promising. In other words, the therapist must be seen by the central ego as an ideal object before the patient can resume the process of development. Early on in treatment, when projections abound, the central ego is not in charge of the patient's inner world; only when the central ego is dominant will the therapist be able to help the patient mature.

The therapist must be willing to be transformed repeatedly and yet remain calm while applying his or her master narrative to the scenario that has just been reenacted between them. The next question is: What aspect of transference interpretation is mutative? The answer, I believe, is the therapist's ability to tolerate the pressure from the patient's projection of one of his internal structures onto the therapist without completely disallowing it, while simultaneously using his central ego to understand what is going on in the relational matrix. The therapist then interprets to the patient what has happened within the relationship and thus attempts to engage the patient's central ego in the dialogue, as Odgen (1990) illustrates:

> In my opinion, it is not possible to analyze the transference without making oneself available to participate to some degree in this form of identification. However, it is by no means sufficient to have become a participant in the externalization of an internal relationship. One must, in addition, be able to understand that which one is experiencing as a reflection of a need on the part of the patient to reduce the therapist to the status of a surrogate for a part of the patient's ego. The therapist must himself be aware that the patient is excluding all aspects of the therapist's personality that do not correspond to the features of the split-off ego with which the therapist is being identified. There is considerable psychological work involved in the therapist's consciously and unconsciously integrating the roles imposed upon him with his larger, more reality-based sense of himself (in particular, his role as therapist). (155)

Here Odgen points out that the psychological "work" of transference interpretation consists of the therapist's acceptance of an unflattering projection of, for instance, the rejecting object onto his person, when, in fact, he is trying to be helpful while simultaneously engaging both his and the patient's central ego. Fairbairn's structural model aids the therapist's central ego by providing him with four basic possibilities that are relatively easy to sort through and then identify which ego or internalized object is dominating the patient's consciousness, as well as the reciprocal ego structure and role that is being forced on the therapist.

Working with a Fairbairnian approach to transference can be more complex and ever-changing than the preceding discussion has implied, as it involves the unconscious structures of the patient as well the reciprocal parts of the therapist (who also has the equivalent ego structures, though hopefully not in the same proportion to his central ego compared with the patient) with whom they are seeking to relate. The therapist must allow the patient to "seek" these parts of him, which may or may not be strongly present, while keeping track of the interaction with his central ego. Using the metaphor of a theatrical production, Davies (1998) describes the ever changing flow of interactions and the constant pressure from the patient's unconscious projection of his inner structures onto the therapist:

> For contemporary relational analysts the transference-countertransference matrix, as co-constructed by patient and analyst, becomes the transitional stage

on which the Fairbairnian cast of characters, in ongoing improvisational interaction with the analysts' complementary troupe of players, can, through projective identification and other projective-introjective mechanisms, begin to tell the story of "multiple selves in interaction". Such character-driven dramas as those which unfold from the tapestry of interactive dialogues between patient and therapist become the substance of a new psychoanalytic agenda. The drama progresses, scene by scene, by dint of what we have come to call enactments, that is, personified embodiments of relationally derived unconscious fantasies as they force themselves outward onto the interpersonally receptive medium of the transference-countertransference experience. (67)

Here Davies expresses the complexity of the transference experience, as one unconscious structure may follow on another in an apparently random manner. The simplest example is the sudden split in the patient from seeing the therapist as an exciting object until the patient experiences frustration, whereupon the patient suddenly dissociates her libidinal ego and replaces it with her antilibidinal ego, which then attacks the therapist. This shift may happen several times within a single session.

Two examples illustrate how therapists fight their way out of a patient's transference projections in different ways. As illustrated in case 4.1, the first therapist uses humor and paradox, which challenges the patient's projection with disquieting information that the patient cannot "squeeze" into his existing relational patterns. In effect, the patient encounters a new object in the room that he does not quite understand. In the second example, the therapist uses a straightforward interpretation of Fairbairn's master narrative and applies it to his and his patient's immediate situation. Clearly, the second therapist is not as tolerant of the patient's transformation of him into a rejecting object, and distances himself from the patient's projection.

The first therapist understood his patient's derivative and quickly put himself into an equivalent role, which brought his patient's projection into sharp focus within the therapy dyad. In this particular case, the therapist was not affected by his patient's hostility and so was able to respond with humor and gentle mockery. All situations do not lend themselves to humor, however, as we will see in the next example, where the therapist was transformed by his patient's inner world to another version of a rejecting object. This therapist simply used Fairbairn's model to understand the relational shift that had occurred and his interpretation allowed him to remain calm and unperturbed in the face of a verbal assault from a long-term borderline patient. His response also "nurtured" the patient by offering her central ego (assuming that some part of it was present) an explanation for her behavior without exposing her to either humiliation or countertransference based on aggression from the therapist:

CASE 4.1

Mr. Frank, a college student, came for therapy and described a father who continually undermined him by playing sadistic tricks on him during his childhood. Mr. Frank produced a derivative during the third session of therapy in which he described a high school teacher whom he greatly admired but who had disappointed him by publishing a short story in a regional literature journal that (he felt) was very similar in theme to a story he had written in class. This was a clear projection onto the therapist of equal (rejecting object) untrust-worthiness from the patient's antilibidinal ego. It originated in the patient's antilibidinal self, because a person in power (the high school teacher) allegedly used his position in a corrupt manner that was against the best interests of his (dependent) student. Rather than slowly interpreting the projection, the therapist responded with the paradoxical statement that *all* his publications were actually rewritten versions of papers originally written by his gradu-ate students, and that his trusting students had no idea that parts of their work had been published. Mr. Frank, his worst fear materializing, looked at the therapist in stunned horror. The therapist was unable to continue the ruse, and so he began smiling broadly. Mr. Frank became momentarily confused, since he was faced with the rejecting object from his inner world that he had projected into the room, yet this "new" rejecting object was peculiar and unfamiliar because he was smiling and seeming to enjoy a private joke, while Mr. Frank was overcome with confusion. As he caught on to the reality that his therapist was playing a role, his projection emerged boldly in the relational matrix.

PT: I had a terrible week. I am so angry at my husband that I could kill him, but I am afraid if I tell him how I feel he will leave me. I needed help with the garden this weekend, and all he did was work on his stupid car. I HATE him for his insensitivity. And I hate you, too.

TH: I knew that was coming. Every time your view of your husband shifts from see-ing him as a good object to a bad one, I get the same treatment. I can see how angry you are right now.

PT: I AM ANGRY. You said something last week that made me mad, but I was afraid to say it in the session. You said that you loved steak, and you know that I am a vegetarian. You were making light of my feelings, and I hate you for that. After the session, I went home and realized that everybody in my life is self-centered, stupid, and insensitive. I can't stand to be with my husband, but I know that if I leave that I will not be able to do any better. And if I leave here I will have to start all over again with another overpaid, insensitive analyst.

TH: Well, I can see that three years of work in here has suddenly disappeared from your memory. I assume that you will not be able to understand that my love of steak is not a mortal insult to you. This sudden shift in your view of me has turned me from the greatest guy in the world to some sort of monster. That's the danger of splitting me. Once you lose sight of my efforts to help you, all the good memories of me disappear and your whole world comes down around you.

This brief dialogue actually minimizes the angry torrent of abuse that poured from this patient. There is absolutely no way that therapists can avoid being "transformed" by their patients, as was true in this example, in that the patient's antilibidinal rage was provoked by an innocent offhand comment. The therapist or analyst who works with patients who use the splitting defense is walking into a minefield of special meanings, most of which the therapist is completely unaware, and when he or she inadvertently steps on one, the patient will respond with an enormous emotional reaction. In this case, the therapist remained (relatively) unperturbed because of his experience with this particular patient over time and his knowledge of the type of projection she was likely to force onto his personal reality. Fairbairn's explanatory model acts as an invisible fence that protects the therapist from accepting the non-legitimate complaints and projections from the patient, and simultaneously supplies a language and metapsychology to explain (in this example) the sudden derepression of split-off aspects of the patient's unconscious. Over time, calm interpretations of this type allow the patient's central ego to start viewing the therapist as an ideal object who has managed to remain outside the projection. In other words, the patient's transference projection is not allowed to completely "transform" the therapist into one of the powerful templates that the patient carries around in his or her inner world. By verbalizing this part of Fairbairn's master narrative, the therapist assured himself (and a small part of the patient's central ego) that he understood what was happening between them and that he was not identical to the patient's inner template of the rejecting object. It is the ongoing struggle between the patient, who is trying to transform the therapist into one of his inner structures, and the therapist's rectification of his personal reality and role that is the one of the powerfully mutative factors in this model.

THE FIRST SPLIT OF THE THERAPIST INTO A REJECTING OBJECT

As noted previously, I have spent countless hours early in the treatment process "pinned" into my chair by self-righteous, vengeful patients whose outpouring of pain was both genuine and seemingly endless. The end of the therapeutic hour was always a challenge with this type of patient, as these individuals would almost always experience the end of the session as a rejection of their needs and frequently would transform me into a rejecting object when I noted that our time was up. I was repeatedly implored for lengthier sessions or double sessions, and every time I enforced the framework I was met by an angry attack. The therapist has to allow the patient to transform him into a rejecting object and risk the possibility that the patient refuses to return—an eventuality that, in fact, is seldom realized. The patient's internal structures, along with her insatiable developmental needs, *insist* that the therapist must be identical to one of the four internal structures, and there is simply no way that the therapist can remain in the role he most prefers—that of the caring helper.

The initial sessions with deeply split patients often revolve around the patient's outpourings of anger and disappointment about her objects. As mentioned in chapter 3, these outpourings could easily be misunderstood as the patient's antilibidinal reaction toward the therapist, but, in truth, they represent a relationship between the patient's libidinal ego and the therapist as seen as an exciting object "savior." The patient hopes that the therapist will provide love and compensation for all the pain and anguish he has suffered. It is not the verbal material that defines the dominance of one ego structure over the others but the relationship between the patient and the therapist that defines "who is talking to whom." At this juncture in therapy, the patient has absolutely no concept of the therapist as a potential ideal object, because *the patient's central ego is not present*; instead, the patient's personality is dominated by his libidinal ego. The patient's libidinal ego wants (expects and demands) love, endless support, and compensation for all the rejection he has endured. As already noted, mere attention to the patient's life story increases the hopes of the libidinal ego, and in many cases the patient will escalate his demand for more and more attention and support for his "cause." It is not uncommon for a primitive patient to demand that the therapist "do" something to the rejecting objects to prove his loyalty to the put-upon patient. The moment the therapist steps out of the observational role and attempts to intercede in the real world on behalf of the patient, he is violating the individual's autonomy and inviting regression. The therapist is already the focus of a chaotic and shifting amalgam of projections, and acting in any concrete way will destroy the observational framework that differentiates psychotherapy from other forms of treatment. The active "helpful" therapist will discover that no amount of "help" is enough, or that the "help" that was offered was not the type that was needed. In other cases, the therapist's "help" will be used to ensnare him into a vengeful crusade against the original disappointing objects, and his position as an observer will be destroyed. The only reason for violating this prohibition against intervention is when the therapist is convinced that the patient (or the target of the patient) is in physical danger. Giovacchini (1984) has addressed this issue:

> As the analyst confronts the patient with organized interpretations of his inchoate, incomprehensible inner world, he is introducing order. The patient often reacts to interpretation by converting timelessness into a sense of "becoming," and in so doing begins to develop ego structure from the initial regressed state. . . . If the analyst maintains the interpretative approach, he is limiting his therapeutic activity to the observational frame of reference. Both he and the patient are looking at disorganization rather than participating in it. If the analyst abandons the interpretative approach and offers "help" for the patient's helplessness, then he

has shifted from the observational frame of reference to another. He has accepted the patient's helplessness as a reality that requires action. (144)

The therapist's refusal to increase the length of sessions or to become involved in the patient's life may be the event that causes the patient to split from his libidinal ego to his antilibidinal ego, thus transforming the therapist from an exciting object into a rejecting one. When the therapist is transformed into a rejecting object, he is faced with a relationship with the patient's enraged and self-righteous antilibidinal ego. It is the therapist's response to this transformation, and his interpretation of it, that begins the process of projection and introjection that is ultimately mutative. The therapist's central-ego commentary on what he or she thinks is occurring in the relationship forms the cognitive component, which is important but less powerful than "living through" the reenactment with the patient. Most commonly, severely deprived patients will demean and attack their therapist for not taking action to help them, and they will threaten to quit if they are not helped is some way. The therapist must remind the patient of the psychotherapeutic process and fit what has just happened into the master narrative, thus modeling dominance of the central ego under intense interpersonal pressure.

Remaining alert to sudden shifts in the patient's demeanor is akin to walking in the autumn woods of Vermont where you know that grouse are hiding in the underbrush. Reminding yourself not to be startled when a huge bird flushes out of the bushes just under your feet and roars off into the forest only goes so far to quell your startle response when it actually happens! Similarly, I was always startled by sudden splits in a patient's perceptions of me, particularly when the patient was aggressively hostile and interrupted a central-ego–ideal-object interaction, as Odgen (1993) has noted:

> When a borderline patient feels angry at and disappointed by the therapist, he feels that he has now discovered the truth. The therapist is unreliable and the patient should have known it all along. What had been previously seen by the patient as evidence of the therapist's trustworthiness now is seen as an act of deception, a mask, a cover-up for what has been apparent. The truth is now out and the patient will not deceive himself or be caught off guard again. *History is instantaneously rewritten.* The therapist is not the person the patient thought he was; he is now discovered to be someone new. Each time I have arrived at this juncture in therapy, I have been freshly stunned by the coldness of the patient's renunciation of shared experience. There is an assault on the emotional history of the object relationship. (62)

In addition to being stunned, like Ogden, when a patient's perception of me shifted, I often found it difficult to contain my annoyance at a patient's malicious accusations when, in fact, I had been doing my best to work cooperatively with the patient. In most cases, when I was sufficiently coherent to respond within my role, I would try to use Davies's (1996) technique of "inviting" the previously dissociated ego structure into the room. For example, during the second session with a female legal professional, who had complained that her previous therapists had found her problems inconceivable given her pleasant self-presentation, I said something (which I do not recall) that so offended her that her emotionality shifted suddenly into an identification with her rejecting object mother. This attractive, petit patient became antagonistic, demeaning, and challenging, and I was transformed into a confused and defensive near-child. I would always try to use humor at these junctures, and in this case I imitated an umpire calling "time out" and announced, exaggeratedly, that someone new had just entered the room, someone I was eager to know. We were both surprised at each other's response, and this formed the basis of several months of exploration and clarification.

CONTINUING THE DEVELOPMENT OF THE NARRATIVE WHILE MAXIMIZING THE INTROJECTIBILITY OF THE THERAPIST AS AN IDEAL OBJECT

This section continues to examine the co-creation of a narrative of the patient's developmental history with an emphasis on the factors that promote the internalization of the therapist into the patient's inner world. This is a very un-Fairbairnian (or even anti-Fairbairnian) concept, as Fairbairn, as I have noted repeatedly, did not believe that good objects are internalized. It has become evident over time, however, that Fairbairn's position is untenable and that, in fact, attachment to, and internalization of, the therapist as an ideal object is an absolute requirement for change. Only when the patient can rely on her inner memories of herself in relation to the ideal object will she be able to let go of her attachment to bad objects. The reverse is also true, in that children who have an established relationship with good objects rely on these good objects when they are exposed to situations involving bad objects. For example, the ten-year-old son of a long-term patient was forced to visit his primitive father each weekend after my patient divorced her husband (who punched her on the courthouse steps on the day the divorce was finalized). His father had remarried, and during one of the boy's weekend visits his older stepbrother pointed a gun at him in order to intimidate him, and soon after he bravely confronted his cruel stepmother, who was slapping her infant for crying. His horrified mother took appropriate steps to protect him, and she asked him how he had been able to tolerate the weekends with his "new" family. He responded that he closed his eyes and thought about her. Thus, by looking into his inner world and remembering the good object, this young boy was able to deal with adversity.

THE FRAMEWORK

Langs (1973) has written extensively on the concept of the therapeutic framework in which psychotherapy takes place. He has explored the importance of physical privacy, reliability, and predictability inherent in the therapist–patient relationship as a fundamental requirement for therapy to begin. He notes that no significant material will emerge until the framework is absolutely secure. In other words, no fundamental truths about the patient will emerge until she feels that communication with the therapist is absolutely private, understood, and free from outside influences. The therapist's establishment and maintenance of this framework is one of the most frequent sources of a patient's transformations of the therapist, almost always into a rejecting object. It is the therapist's responsibility to establish the framework in as secure a way as possible and to enforce the rules when the patient tries to deviate from them. The framework itself plays an important role in the therapist's impact on the patient, separate and independent from the therapist's personal characteristics and from the explanatory model that is used. The long-term goal is to set up a situation that is utterly reliable and impervious to disruptions instigated by the patient and also to random external events so that the personal narrative can develop unimpeded.

The framework is designed to help patients learn that certain appropriate avenues of gratification are completely available to them, whereas others are entirely off-limits. The therapist becomes a powerful model for the patient when he or she demonstrates the clear limits that exist regarding the therapist's use of a patient for personal gratification, the boundaries of the professional relationship, and the commitment to keep the patient's interests foremost in his mind. Once the boundaries of the relationship have been negotiated, the therapist must enforce them regardless of the source of the disruption. Most often, borderline patients or those with severe character disorders are not content to work within the framework even after it has been established, simply because, in their experiences within their families, no real boundaries ever existed. One patient, for example, who was struggling with problems of acting out, asked her therapist if she could bring her eleven-month-old child to the therapy session were she unable to find a babysitter. The well-meaning therapist reluctantly agreed, assuming that the patient's own infant child would not disrupt the established framework. Moments after the patient left, she returned to the consulting room and asked if her sister, who had many of the same problems as she did, could also come to the next session. The therapist realized her mistake and suggested that the therapy should remain closed to all outsiders, including the patient's infant. This case illustrates how patients often test the security of the framework. If the therapist fails to enforce the sanctity of the hour, a spiral of further tests can be expected, as the patient frantically explores other possible open circuits in the relationship. During this testing period, and until the framework is repaired, no progress will be made in terms of the emergence of material from the patient.

When engaged with a patient who may eventually be able to work within the constraints of the framework, the therapist should initially interpret sparingly, as the patient will often be extremely wary until therapy has progressed. This does not mean that the therapist should allow the patient to dictate the terms of therapy but that the therapist ought to allow the patient to use therapy on his or her own terms at the very outset. This suggestion should not to be misconstrued as advocating self-dosing on the patient's part, as it applies only to the patient's attendance, adherence to using verbal communication, acceptance of the termination point of each session, and willingness to pay the agreed-on fee. The therapist's sparing use of observations and the explanatory model is relatively easy to accomplish, as most patients are in a mild frenzy when they enter therapy and pour out nonstop complaints and agony regarding their interpersonal relationships. Over time, the therapist can introduce his particular model and begin the co-construction of a narrative of the patient's life. If the patient cannot conform to the framework after about five sessions, then the therapist is justified in giving up on that particular individual. The following exchange illustrates the initial permissiveness of a therapist in dealing with a chaotic patient who came for therapy for two months, then canceled three consecutive sessions (which she paid for), and finally returned in a crisis. The dialogue reveals a common situation in which the therapist is applying the master narrative to the patient's "story," but the patient seems to be ignoring him, a typical scenario with primitive patients. The therapist is using the model to remain calm and nonpunitive, while demonstrating how an integrated central ego understands reality as he "remembers" the material that the patient has split off:

PT (*crying, desperate*): He left me, I never thought it would happen, but he just could not make a commitment to me. What is wrong with me, I can't find a man that is willing to love me.

TH: As I remember, you have been chasing this fellow for two years, and he has told you from the very beginning that he has trouble committing himself to relationships. In fact, your best friend told you he was a womanizer.

PT (*emphatically*): I love him and will never give up on him!

TH: Let me see now, do you love the fact that he often goes to Atlantic City to gamble, and do you love the women's panties you found hidden in his luggage? It seems to me that you love parts of him—only the parts you want to see. You forget about the parts that you can't love, and then you get terribly hurt when you can no longer ignore those parts. You are splitting him into pieces so you can love him, because you can't bear to see the whole package.

PT: I feel so horrible, so alone. I hate this feeling! I know you have told me that I am looking for a person just like my father, but it doesn't help when I feel like this.

TH: I find it interesting that you have not been here for three weeks and instead have spent your time and money chasing this fellow up and down the East Coast. It seems that you are willing to come back only when you are desperate.

PT: I knew you were going to say that! I don't like normal men, you know that. I can't help myself when it comes to men. But Jim is really killing me. It's true that I forget stuff that I hate when I don't come in here, but I love him more than ever.

This dialogue typifies the long-term struggle involved with a borderline patient who is acting out and initially came for therapy only when she was in crisis. Over time, the patient began to internalize the therapist's calm analysis of her splitting defense as well as his tolerance of her chaotic use of therapy. Her own ambivalence about committing herself to a clear, well-defined relationship to an object was worn away by the therapist's initial permissiveness (allowing her to return to therapy after missed sessions) and by his ability to calmly make sense of her incomprehensible life. Not all patients who resist the imposition of the framework are ultimately able to work productively. Experience suggests, however, that initial permissiveness followed by ever tightening demands allows a large number of characterological patients to make use of therapy.

It is *absolutely* counterproductive, however, to allow a patient to use therapy in an exploitative manner over a long period or to accept extremely disturbed patients in an outpatient setting in the hope of a "heroic" rescue. If the patient continually demands therapy on a crisis basis, then he is using therapy only as a site to discharge tension and is avoiding the ego-developing discipline inherent in the psychotherapeutic framework; such a patient should be terminated until he or she can tolerate the pressure of therapeutic work. Attempting to work with extremely rebellious patients in the outpatient setting will only engender frustration and hostility in the therapist and reduce his effectiveness with other patients. Two examples from my own practice illustrate the type of patient who is likely to frustrate the therapist with little prospect of improvement

James, in case 4.2, was so far away from being an appropriate patient that I did not even begin to negotiate the parameters of our possible relationship. Case 4.3 makes a similar point. The patient, Karen, was sent from another therapist who was having great difficulties in treating her. The referring therapist wanted the patient to investigate switching over to me because the patient (who had been in therapy with a number of different therapists) was continually in conflict with her. I was given no advance information about this patient and was not at all prepared for the rapid splitting, intense emotionality, and extreme aggressiveness that she displayed during our first (and last) interview.

CASE 4.2

James, a tall bohemian-looking artist, swept into my office for his first session and dramatically slapped a twenty-dollar bill on the table between us, saying that he did not know what my fee was but that was all the money he had. He then remarked that I should tell him when the session was over. Thus, by setting the fee himself, he took that aspect of the framework out of my hands. He then described his extremely busy and chaotic life, living partly in Vermont and partly in New York City, a lifestyle that made him unable to attend regular sessions; thus he was unilaterally declaring that irregularly spaced sessions were to become the norm. Finally, he mentioned a new-age treatment that interested him, and he suggested that I use it as my explanatory model in our work. Seldom does a potential patient succeed in violating all the parameters of the framework at once, but James managed to do so! I stood up after twenty minutes, pocketed the money, and, opening the consulting room door, announced that the session was over. Thus I utilized the only aspect of the framework that he left to me—termination of the session. I noted that regularity, appropriate payment, and use of my model were all required if he was to work with me, and, given that he had excluded all three, I saw no possibility that we could work together.

By avoiding patients like James and Karen, therapists sidestep involvements with patients who can tie them up for years in futile struggles that ultimately deplete their goodwill. Some patients with enormously engorged antilibidinal egos or, alternatively, exciting object seducers like Karen present themselves in a way that demonstrates that their desire for unproductive entanglements and endless conflict exceeds their hope of, or interest in, improvement.

Some framework issues are directly linked with the patient's use of the therapist as a stabilizing introjectible object. This was the case when one of my patients drove by my office and spotted me emptying the office trash into the outdoor receptacle. The next session, he complained that he did not like to see me "wandering around outside" with the trash basket—he wanted me in the office, symbolically "on duty," to meet his omnipresent needs. This symbolic disruption also seems to be a source of discomfort to patients when they accidentally see their therapist in the real world. From the patient's perspective, the therapist is breaking the therapeutic framework by operating in life outside the consulting room. The reality that the therapist has a life apart from the patient challenges the patient's need for the fantasy that the therapist is an ideal object who is continually focused on the patient's needs. This need to symbolize the therapist as a good omnipresent object was popularized a few years ago with the concept of "angels" who constantly monitored and protected individuals. Naturally, it is critical that the shame-ridden patient should never be criticized for his or her intense dependency needs; instead, the therapist can, in a matter-of-fact way, note that serving as a new internalized

---

CASE 4.3

Karen began her session in tears, describing her intense conflict over religious issues that had been provoked by her Christian fundamentalist friends who invoked the fear of eternal damnation if she did not join their sect. She was crying and imploring me for help. Within a few minutes, she dropped the issue and turned her attention to an Eastern guru who had a large following and whom Karen also admired. Her affect switched from a desperate suppliant to an advocate of this religious philosophy, and she claimed that this guru had "cured" her. The teary emotions displayed just minutes before were dissociated, and she became aggressive toward me for not knowing anything about this religious leader. This was followed by a discussion of her current work in therapy, which she described as five years of ongoing debate and battles with her therapist on the purpose and value of her being in therapy, an issue that was still unresolved. As our interview went on, Karen switched emotionality from idealizing stances to hostile criticisms about individuals, philosophies, and therapeutic models, including object relations theory, about which she did not appear to know anything. Some of her display seemed to be a hostile reaction to her current therapist's possible abandonment of her, despite the fact that she was dismissive of the past work with that person. Rather than feeling challenged to rescue this complex but misunderstood patient, I saw an individual who was more interested in seducing and destroying therapists. I concluded the interview by getting out of my chair and, standing well away from the patient, removing my first published book from the bookshelf. I noted that most patients chose to come for therapy with me because they had read either that book or articles about the model that I had written and wanted to work within that model. I did not offer the book for her to take in her hands for fear that she would throw it on the floor, which I saw as a real possibility. I then removed a second book that I had written and repeated what I had said. After placing the books back on the shelf, I opened the consulting room door, an unmistakable nonverbal cue that the session was over, and remarked that her ambivalence about being in therapy and her negativity toward the model I worked with gave us little room for a therapeutic alliance. As she left, Karen began to giggle, which I took to mean that she could not believe she was being asked to leave on no uncertain terms. It struck me that her lifelong experiences in therapy had accustomed her to either dominating or seducing well-meaning therapists to her personal cause, which was to repair a complex and interesting patient who ostensibly knew so much about the field. Structurally, her interpersonal display (which I saw as fundamentally genuine) operated as an exciting object "attractor" to therapists who responded with their libidinal egos, which were tempted by the future possibility of approbation and personal success if they cured this complex, exciting object patient.

---

object is part of a therapist's role and that it is not a burden. Furthermore, as time goes on and more and more positive introjects are taken into the patient's ego structure, he or she can be expected to need the therapist less intensely.

A prime characteristic of the framework is the therapist's absolute predictability. All therapists are familiar with the disruptions produced when they go on vacation and "abandon" their patients. Many therapists temporarily transfer their needy patients to colleagues during their absence, on the theory that a replacement object is better than no object at all. In my experience, this may lead to major problems with many characterological patients. Patients are apt to comply initially with the demand that they see someone else, but in their minds this establishes that they cannot get by for even two weeks without the therapist. This point was made by a well-meaning supervisee who suggested to her borderline patient that the patient take a vacation at the same time as she, the therapist, did, so as to minimize the time they would be apart. I winced at this idea, and the supervisee responded, "How did you know that my suggestion would upset her?" The answer is simply that adult borderline individuals are as dependent as young children, and they are deeply ashamed of this aspect of their behavior. To remind the patient of this reality is to insult them. Some of my patients who saw a "replacement" therapist during my vacations reported that they were disturbed to see a stranger in the role of "their" therapist, and it provoked increased grief about my absence. In effect, the new well-meaning therapist inadvertently reminds the patient of how much he misses his treasured object. Therefore many borderline patients may function better during the therapist's absence if they do not see a colleague, odd as that may seem. Patients also resent the feeling that they will have to "start over" with someone else while their own therapist is on vacation.

THE GRADUAL PROCESS OF INTERNALIZING THE THERAPIST

Over time, with most relatively cooperative patients, the explanatory model the therapist uses to co-create a narrative of the patient's developmental history gradually brings therapist and patient into agreement as to the reasons for the patient's emotional predicament. Looked at from the perspective of the patient's conscious defenses, psychotherapy is a long-term disagreement between the therapist's explanatory model and the patient's. Each patient brings a personal theory of his or her problems, which is often defended aggressively during the course of therapy. These "personal theories" are far-ranging, but in my experience almost all of them are not even remotely accurate. They almost universally protect the patient's bad objects or, more accurately, protect the patient's attachment to his or her bad objects. The very discussion of the patient's attachments to bad objects creates anxiety for him, as Fairbairn (1943) noted: "From the patient's point of view, accordingly, the effect of analytical treatment is to promote the very situation from which he seeks to escape" (75). This is true both in patients dominated by their libidinal egos and in those dominated by their antilibidinal egos. The patient comes from a universe in which her explanatory model has failed, and yet she holds onto that failed model with a vise-like grip. Resistance to the therapist's views by the extremely defensive characterological patient who is acting out is unmatched, and so an extremely potent explanatory model is needed to replace the patient's rationalizations for her condition. As mentioned previously, transferences prevent many interpretations from having an impact on the patient, because they are short-circuited by the patient's interior structures that force all external objects into familiar roles. This requires much effort on the therapist's part just to help the patient understand what an interpretation is and how it can be used, as noted by Mitchell (1993):

> The patient's subjective world is organized like a prism whose facets refract and disperse entering illumination into customary and familiar wavelengths. The analyst, from the beginning, would like to reach the patient directly, would like his understanding to expose for consideration the very structure of the patient's prism of subjectivity itself. This is not possible for the patient. . . . The light that the analyst shines on the prism invariably enters it and is dispersed into familiar categories of experience: old dreads, old longings, old hopes. For the patient to be able to hear the interpretation as an interpretation . . . the patient would already have to be able to recognize an analytic interpretation as something different from anything in his previous experience.   (212–213)

The following exchange between patient and therapist illustrates this process, which consists of interpretative attempts by the therapist to understand the patient's externalization and enactment of her inner structures with objects in the external world. The patient was an educated and relatively nondefensive thirty-five-year-old woman who had a history of severe childhood deprivation. As an adult, she went from one unsatisfying relationship to another, and the therapist offered the following interpretation in her fifteenth session:

PT: I met a Broadway actor who is up here for a semester teaching at the university, and I agreed to visit him in his apartment tonight.

TH: Well, you really seem to be jumping into things in a big way. Is this fellow more or less exciting than the man that you brought home from the office last week?

PT (*laughs*): That Larry fellow is a real loser. I know what you are going to say about this sudden change, but this is how I really feel.

TH: Oh, I do not doubt for a moment that this change is how you really feel. I am reminded of how you used to wait for your father to come home. Didn't you tell me how you would dress up in your roller-skating tights and greet him on the driveway with a new trick that you were perfecting when he got there? And didn't you throw the purse he had given you into the woods when he failed to come home. Wasn't that a sudden change of feeling as well?

PT: I can't remember how this business is supposed to fit together. I really don't know if it has anything to do with today.

TH: Let me see if I can help you out. You actually had two fathers, an exciting one who filled you with hope and expectation and an unreliable one who let you down time and again. When you were waiting for the exciting one to come home, you couldn't remember his unreliable side. Your actor friend is the new version of the exciting side of your dad, and you can't see any other possibility. Larry, your exciting friend from our last session, is now equal to the unreliable side of your father, and you are not able to see any good in him.

PT: I really hope that this isn't right. I hate to think that I am so simple.

As I mentioned, the patient in this vignette displayed a moderate to low level of defensiveness and was therefore unusual, in that most patients who had attended only fifteen sessions would reject this relatively early interpretation. This patient was a university faculty member and prided herself on her intellect; she had made it a point to understand the concepts of the master narrative presented in the prior sessions. The therapist's interpretation offered this patient an explanation for her lifelong behavior, which, up to that point, had been filled with unexplained inter-personal chaos. She disliked acknowledging that the therapist's explanation was possibly the correct one, as that would mean the loss of her romantic view of herself as well as force a reexamination of her attachment to her exciting\rejecting objects. Note that the therapist in this example began his explanation with the patient's inner experience, and he was careful not to contradict the patient's initial perspective. By starting with the patient's subjective reality—that she felt very differently about the men she encountered from week to week—he opened the door to using his model when he explained *why* the subjective shift in her perceptions took place according to Fairbairn's metapsychology. The explanation was aimed at the patient's central ego and was designed to help her understand the particular form of her inner experience. As Mitchell (1993) noted, patients are not ready to see interpretations for what they really are, but, over time, the therapist who consistently uses his "master narrative" to understand the patient's life (or to understand the patient's transferences) will gradually help the individual make use of this new way of seeing herself.

It appears at times that all the understanding in the world, even when it is overtly accepted by the patient, has little immediate effect on the parallel universe of self and object representations in the patient's inner world. In this example, the insight from the explanatory model did not appear to make much difference in the patient's behavior in the external world. Only gradually does the patient "catch on" to what an interpretation is and, equally important, who the therapist is in reality. The therapist's use of a consistent explanatory model is only the cognitive part of his therapeutic effort; it must be accompanied by an active working through of the projective aspects of the transference. Second, and most important in my view, the patient must gradually internalize the therapist as a good object, and this attachment will act as an alternative to the patient's attachments to his or her bad internalized objects.

The therapist's explanatory model not only protects her from a patient's aggression, but also challenges and ultimately excludes the patient's defensive explanations for his condition. As the patient begins to accept the reality that his losses are an ineluctable aspect of his family history, he is faced with pain that no technique or model can soften. It is the patient's attachment to the therapist, along with the support the therapist provides, that will allow the patient to face what appeared at the outset of therapy as completely unendurable, as noted by Mitchell (1993): "Understanding does not provide much solace for, among other things, real loss, grief over lost opportunities, irreconcilable conflicts, and, ultimately, death. The analyst's understanding, no matter how powerfully transformative and also comforting it may be in some respects, is incapable of warding off or of providing restitution for those losses, conflicts and limitations" (213).

It is the therapist's humaneness and openness to attachment that offers patients an alternative to their rigid relationships with their internalized bad objects. The harsh reality is that, at the end of the session, the patient goes home and the analyst goes home. In my practice, many, if not most, of my characterological patients lived alone, which meant that after each profoundly disturbing session they had to go home to an empty house. It is not surprising to find, therefore, that patients *must continue* their attachment to their bad objects, which they have come to depend on for support (thus preventing an abandonment crisis), as they simultaneously gather memories of the relationship with the ideal-object therapist in their interior world. In the following quote, Winnicott (1986) describes an "empty" patient—that is, one with an exceedingly underdeveloped central ego—which in my experience is a common type of character disorder that is often based on parental indifference and abandonment rather than on abuse. Her tenuous ego structure required that she see the therapist three times a week in order to keep her central-ego memories of him alive in her interior world:

I have a patient at the moment; she is fifty-five years old and she can keep the image of me alive if she sees me three times a week. Twice a week is just possible. Once a week, although I give her a long session, is not enough. The image wilts and the pain of seeing all the feelings and all the meaning going out is so great that she will say to me that it is not worth it, she would rather die. So the pattern of treatment has to depend on how the image of the parent-figure can be kept alive. (147)

Illustrated here is the reality that the therapist who deals with central ego–deficient patients must expect them to become enormously dependent on the therapist until such time as his or her image is firmly internalized in their inner worlds. Other patients who are attached to powerful bad objects, as opposed to Winnicott's "empty" patient, cannot be condemned for remaining loyal to their bad objects because they simply cannot live without their attachments, as Fairbairn (1944) noted: "Even if they neglect him, he cannot reject them: for if they neglect him, his need for them is increased" (67). The therapist's "introjectibility" as an ideal object is increased by providing clear (and often repeated) observations about the patient's life that the patient can use as organizing principles when he or she is not in the therapist's presence.

In order for patients to internalize an integrated view of the therapist as an ideal object that will promote a well-differentiated and integrated central ego, they must resolve their transformations at some point, which will then allow them to see the therapist for who he or she truly is. These two events are related in that patients will not internalize the therapist as an ideal object when they are still transforming him or her into something that he or she is not. Only after this internalization has taken place will patients be able to tolerate relinquishing their internal and external ties to their desperately needed bad objects. As discussed earlier, this is clearly *not* Fairbairn's position. Because Fairbairn assumed that internalization was a distinctly defensive act, he believed that the good object remained in the external world and helped the patient mature from the outside. In the light of current knowledge, we simply must let go of his position. As noted previously, Fairbairn placed too little emphasis on the role of good objects in normal development, a point also noted by Greenberg and Mitchell (1983): "Although Fairbairn argues that good relationships are longed for and required for healthy development, he does not account for the residues of good experiences and gratifying relationships, the establishment of healthy identifications, authentic values, and so on. There is no place for good internal objects which function apart from defenses against bad internal object relations" (180).

Greenberg and Mitchell's criticism of Fairbairn's original work is appropriate and deserved, but if we set aside Fairbairn's incorrect assumption that internalization of objects (good and bad) is a strictly defensive process, then his model does afford a view of how change takes place. His structural model (1944:129–130) states that the central ego must take over "territories"—split-off parts of the internal world—that were formerly occupied by antilibidinal or libidinal subegos. The problem with this conceptualization is that it makes no provision for *new* material to be added to the central ego. In some ways, this appears to be related to Freud's energetic model, where a finite amount of libido was divided into three structures in different proportions, given the level of psychic development. Here Fairbairn's model uses a similar metaphor in that his position sees the central ego retaking the "territories" that have been lost to the subegos. It implies that there is a fixed amount of "psychic territory" that simply changes hands. In fact, the only way that the central ego can grow to the point that it can tolerate dissociated memories (i.e., libidinal and antilibidinal memories of the exciting and rejecting object) is to increase its size (and security) by adding memory after memory of a positive emotional relationship with the ideal object. The security of this relationship will allow the splitting defense to subside, as the patient will no longer have to hide from the badness of his objects. The expanded and strengthened central-ego–ideal-object relationship, which originated with the "fragment" of the good object left in the patient's interior world, after the exciting and rejecting aspects were dissociated, grows and forms the substrate of the personality that gives it strength under duress and offers the developing patient an alternative attachment to his bad objects. This new attachment to the therapist is the "new material" in the patient's central ego, which Fairbairn does not mention, that allows the central ego to see the bad objects for what they are.

The patient is also presented with the therapist's central-ego style of operation, which serves as a model for him to internalize. There are numerous nonspecific aspects of the therapist's ego processes that the patient unconsciously introjects and ultimately imitates. Druck (1989) has commented on both the specific and nonspecific aspects of the therapist's ego functions that are introjected by the patient: "He is steady, reliable, empathic, neither corrupted nor corrupting. He confirms the patient's inner reality and performs certain educative functions in the arena of the patient's subjective life. He models thought, reflection, anticipation, delay, introspection, and a host of ego functions" (33). The process of psychotherapy confronts the characterological patient with a good object whose central ego operates in a very different manner from the way the patient's ego normally functions. Feelings are understood, explored, and investigated, and the discharge of tension is never condoned. Thus it is both the new explanatory model that the therapist offers and the nonanxious, concerned manner in which he reacts to the patient's problems that promotes both increased comfort and increased ego structuralization. Searles (1965) has looked at the issue of ego structuralization in a different but related diagnostic group, schizophrenia. He hypothesized that ego structuralization occurs as a consequence of introjection by both parties in the therapeutic dyad. There are clearly differences in severity between schizophrenic and borderline patients, but the processes by which patients in both diagnostic categories gain ego strength appear to have much in common. Searles notes that the therapist introjects the patient's conflicts and then works on these conflicts intrapsychically, with the full force of his healthy ego. The patient then re-introjects the newly solved, less conflicted result:

I refer here to the seeming circumstance that the therapist, at the deepest levels of the therapeutic interaction, temporarily introjects the patient's pathogenic conflicts and deals with them at an intrapsychic, unconscious as well as conscious, level, bringing to bear upon them the capacities of his own relatively strong ego, and then, similarly by introjection, the patient benefits from this intrapsychic therapeutic work which has been accomplished in the therapist.

(Searles 1965:214)

The therapist who works with borderline patients applies similar but more conscious techniques than does Searles with his schizophrenic patients. The therapist applies his healthy ego and his explanatory model to the patient's difficulties with attachments to bad objects. The patient then gradually re-introjects the solutions that the therapist has produced. This process is aided by the fact that the therapist is simultaneously providing the patient's unconscious with positive images of him- or herself as an ideal object that increase the strength of the patient's central ego and thus reduce the patient's dependency on bad objects.

PROJECTING LOVE INTO THE PATIENT

The therapist, almost inadvertently, projects love into the patient's inner world, as expressed through his empathy, concern, and efforts to help. The psychotherapeutic framework, the explanatory model, and transference interpretations all help therapists penetrate their patients' "closed-loop thinking," so that the therapists have a chance of becoming the ideal objects in relationship to their patients' central egos. Once patients recognize the therapist's efforts in this regard, the therapist will have a greater probability of being introjected as a good object into the patient's inner world. It is up to the therapist, and the inherent powers of the therapeutic situation, to reorient the patient to the reality that outside objects can be caring, calming, trustworthy, and supportive, all behaviors that can be summed up as "love." Hamilton (1988) has described the power of "positive projective identification": "Projective identification is the basis for our deepest affections and attachments. Lovers describe themselves as giving their love. They give their selves and hearts to each other. These common expressions of love are examples of projective identification—imagining a loving aspect of oneself to be actually inside the other person, and acting accordingly" (96).

The therapist metaphorically becomes the patient's lover by projecting his love onto the patient—despite the patient initially being quite unlovable. Searles (1965) has described the zenith of this projection as the stage in the therapeutic process he calls "therapeutic symbiosis." During that process, the therapist splits the patient into an all-good object while dissociating the patient's frustrating aspects. The patient becomes the recipient of this love and is pressured both internally and externally by these projections to conform to the positive emotionality that he or she is receiving. The therapist's projection of love (ideally) starts long before the symbiosis stage, but many characterological patients cannot accept the therapist's goodness and thus initially fight off the early positive projections. As previously noted, patients who have been treated extremely badly as children cannot give up the idea that they will be abused or abandoned and often test the limits of the object who offers help. Once again, Winnicott (1986) describes this problem: "If you start to love a child who was not loved in this preverbal sense, you may find yourself in a mess; you find yourself being stolen from, windows broken, the cat being tortured, and all sorts of frightful things" (148).

Sadly, the same general dynamic is true for many abused, abandoned, and manipulated adult patients who cannot believe that they are going to be treated in an honest and forthright manner. All the patients' experiences indicate that there is a trade, trick, or unforeseen consequence behind the apparent offer of attention and understanding. These patients try every deception and manipulation that they developed in relation to their original objects on the new object-therapist. The patient discussed in chapter 3 who came into sessions high on drugs and later would berate me for not detecting her condition is a good example of the lack of belief in the goodness of others. The therapist's extension of love, coupled with his or her ability to contain the patient's chaos, acts as a nonverbal demand that the patient relate to the therapist in a way that the patient has not yet experienced. The therapist, as an ideal object relating to the patient's central ego, sets up an entirely new standard of communication, respect, and attention.

Another powerful aspect of the therapist's projected goodwill is his or her availability to become emotionally involved with individuals who have been discarded and misused throughout their developmental histories. The therapist's willingness to become invested in a long-term relationship with the patient places great burdens on both parties. The relationship demands discipline, the control of aggression, and the loss of autonomy (for both members of the dyad) until the task is completed. Many dependent characterological patients have spent a lifetime conforming to the needs of a variety of bad objects, and they are now confronted by a person who is willing to lend him- or herself to meet their unmet needs. These sacrifices may go unnoticed for long periods by the patient in therapy, but the pressure from the therapist's goodwill and the implicit demand for reciprocity eventually penetrate most individuals' awareness.

PROVIDING PATIENTS WITH AN ACCURATE VISION OF THEMSELVES

Another area of the patient's central-ego weakness that the therapist must deal with directly is to provide the patient with a reasonably accurate reflection of the patient's characteristics and potential. Most characterological patients have weak central egos, and the process of psychotherapy is critical in helping them discover who they really are. Borderline individuals have experienced so many contradictory and inaccurate views of their personal reality projected onto them by faulty objects that, in many cases, they have not been able to develop a clear identity. This lack of a central-ego view of the self is also owing to the fact that borderline patients have subegos that appear and disappear unpredictably, sweeping away prior understandings and destroying relationships. Before the patient's development of a consistent central ego, he or she must rely on an external guidance system in the form of the therapist's ego. The therapist must offer the patient feedback as to his current functioning, as well as his future potential, that can be incorporated in the patient's central ego. Loewald (1960), a classical analyst of impeccable credentials, has described this aspect of the therapist's task (which was not acceptable to most analysts of his day), which consisted of gently guiding the ego development of the patient by giving the patient a vision of the future:

> The parent–child relationship can serve as a model here. The parent ideally is in an empathic relationship of understanding the child's particular stage of development, yet ahead in his vision of the child's future and mediating this vision to the child in his dealing with him. This vision, informed by the parent's own experience and knowledge of growth and future, is, ideally, a more articulate and more integrated version of the core of being which the child presents to the parent. This "more" that the parent sees and knows, he mediates to the child so that the child in identification with it can grow. The child, by internalizing aspects of the parent, also internalizes the parent's image of the child — an image which is mediated to the child in the thousand different ways of being handled, bodily and emotionally. (20)

The task of being a good object in terms of this version of Fairbairn's model involves teaching, providing support, and re-parenting, in addition to interpreting transferences and co-creating a narrative of the patient's history. In terms of the therapist's responsibility, this approach places a larger burden on the therapist than does the classical analytic task of resolving the transference neurosis. Fairbairn's theory, with its focus on developmental deficiencies in the patient's life, assumes that the wholeness of the patient has been compromised and thwarted, and has to be restarted by the therapist's empathy and support, thus allowing development to resume from the point where it stopped. The gratification of appropriate patient dependency needs, even within the parameters of the framework, have been negatively regarded by classical psychoanalysis; within Fairbairn's metapsychology, however, it is central to reducing their force over time. Many therapists fear the intensity of the patient's dependency needs and assume that by gratifying these needs the patient will become greedy and regress. This is not the case either in normal development, where appropriate gratifications produce healthy, individuated children, or in the therapeutic re-parenting process. Therapists who gratify their patients' legitimate needs and simultaneously set and maintain firm and clear boundaries will succeed in developing a mature central-ego structure in their patients. Patients will absorb what is needed, and at a certain moment their inner void will be sated, their bad objects released, and their dependency reduced.

GRIEF AND THE ACHIEVEMENT OF AMBIVALENCE

As the alliance between the therapist as an ideal object and the patient's central ego develops and matures, many patients begin to watch how their external bad object manipulates others and they often become quite expert in assessing their bad object's specific techniques. During this time, many patients become fascinated with this question: Are my objects bad people who are acting "good" and who are therefore fooling me, or are they "good" people who are acting "badly"? As the central-ego–ideal-object relationship prevails, the patient characteristically becomes increasingly certain that his or her frustrating objects are indeed frustrating. The patient may take steps to engage and challenge the parental object (or displaced object) and become embroiled in real conflict with the once feared and respected object. If the tone of the conflict with the bad object is accusatory (dominated by the patient's antilibidinal ego), then the patient is still holding out hope that he or she can somehow correct or modify the rejecting object or, alternatively, experience a measure of revenge over the powerful object. There can be enormous force and aggression in these interactions between the patient and the rejecting object, but underneath the antilibidinal rage there is still the libidinal hope that a loving parent may suddenly reemerge. Real success can be achieved only when the patient gives up this unrealistic libidinal-ego hope of the existence of a gratifying object. During this intense period, the patient may have a number of victories over the bad object to savor. These victories are an intermediate step in the patient's maturational process, because the patient still regards the external rejecting object as a significant individual. With the therapist's insight, patients will recognize that children (of whatever age) should not have to be constantly fighting for their psychological life with their objects.

The gradual process of developing a narrative of the patient's unique history, based on Fairbairn's metapsychology, is designed to strengthen the central ego and erode the subegos that are filled with the fantasy of bigger-than-life objects. As the dissociated material in the subegos is slowly tolerated by and integrated into the central ego, the parental objects become viewed as flawed, imperfect, and, in many cases, hopeless as parents, both in the past and in the future. As the central ego is able to tolerate greater ambivalence about the once split objects, the two subegos lose their purpose in the inner world. Over time, the hate and fear of the antilibidinal ego toward the rejecting object(s) lose all their potency, as the rejecting objects are seen as pathetic and not important enough to fight with. The experience of integrating a single view of the (mostly good) therapist into the patient's central ego also allows the patient to hold onto a single view of the bad objects as sadly disappointing rather than enraging or tempting. The new central-ego–ideal-object relationship between the patient and the therapist becomes the template for all relationships, and the patient's sense of self gradually stabilizes over time in response to the single consistent view supplied by the therapist. The dependency that was experienced toward the original object is now focused on the therapist, where it is appropriately gratified by the therapist's emotional contact. The result of the integration of the exciting and rejecting parts of the bad object into a single view produces grief for the lost object who was not human enough to love the patient or bad enough to attain the status of a monster.

The ultimate goal is to have the patient operating out of the central ego, which will experience the patient's failed objects with ambivalence, grief, and resignation. The central ego will be able to accept the reality that he or she was neglected, not because of individual badness but as a consequence of being a human being who is vulnerable to the chaotic vagaries of fate. The patient, supported by her therapist's positive introjections, can face the realization that no matter what she did or failed to do as a child, her objects were completely bankrupt and any hope of being blessed and released into adulthood by them was nonexistent.

The further the patient gets from the smothering grip of the frustrating object, the more acute his appreciation of just how much he has really missed in life. This point was made by a patient who was raised in southern poverty by a mother who believed in evil spirits and suffered from occasional episodes of psychosis. His childhood strategy was to close down all his emotions and slip through life, waiting for death. After he recovered his emotionality (and, to a large extent, his dormant intelligence), he was awestruck by the true dangers of his childhood. His violent and psychotic older brother (who often threatened to kill him) ultimately was hospitalized for schizophrenia for the duration of his life. The patient likened his experience of living inside his defenses against the fear and confusion of his childhood to "walking through a roaring fire and not even knowing it." This type of realization often provokes an upwelling of grief, so profound and deep that it is identical to the grief at the death of a beloved object, for it is the death of hope and illusion (structurally, of the libidinal-ego–exciting-object constellation), since the still living parent is completely lost to the individual. This sad moment is actually the beginning of a new life for the person who comes this far. This can occur only when the therapist is firmly implanted in the patient's consciousness and serves as a steady and reliable good object. Surprisingly, this point can be reached with many characterological patients, given enough time and provided that the therapist has great patience.

SUPPORTING CENTRAL-EGO GAINS

An effective method for keeping a vision of the patient before both members of the dyad is for the therapist to retrace the patient's history as part of the therapeutic narrative. In effect, the therapist remembers and recounts the different stages that she and the patient went through during the co-creation of the narrative of the patient's developmental history. It is similar to a parent telling teenage children stories of their childhood that they only vaguely remember. The therapist can begin with his memories of the patient as the latter first entered therapy, and then progressively trace the patient's development up to the current status and next project it into the future. This is easily done if the therapist uses the patient's choice of objects as an indicator of increased inner structure as well as the patient's level of attachment to bad internalized objects. Because object choice is nearly a mirror image of the patient's inner structure, the patient easily understands his or her own progress. The following clinical vignette illustrates this technique:

PT: I am really tired of this therapy stuff. We seem to go over the same topic week after week. When am I going to finally get better?

TH (*mildly*): Well, I think you are much improved. When you first came in several years ago, you were about to quit your job and sue your employers whom you hated, and become (*smiles*) let's see, an accountant, or a biologist specializing in marine mammals, or a graphic artist. For the life of me, I couldn't see any connection between these jobs, or any real long-term interest in any of them on your part. You also had a regular army of "friends" who called on you only when they had a favor to ask of you, including a woman friend of your wife's who lived in your house and demanded that you cook her vegetarian meals. I can't quite remember her name.

PT (*laughs*): The infamous Sandy, queen of the rutabagas. How could you forget her!

TH: Ah yes, boiled vegetables morning, noon, and night. I also seem to remember that you were so ambivalent about your wife in those days that you were having an affair with a woman whom you met. As I recall, you ran into her husband one day . . .

PT: Boy oh boy, you don't forget anything, do you? I can now see that the whole deal was ridiculous, but I had almost forgotten about it. Your memory won't let me forget anything.

TH: I must say that somehow you got more realistic along the way and started your business, which had nothing to do with that odd collection of jobs you used to talk about, avoided your pain-in-the-neck friends, and found your way back to your wife. I suspect that you are going to be able to tell who your real friends are from now on, and manage to make a living as well. It seemed to me that you were wasting your time daydreaming about all those jobs, while you were ignoring the fact that you had talent as a draftsman and designer. It took a while to get going, but it seems to me that you are well on your way.

PT: I think so, too.

Clearly this therapist was well aware of how the changes in the patient occurred (within the limitations of the specific model used), and also realized that describing to the patient how the changes probably came about was completely unnecessary. This particular patient was fragmented and grandiose when he entered therapy, and the therapist's repeated vision of his real potential was conveyed to him in a manner that allowed him to develop organically. This example illustrates the central ego organizing potential for the patient of an ideal object therapist who behaved consistently over a long period. Classically oriented therapists try to adhere to the ideal of the "neutral screen" in order to avoid contaminating the patient's projections. This is a major technical error when dealing with internally empty characterological patients who can lose themselves when there is no clear object around which they can organize their central ego. The therapist who misapplies the neutral screen with central ego-deficient patients risks being confronted by a patient who is in a panic, who becomes more and more demanding and aggressive, and who may decompensate. This point was made by Fairbairn (1958) when he noted that free association, with its lack of visual contact, reproduced the isolation of the individual's childhood.

TERMINATION

Termination is a natural outgrowth of the success of the introjection process. The key change in a patient's behavior that indicates that the patient has internalized the good-object therapist occurs when he or she pursues and interacts with good objects and avoids prior frustrating/exciting objects. I have seen this shift take place in two stages. Many improved patients are able to avoid frustrating objects long before they are able to approach good objects. Even the avoidance of frustrating/ exciting objects can occur in stages. One patient had a series of "diminishingly" bad-object boyfriends, each better than the last until she was able to cope with an actual good object. As the frustrating objects are abandoned, the patient will focus even more intensely on the therapist, a situation that can remain relatively static for several years. Many patients remain in this position as they slowly gather central-ego strength before they are able to reenter (or enter for the first time) the world of good objects. Good objects are feared because they have the potential of "discovering" the patient's hidden badness, and because they put a far greater strain on the patient's central ego than do frustrating objects. Good objects will not tolerate acting out, disloyalty, or expressions of hate, whereas other characterological partners will accept such behavior as normal. The demand for consistency is often too much for the discharge-prone patient to face until he or she has made great gains in therapy. For instance, borderline women commonly hide their own erratic and discharge-prone behavior behind the more flamboyant and obvious acting-out behavior of their partners. Their own pathology comes to the fore when they seek out better objects and cannot control their aggression or act consistently when confronted with a well-modulated partner.

The therapist can tell when the patient is entering the first stage of this process (avoidance of bad objects) as his patient will suddenly become critical of the infantile demands placed on him by "friends" whom he no longer needs to depend on now that the therapist is beginning to be internalized. The following vignette illustrates this change:

PT: I was visited by my friend the sculptor from Baltimore this weekend.
TH: I remember her, didn't she invite two other artist friends of hers to stay with you last time, and not mention it to you until they showed up on your doorstep?
PT: Yes, and one of them used my spare bed to have sex with this creepy neighborhood guy and then lied to me about it.
TH: I don't seem to remember that.
PT: I was afraid to tell you about it back then. I knew something was going on in my guest bedroom because I heard them, and then saw the creepy guy jump out of the window and run across the back lawn.
TH: How inspiring.
PT: I didn't want to face you because I knew what you were going to say, so I didn't mention it. This time things were different. She came with some half-finished pottery, and I told her she couldn't mess up my place with her clay.
TH (*archly*): Don't you appreciate fine art?
PT (*delighted*): That's exactly what she said! I can't believe that she used to trap me with that baloney. I told her to keep her pots in their cardboard box and not mess up the place. If I want to see fine art, I will go to a museum.
TH: So, how did the rest of the visit go?
PT: Things got worse rather than better. I was talking on the phone to my daughter, who is visiting with her father in California. When I got off the phone, Tanya [the house guest] yelled at me for spending so much time on the phone,

and ignoring her. Then she said it was a big therapeutic breakthrough for her to be able to yell at me and not repress herself.

TH: Well, it sounds like a breakthrough all right, but of acting out. It reminds me of your outbursts in the old days.

PT: That's why she really upset me. I had forgotten what it used to be like in my house, but it all came back to me during this visit. I was so shaky after her outburst that I didn't know what to do. I was so scared and mad that I couldn't sleep, and then I decided that I would rather be alone than put up with her. So next morning I told her to leave.

TH: How did she take the news?

PT: She started crying and then told me I was the meanest bitch she ever met. She told me she never liked me, that her friends thought I was a snob, and that she would never come back.

TH: Sounds like quite a scene.

PT: I got scared again and began to tremble inside, but I didn't cave in, and she left.

This scene is typical of what is likely to occur as the patient begins to rely on the introjects of the therapist for inner support rather than on his or her frustrating objects. Bad objects lose their allure for a number of reasons, many of which have been mentioned previously. The relationship with the therapist has introduced the patient to higher standards of interpersonal behavior. The "normal" explosive, chaotic style of relating is no longer acceptable. The patient also begins to experience objects as whole- rather than part-objects, and is no longer seduced by promises of hope generated by her libidinal ego. The improved patient also has a greatly attenuated internalized rejecting object, and therefore abuse or rejection from an external rejecting object is no longer congruent with the patient's inner world. In other words, the patient no longer seeks rejecting, punishing interpersonal relationships to supply her antilibidinal ego with a rejecting object "sparring partner." Finally, and most important, the patient has, for the first time in her life, an alternative to the rejecting/exciting object. The process of therapy has allowed the patient to shift her dependency needs onto a good object, and, in so doing, she has resolved part or most of her developmentally unmet infantile needs.

At the outset of treatment, patients are unable to accept that their difficulties are a result of their choice of objects as well as the fact that their behavior brings out the worst in others. Toward the end of therapy, the patient's ego is sufficiently robust to tolerate these unsettling truths. Once patients can accept the reality that they are the source of anger and cynicism, then they can see why they were once limited by their attachment to objects that inhabited the primitive end of the spectrum of human behavior. Within Fairbairn's metapsychology, the abandonment of frustrating objects and engagement with consistent good objects is the final sign

that therapy has succeeded. The choice of good objects is the most important diagnostic sign that the patient is no longer attached to internal bad objects. During
the transition period, when the patient either is pursuing "less bad" objects or is in
a relatively objectless state, the therapist must sustain himself with the knowledge
that the patient is reorganizing her inner world with memories and images of him
as the ideal object. Only when this task is complete will the patient be able to
consistently pursue good objects. Prior to this point, the therapist will have to wade
through endless avoidances on the patient's part regarding the lack of availability
of good objects, a lack of interest in good objects, and—the most common complaint—the dullness of good objects. The attachment to the good-object therapist
offers the patient a window onto a new spectrum of enjoyment based on intimacy
and interpersonal connectedness that allows her to metabolize the ordinary goodness from new external objects which is central to normal human relatedness.

When the process of introjection is completed, the tone of the material that
emerges in the therapy hour begins to fall flat. The patient seems to have very
little to say, and there is little or no tension between the patient and the therapist.
The patient may struggle to bring up material that seemed important a few days
earlier, but by the time the session takes place the issues have wilted away. The
internalization of the therapist, and of his techniques for solving problems, allows
the patient to solve problems internally, outside the therapy hour. Very often the
feeling that there is nothing more to say emerges from one or both members of the
dyad. Termination in most cases seems to be a natural, appropriate, and inevitable
event. Rather than setting firm dates, it is best to allow characterological patients,
who have been traditionally horrified about separating from objects, to set their
own pace. This is perhaps the only point where self-dosing in the treatment of
the patient is both permissible and appropriate. Schedules of decreasing frequency
often give the patient enough contact to feel secure while continuing to progress
with their lives. Many patients rely on one session every other week as they merge
back into life. Finally, even the occasional session becomes a burden to patients
who would rather be doing other things with their time and money.

Little has been said so far about the time frame for the introjection of the therapist. Experience suggests that the key factor in terms of patient pathology is the
strength of the patient's emotional deprivation, the maliciousness of her internalized rejecting object, and the extent of dependency on compensatory exciting
objects. In terms of therapist variables, the ability to use an explanatory model
that challenges the patient's defenses and the therapist's skill in maximizing his
"introjectibility" seem to be the most significant factors. Most characterological
and borderline patients improve, using the principles outlined here, within five
years while attending therapy sessions once or twice a week. There are exceptions,
of course, but in my experience the five-year frame seems to cover the majority of
borderline patients.

CHAPTER 5

WORKING WITH THE BORDERLINE PATIENT
AND THE BATTERED WOMAN

THERE ARE MANY COMPETING definitions of the borderline personality disorder, and each comes from a school of thought that emphasizes one clinical characteristic over others (Druck 1989). Sadly, Fairbairn's work is infrequently mentioned, even though his basic model of development and the splitting defense are a nearly perfect and timeless description of the borderline personality disorder.

The previous chapter detailed the mutative factors within Fairbairn's metapsychology, and this chapter compliments it by focusing on the "mechanics" of dealing with borderline patients. What I mean by the word "mechanics" are issues of technique, description of typical interpersonal situations, and strategies for working with patients when, for instance, members of their families are trying to actively sabotage the treatment process. The second section of this chapter fleshes out, using clinical examples, the many observations Fairbairn made in his first four theoretical papers. Finally, the last section reviews a Fairbairnian approach to the battered woman, who is the ultimate example of both splitting and attachment to bad objects. Many examples will overlap, as Fairbairn returned repeatedly to the same issues in his papers. The intention of this chapter is to give clinicians a feel for working with the borderline personality disorder, as well as with other characterological disorders, so they are prepared for many of the challenges and clinical dilemmas that will confront them when working with these patient populations.

THE CLINICAL MANAGEMENT OF THE BORDERLINE PATIENT

INITIAL INTERVIEW STRATEGIES

The task of applying a particular metapsychological model to the patient's issues and co-creating a narrative acceptable to a patient population that can be hypersensitive, irritable, opinionated, fearful, grandiose, illogical, attacking, and counter-dependent is one of the necessary skills of the psychotherapist who works with this difficult clinical group. The therapist must use her model to explain the patient's baffling and repetitive self-destructiveness and be able to link new observations with her particular master narrative. The therapist must expect the patient to attack her explanations, particularly when they involve an unacceptable view (to the patient) of his destructive attachments to bad object(s) without complaint. When these complaints are voiced, the therapist must be ready to abandon her line of inquiry temporarily without comment or a sense of defeat, and then return to it when the patient can tolerate the loss it implies. Finally, the therapist must tolerate transferences that remake her into either a malicious or a seductive object who has no relation to her person or role. During all this activity, the therapist has to continue developing a narrative of the patient's developmental history using a single "master narrative" that remains invariant throughout the course of therapy.

In the initial sessions, the therapist's first task is to assess the level and intensity of the patient's attachment to his frustrating/exciting objects. This assessment should be done in the spirit of curiosity, without any hint of condemnation, because the patient has been exposed to many realities that have already informed him that he is excessively attached to his frustrating objects. The inquiry should include the frequency and duration of visits to the parental home, the number of phone calls, the financial ties between the patient and the parents (or displaced frustrating objects), and an assessment of the patient's developmental maturity. This assessment must be done as a matter of course, after acknowledgment of the patient's presenting complaint. Generally, the patient will be willing to talk endlessly about his frustrating objects (given a neutral tone of therapist curiosity) since rejecting/exciting objects are the center of his life. All validation of the patient's worth comes from the now internalized object's views of him (whether or not that object is currently alive), so it is counterproductive for the therapist to say anything negative about these cherished objects at the outset. If the patient suspects, at this early stage of work, that the therapist is going to suggest that the patient separate from his objects, it will cause the patient to flee from therapy. At the end of the very first session, I often present a sketch of Fairbairn's model with comments regarding what I think happened to the patient during his development, including general concepts of psychic maturity versus chronological age and the concept of unresolved dependencies. These individuals are so often misinformed about why they are the way they are that a general and accurate assessment is a relief to them, assuming it does not run headlong into their personal explanatory model. It is the one aspect of the process in which the therapist becomes a good "introjectible" object, simply by knowing something and presenting it in a way that is helpful. Havens (1976) spoke about the skills Sullivan demonstrated in this regard: "Sullivan saw his first job as showing the patient that he could make sense of incomprehensible matters. . . . In a field largely without the anesthetics of other medical specialties, this ability to operate quickly and relatively painlessly is a prime mark of the expert" (37).

During the initial interviews, it is best for the therapist to keep an open mind as to how and why the patient developed serious defenses and fixations on bad objects; I usually emphasize to the patient that it is not at all clear how this could have happened. However, after a number of years of working with extremely dependent, enmeshed borderline patients, it often became *abundantly clear* just how this happened; sometimes it was blatantly obvious in the very first session, but it is absolutely counterproductive to say anything in the initial sessions. At that time, the patient is probably so poorly separated from, and dependent on, her objects that any hint of condemnation directed toward the objects condemns the patient as well. The patient's reaction to this assessment will give the clinician a good idea of the patient's readiness to accept input from a new external object.

DEFEATING THE PATIENT'S THEORY OF HIS PERSONAL BADNESS AND GUILT

One area that earns considerable discussion during the co-construction of a narrative of the patient's developmental history revolves around the patient's assumptions of personal "badness." Most patients enter therapy and present themselves to the therapist from the position of their libidinal ego (with the exception of grandiose and narcissistic patients), seeking support, validation, and love as compensation for all the pain they have suffered. They feel maligned and aggrieved, and yet they appear to be (and in many cases are) underachievers who are socially isolated, fearful of the world, and intensely critical and envious of others. This self-view is a consequence of the long-term relationship of their central ego with the tolerable (non-dissociated) appraisal of their value by the rejecting object and their childhood rationalization of badness from the moral defense. The most extreme incidents of pain, rage, and self-contempt must remain in the unconscious, known only to the antilibidinal ego, as those repressed realities are still intolerable to the central ego because it reveals too much truth about the badness of the rejecting object. I must also qualify my use of the concept of the moral defense to mean the patient's use of the rationalization that he was treated badly as a consequence of his parents putatively "legitimate" reaction to his essential "badness," and not Fairbairn's dynamic explanation for self-blame. A large part of the co-constructed narrative that is developed between the patient and the therapist is a careful reassessment of whose viewpoint is valid; that is, is the patient as bad as he was portrayed to be by his parents? The therapist must sort out what is real versus what has been imposed and projected onto the patient. Therapists must help their patients locate the "badness" in their original objects while simultaneously not discouraging patients from remaining attached to them—a tricky proposition.

A therapeutic strategy that addresses this problem is for the therapist to listen carefully to descriptions of the patient's past history and point out when and how the patient assumed that she was somehow responsible for all the deprivation and punishment that befell her. The patient was likely blamed for many "family" problems, and over time she learned to accept and incorporate this view, which was supported by the moral defense. When engaged in developing this part of the narrative, it is best to remain in the past, for if the therapist focuses on current relationships with frustrating/exciting objects, the patient can assume that something must be done immediately about the situation. In terms of confronting the patient's conclusions about herself, the therapist simply has to reconstruct key past events from the patient's life and contrast the conclusions reached by the "family" regarding the patient's culpability with his conclusions. For example, one of my patients was often physically abused by her poorly controlled father. Her mother would blame her after each attack for having provoked her father. The most egregious example of this occurred when her father pushed her down a flight of stairs and was pummeling her on the landing. Her mother got down on her hands and knees during the beating and yelled in her face, "Stop making him mad!" The therapist's reaction to this type of information can change over time from surprise and mild condemnation during the initial stages of therapy to appropriate outrage at the injustice of the undeserved abuse, the latter only after the patient and therapist have moved into a relationship between the patient's central ego and the therapist as the ideal object.

The therapist must keep in mind that defeating the patient's attachment to frustrating objects is a long-term struggle fraught with extreme anxiety for the patient. As the therapist calls into question the patient's rationalized "badness," the patient may act out hatred of displaced "bad objects" that are safe. The safe "bad objects" are almost never the patient's actual parents. This is understandable, as many severe borderline patients continue to live with their original objects or cling desperately to idealized views of them that are mediated by the libidinal ego. For many borderline individuals (but not all), it is too dangerous to express the level of hate they have toward the parental objects directly, as it would threaten their continued dependency, a point Fairbairn made repeatedly.

Another source of personal "badness" is guilt experienced by individuals with borderline structures stemming from the child's sense of duty to, and responsibility for, the abusing/abandoning object. Frequently, the patient as a child had a split perception of his objects as both abusers and pathetic infants. This is based on the parents' conscious or unconscious demand that their child comfort them (rather than the reverse) when they were in distress (Liotti 1992). The patient's sense of guilt regarding his abandonment of the pathetic aspect of his objects can be countered only with mild confrontations after a strong alliance has been formed between the

---

CASE 5.1

A patient who was struggling to separate from his massively intrusive, guilt-inducing, and infantilizing mother described a dream in which his task was to run as fast as he could along a road in order to escape an unnamed danger. He realized that running that fast was extremely difficult, but he could manage to outrun the threat. His success was foiled by a pack of dogs unleashed by an unnamed force that turned out to be his mother. He recognized that he could have succeeded in his escape if the dogs had not been added to the already difficult task. In desperation, he climbed a tree to escape from the harassment of the dogs. One dog climbed after him and was about to bite him when he kicked it, and it fell to the ground, paralyzed by the fall. He was overcome at this point with waves of contrition for hurting the dog, which he recognized as the embodiment of his mother.

---

patient's central ego and the ideal-object therapist. The therapist must remind the patient again and again of the active abuse perpetuated by the frustrating/exciting objects. In case 5.1, my patient had been told many times that separation from his family would be a selfish act that would emotionally kill his mother.

Working against the level of guilt described in this example requires a strong relationship between the patient's central ego and the ideal-object therapist, who must be internalized as an alternative relationship to the bad object so the patient can separate from the bad object without misgivings. Naturally, guilt is strongest in the early stages of therapy when the patient still assumes that his objects were less "bad" than they really were and, conversely, that he was less "good" than he is in reality. It is no wonder that work with the dependent borderline patient is so slow, since many factors are aligned against the emergence of the individual into adulthood.

The feelings of guilt that dependent borderline individuals experience is of a different magnitude from that associated with less severe disorders. A slightly different variation on the guilt scenario comes from families that have an unspoken expectation that their children are responsible for the parents' happiness and therefore the success of the family enterprise. Children can be gradually convinced that they are responsible for their family's well-being by the simple expedient of being blamed whenever events in the family go awry, and by being assigned tasks that are supposed to ensure the parents' well-being. This process of shifting responsibility to the children occurs gradually, year after year, until, finally, the children are held responsible for events that are completely beyond their control. Many children who are burdened in this manner become hypercompetent at protecting their objects from exposure. Although they become experts at negotiating with adults in the external world, their internal world is one of frustration and emptiness since their own developmental needs have been completely neglected. Case 5.2 illustrates, once again, Fairbairn's recognition of the unconditional nature of the child's dependency on his

CASE 5.2

Warren described a desolate and empty childhood in his working-class family that revolved around his psychologically disabled mother. She was so fragile that she usually remained in bed, unable to bear up under the strain of raising her two children. Warren and his younger sister were charged with the task of making elaborate breakfasts for their mother, and their fate for the day depended on this performance. The expected level of the effort was far beyond their developmental ages, yet, over time, they mastered nearly professional levels of skill. If they presented a pleasing enough performance, their mother would get up and "care" for them during the day; if they did not meet her expectations, she remained in bed.

objects. There is no other choice for the unfortunate child, and he must do whatever is in his power to meet the needs of the object in the hope that his parents will eventually improve and take care of him.

The patient, Warren, was pseudo-mature in that he had mastered skills that were ostensibly nurturing to others, yet his own dependency needs were almost completely unmet and he became hopelessly entangled in dependent relationships with women who, on the surface, seemed maternal. His constant companion was a wave of guilt that overcame him whenever he was reminded of his mother, whom he finally "abandoned" without repairing her to the point where she could function. Another aspect of his repetition compulsion that emerged at his job (as a social worker) was to become involved in "projects" involving the attempted rescue of one dysfunctional client after another.

CHALLENGING THE PATIENT'S EXTREME ANTILIBIDINAL STANCE

Borderline patients are so hostile and contentious that they often are involved in disputes with a number of individuals at the same time. These battles with others can interfere with the therapeutic work with ego-deficient patients. Many patients have antilibidinal subegos so extreme that this structure causes them continual interpersonal trouble. The therapist can challenge the antilibidinal subego's certainty of its position by comparing the patient's antilibidinal vision of the external object as totally rejecting with his previously expressed central-ego view of the same object. This technique is not essential to the development of the narrative, but it can be very helpful in reducing the unnecessary and self-defeating interpersonal tangles that the borderline patient typically gets himself into with friends and colleagues, entanglements that can eat up enormous time and energy. For instance, if the patient goes into a blind hate-filled rage after being rebuffed by an object in the external world that was previously seen as a good object, the therapist can begin to explore the possibility that the rejection was either inadvertent or even illusory. After the patient's antilibidinal outbreak has subsided, the therapist can cite instances in the past where the same object behaved in a gratifying manner, thus confronting the absolute and unrealistic position of the antilibidinal ego with the patient's previously expressed central-ego position. The therapist must stay very close to the material that the patient produced in prior sessions in order to justify her contrast of the opposite positions. As mentioned previously, any statement the therapist makes that is not exactly in tune with the needs of the borderline patient is experienced as abandonment, particularly during the early stages of treatment. This technique can therefore be used only with patients who have established some relationship between their central ego and the ideal-object therapist. The therapist's position can be that of a puzzled but neutral observer who mildly confronts the patient with a different reality. The therapist's central-ego correction of the patient's extreme perception will be less objectionable than it might originally have been, since it contains material that the patient has previously presented herself, as illustrated in case 5.3.

CASE 5.3

Irene was physically battered by her wealthy alcoholic mother, who was insulated from reality by her money and extreme defenses. She and her mother were linked together by guilt and spite, and seemed to be in an endless competition to discredit each other. Irene was supported by a considerable inheritance and was able to live a nomadic "eternal student" life, switching from one college to the next, taking continuing education courses that did not require her to be a full-time matriculated student. She roomed with other college students, and many of our therapy sessions consisted of a continuous monologue of hatred, envy, and spite directed at her roommates. She described how they abused her, made fun of her, borrowed her clothes, and ignored or otherwise humiliated her. The therapist recognized that Irene was experiencing the world from the perspective of her enraged antilibidinal ego and silently listened to the material, since Irene had no ability to tolerate any statement that contradicted her views. Week after week, the therapist offered his interested attention. If, in reality, anyone had truly believed Irene's extreme statements regarding the behavior of her three roommates, the roommates would have been *imprisoned* at the very least! Finally, an opening appeared for the therapist to interject a central-ego view of the same situation. Irene was failing the single course she took that semester, and her roommates made numerous suggestions for changes to a paper that she had written, downloaded study notes online, and provided her with their class notes from prior semesters for the upcoming final examination. Irene attempted to hold onto her hostility toward her roommates, because now she felt that they saw her as a pitiful "basket case." The therapist proposed a central-ego view of her roommates' behavior as being motivated by goodness. He then questioned why such hateful, vindictive, and malicious people would go to such lengths to help her out. This provoked a slight shift away from the extreme antilibidinal view toward a more central-ego view, although, naturally, Irene questioned my loyalty to her.

The repeated technique of waiting for an opportunity to cut back toward reality can, over time, strengthen the patient's central ego. This is one of the possible cognitive interventions for times when the therapist is not fighting his way out of a patient transference, and though it is a peripheral technique, it can be quite handy.

As mentioned earlier, it is far more dangerous, and usually futile, to use the reciprocal structures in this procedure. In other words, it is not advisable to compare the patient's libidinal-ego view that the possibility of love exists in her exciting object with the therapist's central-ego view of the same individual as empty, uncaring, or manipulative. Based on my experience, if the therapist attempts to "correct" the fantastic view of the patient's libidinal ego regarding the potential for love from the exciting object, he will simply create increased resistance and conflict. The very fact that the libidinal ego is dominant is a clear indicator that the patient feels in danger of losing her object. Since the only function of the libidinal ego is to protect the patient from an abandonment crisis, the patient will hang onto that attachment regardless of what the therapist says or does. Therefore, it is best to allow the patient to wax hopefully about the assumed love contained within the exciting object without the therapist interfering by interjecting his integrated, central-ego perception of that object.

SUPPORTIVE BEHAVIORS THAT FOSTER SEPARATION FROM EXTERNAL BAD OBJECTS

Another aspect of the relationship between the therapist as an ideal object and the patient's central ego is support for the patient's differentiation from his bad objects, as well as support for more mature levels of relationships with others. This puts the Fairbairnian approach outside the boundaries of classical psychoanalysis, which prohibits the analyst from offering any advice or support whatsoever. Fairbairn (1958) stated his position clearly:

> It should be added that what I understand by "the relationship between the patient and the analyst" is not just the relationship involved in the transference, but the total relationship existing between the patient and the analyst as persons. After all, it is on the basis of the relationships existing between the individual and his parents in childhood that his personality develops and assumes its particular form; and it seems logical to infer that any subsequent change in his personality that may be effected by psycho-analytical treatment (or any other form of psychotherapy) must be effected primarily on the basis of a personal relationship. (379)

The Fairbairnian approach offers a major advantage to the psychotherapist working with ego-deficient patients in that it gives the therapist permission to encourage separation from the frustrating/exciting object. There is no ban on active support or teaching since the model does not share the belief that the patient is a complete, but conflicted, psychic entity. Rather, the patient is seen as caught in a developmental time warp, empty, lost, and clinging to the bad object for fear of complete annihilation. I am not suddenly advocating intervening with external objects on the patient's behalf; instead, I suggest that "active support" means offering both support for the patient's pursuits and psychological education regarding the patient's understanding of himself and the probable motives and interpersonal tactics of others in his environment.

Once the patient overcomes his antilibidinal wariness of the therapist as a good object and a sound central-ego–ideal-object relationship is established between them, the therapist can move more forcibly against the external frustrating/exciting objects. Here I must emphasize, however, that *forcefulness by itself* cannot and will not motivate the patient to do anything new until his attachments to his bad objects have been eroded by his internalization of the ideal-object therapist into his inner world. Strengthening the patient's central ego through psychological education aims to modify the patient's interpersonal responses to the parental objects (or the new, displaced bad objects) by internalizing the therapist's techniques for handling external objects. To begin this process, the therapist should carefully assess the patient's interpersonal functioning with the still living parent or displaced objects, with an eye toward strengthening the patient's responses to repeated self-defeating or humiliating interactions. Very often, the patient will describe discussions, battles, or confrontations in which he was overwhelmed by the power of the rejecting object's anger, abuse, or condemnation. Most typically, a patient's antilibidinal ego tries to defend itself from the accusations aimed at it by the rejecting object and most often fails miserably. This attempt on the part of the patient fails because the patient is convinced of his own badness and at the same time assumes that the frustrating object sees something in him that is valid. Second, the patient dare not win, for if he does, he will endanger his dependent relationship with his frustrating object. The patient does not understand that the very act of fighting back against the accusations from the frustrating object validates the attack. The borderline patient's overvaluation of the importance of the parental object, or displaced object, results because these objects are internalized in structures that were formed at an earlier time in life and are unchanged by experience.

In terms of interpersonal tactics, it is relatively simple to teach the patient not to respond to the attacks and to explain the rationale for containing the ineffective responses. As the patient's central ego develops, the therapist can explain the probable motivations of the frustrating object's quest to keep the patient in a submissive position. When the therapist focuses on the motivations of the frustrating object, the patient will begin to understand, via his central ego, how he has been manipulated. This aids in the development of the patient's central ego, and over time the once omnipotent and terrifying rejecting object becomes manageable through his own efforts. Almost invariably, the frustrating object does everything in her power to keep the patient in the dependent and insecure position, and will actively work against the patient's increasing autonomy. This emphasis on the active opposition of the external object does not deny that there is a simultaneous battle in the patient's inner world regarding his continuing need for, and loyalty to, the frustrating/exciting object. The therapist's support of the patient's central ego promotes the patient's attachment to the therapist as an ideal object who is attempting to protect the patient from further abuse. As the relationship between the central ego and the ideal object flourishes, the therapist can note just how aggressive and demeaning the parent (or current frustrating/exciting object) is to the patient and how destructive it has been to the patient's growth, without fear of counterproductively triggering the patient's libidinal ego. Consider case 5.4, in which a small success occurred because the patient gave up hope that his father would ever support or approve of him. Naturally, this realization takes some time to achieve, but most dependent borderline patients are in active contact with their frustrating/exciting object, so opportunities arise to support the patient so he can achieve better and better results.

A second beneficial consequence of this technique is that the patient's central ego will begin to realize that the frustrating object's tactics, which once impressed and overwhelmed him, are not so much a threat as they are an illusion, a chimera, that he can defeat by adopting the new information his therapist offers. This revolutionary view of the parent usually occurs after the patient's central ego has

---

CASE 5.4

A young man described how his wealthy and powerful father, who owned many buildings and for whom he worked as a member of a maintenance crew, would toss lunch money on the floor for his son in front of other employees. The therapist noted how sadistic and cruel his father was behaving, a concept that was new to the young man and not supported by anyone in his interpersonal universe. The patient was surprised that the therapist was actively taking his side and said that it was the first time he could remember being helped by an adult. The therapist suggested that the patient bring his own lunch money to work, which forced the patient to confront his stubborn and dependent demand that his father support him. The patient began bringing his own lunch money, but his father continued to seek him out at noontime to repeat the humiliating scenario. These developments changed dramatically when his father, sensing his son's defection, escalated his attempts to embarrass him in front of the other employees by throwing a twenty-dollar bill on the floor, ostensibly for his son to pick up. When the young man ignored his father's attempt to humiliate him and walked away, one of the employees picked up the money and handed it back to the now thoroughly enraged father.

developed sufficiently to recognize how predictable (and pathetic) his once invincible rejecting object now appears. This shift in perception signals the shift in the patient's inner world from dominance by the antilibidinal ego, with its fear and hatred of (and respect for) the rejecting object to the emergence of a stronger central ego, which is the structural goal.

In this example, the young man was able to see how petty and manipulative his once feared father now seemed as his own central ego became increasingly dominant. This patient relied on the internalization of the good-object therapist to give up his demand that his father take care of him (via the lunch money) and moved into a more differentiated position in relation to his bad object by substituting his new attachment to the good-object therapist. The therapist must be aware of which ego he is dealing with when supporting differentiating behaviors with any given patient. If the patient enjoys the sadistic pleasure of defeating the once potent object, then the therapist can assume that he has been relating to the patient's anti-libidinal-ego–rejecting-object constellation without engaging the central ego. This signals that the patent has identified with his internalized rejecting object and has learned to force the once feared parent into the antilibidinal position, a situation I have reported on previously (Celani 2005). This is not an uncommon shift, and the therapist must engage the patient's central ego through the interpretation that the patient has become identical to his rejecting object, an interpretation that usually quickly corrects this error. In other words, a clear confrontation of the patient indicating that he is imitating his sadistic rejecting object will usually be potent enough to stop the identification.

MANAGING COUNTER-STRATEGIES IMPLEMENTED BY THE PATIENT'S OBJECTS

Over the past hundred years, mainstream psychoanalysis has dealt with patients as if they lived in a one-person universe, engulfed in their self-created fantasies as they struggled with destructive id-based derivatives from their (assumedly) inherited instincts. Fairbairn's metapsychology offers clinicians a completely different view, one that includes the importance of external objects who impact the patient continuously. Parents can become threatened when their offspring (regardless of age) enters therapy. Some parents become angered by the new reality that they no longer exercise complete dominance over their psychological child, who is simultaneously an adult patient. Part of the support that the ideal-object therapist can offer to the patient's central ego involves predicting the parents' next interpersonal "move" against the ongoing development of the patient's autonomy. Typical moves by frustrating/exciting objects include fast shifts in strategy as they sense that their child is no longer intimidated by them, as in the case of Connie, described in detail later in this chapter, when she challenged one of her father's threatened assaults. These threats were common in her childhood and caused her to freeze in terror, but after several years of therapy, she stood up to one of his threats with counter-aggression of her own, and her father instantly switched to bribery. In other cases, the parental objects may begin favoring another sibling (or a nonfamily member) in order to reactivate the patient's libidinal-ego–exciting-object constellation. Other behaviors that counter the patient's differentiation include the parents' gross condemnation of the therapist or "stonewalling" (ignoring) the patient's efforts toward autonomy in the hope that the patient will collapse into an abandonment depression before the family does. Guilt-inducing manipulations are also common and include sending the patient baby pictures, baby books, or other memorabilia designed to activate the patient's libidinal ego. An example I have used previously (Celani 1993, 2005) involved Susan, a young single woman, who came to me for help in the process of separating from her family. Note that her splitting of me from an exciting object to a rejecting object, outlined in case 5.5, is reminiscent of Odgen's (1990) passage, quoted in chapter 4, regarding the destruction of a previously agreed-on reality.

Over her time in treatment, Susan was once again able to accept a central-ego view of her family situation, as she modified her excessively hateful antilibidinal perceptions of her father back into an integrated view. This is a *critical change*, as antilibidinal hostility toward the rejecting object can keep the patient passionately attached through the hope of vanquishing the rejecting object. Susan's case also illustrates the fact that patients who have strong antilibidinal egos are unable to separate from their frustrating objects and operate in the world alone, regardless of how angry they might be at their objects. Developmental progress can be made only when the antilibidinal ego and its attachment to the rejecting object is supplanted by a central-ego attachment to a good (ideal) object. Susan gradually began to relate to me from her central ego, and once again she saved money for another security deposit and found a different apartment. I attempted to prepare my patient for another card from her father designed to reactivate her libidinal ego, and she assured me that she was *absolutely* immune to that possibility. Not surprisingly, a second card arrived from her father professing his love for her, and once again my patient split into a libidinal-ego view of him and of her life back in her family. This second time, however, the splitting was less severe, and Susan's central ego was strong enough to prevent her from moving back home. Still, her longing for her father was clearly painful.

The most dramatic attempt by a family to prevent differentiation of an adult child that I experienced as a therapist was a "family ambush" of a patient who was becoming increasingly autonomous, as recounted in case 5.6. The positive outcome of this strange event was based on the length of time my patient had been in therapy and the advanced stage of internalization of me in her inner world as an ideal object.

Cases 5.5 and 5.6 emphasize how active the original frustrating objects can be in thwarting the patient's development. They are more than internal objects or

Susan, twenty-four years old, was living at home with her parents and two older brothers while working at her first job as a receptionist and secretary in a law firm. When she began therapy, she described her father from an antilibidinal-ego position as a monster of a human being who exploited the whole family mercilessly. In contrast, it appeared to me that my patient and her mother were caught in a traditional lower-middle-class family and were being treated as if they were inferior to the males by the dominant husband, who favored his two sons, both of whom worked with him in the family auto-repair business. Susan reported that her father seldom addressed her directly but expected her to help her mother prepare lunches for him and her two brothers every day, even though she had to ready herself for her new job. Similarly, after returning from work, she was expected to help prepare dinner and clean up the dishes every evening, while her father and brothers conversed in the living room and watched television. Her mother had developed a severe drinking problem over the years, and one of her unspoken tasks within the family was to help put her mother to bed most evenings when she collapsed from too much alcohol. Her description of her father was antilibidinal, as it portrayed him as one of the worst villains of all time, though, as I have pointed out, her presentation of this material placed her in a libidinal-ego–exciting-object relationship to me as a potential savior. In the past, she had tried to rescue her mother from her situation (who rejected all suggestions) and repeatedly complained about how she herself was being treated to relatives whom she asked to intervene, but they were indifferent to her plight.

Her life at home contrasted sharply with her ever improving relationships at work and the beginnings of a serious romantic relationship. Frustrated by her long-term, unmet dependency needs, she became fixated at an earlier stage of development when she was unable to separate and live on her own despite a year of twice-weekly psychotherapy sessions informed by Fairbairn's model. During the second year, she had modified her antilibidinal perceptions of her father to the point where they were part of her central ego. Her increasingly powerful central ego allowed her to separate from her family, and she rented an apartment of her own despite considerable guilt at leaving her hapless mother at home, without an ally. Within a week, she received her first card (ever) from her father, which was filled with protestations of his love for her, saying that their home was not the same without her. She brought the card to the session and read it to me, tears streaming, saying that she always knew her father loved her and that she planned to move back home as soon as she could move out of her new apartment. This clever ploy on her father's part had reactivated her dormant libidinal ego, which repressed the now less powerful central ego, and she suddenly saw her father as an exciting object, filled with the potential to love her. She also switched her view of me from an ideal object to a rejecting object, believing that I had convinced her to leave her "loving" family. I tried to review both her antilibidinal statements and her later central-ego statements about her father, but she threatened to leave if I said anything negative about her family—a common situation when dealing with borderline patients who suddenly split into a strong libidinal-ego position. After moving back home, there was a brief reunion, but, not unexpectedly, the situation soon reverted to the old pattern where she was expected to serve her father's and brothers' needs while they totally ignored her. Her perception of her father split once again from a libidinal view of him as an exciting object to an even stronger antilibidinal view of him as both a tyrant and a shameless trickster.

CASE 5.6

Amy was the daughter of immigrant parents who had engulfed and controlled her until she fled the family home after graduating from high school. She was considered a disgrace to the family because she left home to start a career while still unmarried. Her siblings spent every weekend with her parents, moving their families back to the parental home. In therapy, Amy described a bleak and loveless family that was centered on the acquisition of money in the never-ending quest to appear wealthy and successful. Her parents were extremely upwardly mobile, and yet her father worked a second job as a janitor in a department store, where he could be seen cleaning at night by passersby. The children were taught never to mention that their father had a decidedly déclassé second job and to deny it if someone asked them directly. Amy thrived in therapy because it provided her with a more genuine and personal relationship than she had experienced in her family. After managing to stay away from all her family members for a year, she was lured back by a sister who had recently given birth to a daughter. Amy insisted that her sister keep her visit a secret from her parents, but after visiting with her in her (sister's) home for half an hour she was confronted by her parents and brother, who had been hiding in an unused bedroom! Her mother began a tirade against her, demanding an explanation for her desertion from their "perfect family" in which she had been given everything a daughter could want. Her sister began to scream that Amy was killing their parents and that she would be entirely responsible if they died. Amy reported that she went into a mild state of shock, but she had developed a strong enough central ego to remain separate and to experience her family's grotesque behavior as completely alien and unrelated to her. She tried to leave, but they forcibly blocked the door. She and I had role-played past family scenes, with all their exaggerated, manipulative emotionality, and she was able to employ a facsimile of those experiences as an escape. She confessed her undying loyalty to the family in a very sarcastic manner, but to her complete and utter amazement, her parents and siblings were so eager to hear the message that they were oblivious to her sarcasm. She reviewed the conversations we had had about the emptiness of her childhood and replayed them in reverse, praising her parents for the emotional richness of her childhood and for their love and support. The eagerness with which her parents accepted this utterly fantastic view of reality reinforced her awareness of how pathetic they were. She left unimpeded, returned to her home, and remained separate ever since.

---

fantasies; they are *active agents* in the external world who attempt to influence the patient in any way they can.

CONCEPTS FROM FAIRBAIRN'S PAPERS THAT APPLY TO THE TREATMENT OF THE BORDERLINE PATIENT

This section illustrates typical behaviors encountered in the treatment of borderline patients that are clinical examples of concepts from Fairbairn's original papers. Notably, most of the behaviors that Fairbairn described as typical of the "schizoid" personality eventuate into resistance to the therapist's impact as a good external object.

RESISTANCE FROM FOCUSING EXCESSIVELY ON THE INTERIOR WORLD

One of the very first observations Fairbairn (1940) made regarding "schizoid" patients was their excessive focus on their inner world. Despite this focus, logic would suggest that the "introjectively insufficient" type of borderline patient (Adler 1985) would greedily grasp at and internalize external objects, but many seem oddly uninfluenced by these external objects. On the surface, the "empty" borderline patient appears to be desperately dependent, and yet, despite earnest and heartfelt interaction with the therapist, still complains that she experiences inner emptiness. This suggests that her inner world is almost immune to the impact of external objects, a point Fairbairn (1958) made when he termed the inner world a "closed system." This lack of experience with a good object, with the resulting impoverished central ego, was previously referred to as the "structural deficit" by Seinfeld (1990): " From the perspective of the structural deficit, the therapist as a potential good object is perceived as alien, strange and unfamiliar" (12). These adult individuals currently experience their inner world in exactly the same way as when it was established during their childhood development. Adult borderline individuals with particularly toxic or empty histories are less trusting and tend not to embrace external objects very firmly, even though they need them desperately. Typically, patients who report the experience of inner emptiness are the type of borderline patient who indiscriminately pursues one object after another. A great paradox is that these patients, who seem so utterly dependent on external objects, are so *under-influenced* by them in terms of building internal structure or of developing a lasting sense of security. The interior world of many borderline patients is a consequence of so many historical abandonments that their antilibidinal ego assumes that all objects, despite their initial libidinal allure, are ultimately rejecting. Therefore, the therapist's impact is shunted into one of the preexisting internal structures, and the patient's central ego remains undeveloped. No matter how great an effort the therapist puts into the relationship to make the patient feel secure, many borderline patients continue to feel constant trepidation, even panic, because they are paying excessive attention to their inner rather than their outer reality, as case 5.7 illustrates.

The imperviousness of the patient, Anne, to well-meaning objects, as demonstrated in this example, is often accompanied by extreme sensitivity to rejecting objects, often described as "borderline empathy." This apparent contradiction between hypersensitivity to certain objects and a complete lack of sensitivity to others is resolved by the clinical observation that the imperviousness to others is most

CASE 5.7

Anne came for a consultation in a near panic attack because her husband of seventeen years had left, saying that he had waited long enough for her to calm down and accept the reality of his love, but nothing he did or said made any difference to her. She appeared to be as fearful of abandonment after years of marriage as she was on the first day of their relationship. Anne was also similarly panicked by the fact that she had so few "good" friends. In fact, she was surrounded by several individuals like herself who exploited one another with the zeal that only the undifferentiated can muster. Therapy lasted for five years and was characterized during the middle years by increasing waves of panic and rage at being abandoned both within the context of therapy and regarding her external objects, regardless of the reality of these relationships.

often in the direction of an inability or a resistance to internalizing good objects. Borderline empathy, on the contrary, is the tendency for the ego-deficient borderline patient to sense the needs of rejecting objects and to modify his or her own behavior to meet the rejecting object's unexpressed needs.

RESISTANCE TO THE THERAPIST'S IMPACT
BASED ON UNMET NEEDS

The tendency to experience objects as part-objects is based on the loss of hope in the goodness of objects, which turns the child's focus toward "partial objects." Fairbairn (1940) saw this as a consequence of deprivation. The deprived child focuses on the most important aspect of the object, which is determined by the child's pressing needs, and thus objects are valued only for what they bring to the deprived individual. The emotionally supported child looks for whole-object relationships and regresses to part-object relationships only when he or she is deprived. Fairbairn noted this type of regression, which he termed an "early oral orientation," in many of his patients, and defined it as an attitude of need without an awareness of the characteristics of the object who was meeting the patient's needs. Case 5.8 illustrates a borderline patient, Tim, whose unmet needs greatly overpowered the beginnings of a central-ego–ideal-object relationship that he was slowly developing with me.

The pattern of moving from one dependent, mutually exploitative relationship to another—while resisting the impact of the therapist, who is no competition for the allure of a new object—can be seen in both men and women. The severity of the early deprivation reduces the borderline patient's discrimination, and any object that produces a sense of immediate gratification and safety suffices. Tim could not live alone because he had not sufficiently internalized me as a

CASE 5.8

Tim was the only child of silent, unresponsive parents. He was continually neglected as a child and remembers all the family members retiring to their own rooms after the evening meal. He spent hours alone in his room writing stories and, over time, developed into a remarkable poet and writer. Despite his obvious talent, he spent his young adulthood drifting from one relationship to another, seeking to fulfill his unmet needs, while his talent languished. He developed a pattern of becoming involved with women who had established homes, and he would move in with them, often acting as a father to their children. This obvious exploitation of these women was overshadowed by the masochistic position he would take in relationship to his partners. In each case, Tim was exploited for his money by women as dysfunctional as, but more aggressive than, he was. During one relationship of three years' duration, he compliantly took care of a horse-boarding farm while his partner went on an extended tour of Europe with her children—this in addition to his regular job and against his wishes. He was fearful of and uninterested in horses, and fumed silently that the time he had set aside for writing was largely taken up by his duties on the farm. His relationship with his partner was blatantly a part-object relationship; it emerged, in fact, that his needs were more focused on her homestead than on her person. As therapy progressed, Tim became more aware of how much he actually disliked his partner (a likely repetition of his early relationship with his original objects), and yet, despite his conscious antipathy, he remained with her for another year. When he finally separated from this object, it became clear that he had not internalized me as a good object, as he was unable to live alone. Immediately after leaving this latest relationship, he returned to the chaotic woman (who took him back without question) with whom he had lived just prior to the woman he was now leaving.

---

good object to sustain himself independently. He needed a tangible object within immediate reach to reassure him that he was not alone. In Tim's case, it was not only the object that gave him the sense of security but the actual house and sense of family that accompanied these particular women. Notable as well is that he was also exploited in these relationships, in that he chose women who lived in the world of part-object relationships as firmly as he did. His relationship with me was shadowy and impotent in the face of his unmet developmental needs that pressed for immediate and tangible gratification.

THE PROFOUND FIXATION ON, AND RETURN TO, THE EXCITING/ REJECTING OBJECT

In his first theoretical paper, Fairbairn (1940) noted that emotionally abandoned children became increasingly attached to the objects who had failed to meet their needs, "that, influenced by a resultant sense of deprivation and inferiority, they remained profoundly fixated upon their mother" (23). A lifetime of abuse does not reduce this heightened need for, and attachment to, the rejecting object. This attachment is often evinced by the borderline patient's attempts to woo back the rejecting but exciting object. An extreme example of this was the case of a forty-five-year-old female patient whose mother so rejected her that she permanently banned her own daughter from the house. The only arena in which her mother would allow contact was in restaurants where the two would occasionally dine together. Despite a lifetime of abuse and rejection, this adult woman would send her mother expensive and elaborate flower arrangements on her own birthday as a gift to the mother for having given birth to her.

Many borderline patients assume that the intensity of their needs is causing their desperately needed object to reject them. These patients report, almost universally, that they attempted to cling to the rejecting object by suppressing their needs and adapting themselves to the needs of the object, which is the basis of the previously mentioned borderline empathy. This was the dynamic in the case of the unloved daughter who bought her mother flowers for having given birth to her. My patient suppressed her needs in the hope that by catering to her mother's needs, she would ultimately be accepted. One consequence of this strategy is that when the frustrating object rejects the dependent borderline once again, the resulting rage is either poured out on a "safe" object or redirected toward the patient's antilibidinal ego. In either case, it is far too dangerous for the individual to express her frustration and rage directly toward the needed object. If it were expressed toward the already unloving object, increased abandonment would likely follow, as Fairbairn (1944) noted. When self-hate that is contained in the rejecting object is turned against the borderline's antilibidinal ego, this further diminishes the individual's sense of potency and value, as Armstrong-Perlman (1991) notes:

> They often assume that if only they can repress the intensity of their own needs and adapt themselves to the needs of the other, the relationship offers hope, whatever the costs of personal submission. The rage consequent to the frustration and humiliation, when this hope is not fulfilled, may be totally repressed, or converted into anxiety, or into somatic symptoms, or deflected onto others, or turned against the self for not being able, as they see it, to submit enough or wanting too much. (345)

Borderline patients' "fixation" on the rejecting object does not lessen over time. They wrongly assume that they are to blame for the rejection, and their solution is to give more and more to the rejecting object. Many middle-aged patients can still be seen attempting to win their elderly parents' approval using the same submissive strategy, year after year, to no avail. This is often the case, though not universally true, as we saw the reverse situation in the case of the young man, described in chapter 2, who "accidentally" destroyed his father's prized possessions. That individual could not contain the rage in his antilibidinal ego against his rejecting-object father, but later in life his attempts at attachment reasserted themselves. This same individual took care of his father when the father was dying, and later had his father's clothes retailored to fit him.

The borderline patient's physical return to her actual or displaced frustrating/exciting objects is, of all the behaviors cited, the most typical of all pathological behaviors. From the borderline's perspective, the bad object is seen as the only possible source of nurturance and validation, and, as a result, other potential "good" objects are ignored. This occurs, as Fairbairn noted, because the infant is focused on a single object and is unable to give any credence to other objects. In a similar vein, Seinfeld (1990) has pointed out that the borderline patient reverses the normal process of going toward good objects and away from bad ones. The focus on, and overvaluation of, the bad object causes the borderline individual to depend entirely on the bad object for self-definition. Tragically, the bad object almost universally has a negative assessment of the borderline's worth as a person. The more negative an evaluation the borderline individual receives, the harder she tries to change the frustrating/exciting object's opinion of her. Consider case 5.9.

CASE 5.9

Connie, a nurse, was single and twenty-five when she came for an initial consultation. She described her life as chaotic and told me of her involvements with marginal, alienated friends who were socially and professionally inferior to her. She also suffered from bulimia, which had increased in frequency to the point that it was beginning to compromise her ability to work. Her dependency on her bad objects was remarkable: almost every weekend, she returned to her parents' home, some hundred miles away, to do their housekeeping. During the long drive, she would anticipate impending love and appreciation, but invariably these libidinal hopes would alternate with fear and dread. Often she would eat soft bread and drink milk before leaving and purge a number of times before reaching her parents' house. She would immediately set to work cleaning their house, which, from her perspective, was always dirty and in need of cleaning. Her efforts were inevitably demeaned, as her mother went from room to room pointing out real or feigned failures in her cleaning job. Typically, her father would become increasingly jealous of her presence in the house and find any excuse to yell at her for her selfishness—actually a projection of his own self-centeredness. The most dreaded ritual, which had occurred regularly ever since she was a child, was a car ride her father insisted she and he take, at which time he would discharge near psychotic accusations at her until she was reduced to a screaming rage. While visiting her parents' home in adulthood, she tried to visit childhood friends still living in the area, but she had to give up these visits because, on her return, she was greeted by a barrage of paranoid accusations and questions from her father that often reduced her to tears. Despite this shameless abuse, and despite being in therapy, she continued to return to her parents' house nearly every weekend for three years.

The patient, Connie, typifies borderline individuals who return to their bad objects, who seem (to them) to possess the emotional supplies they so desperately need. As noted earlier in this chapter, Connie's central ego developed over time, and she began to challenge her father when he threatened to hit her. One time, she stood up to his threat (she was twenty-eight years old at the time) by forcefully pushing him backward when he approached her. After first complaining that she had a terrible temper, her father offered to buy her a new car.

The untreated borderline is fixated, frozen in developmental time, seeking to win a positive response from the frustrating/exciting object. Fairbairn (1941) described the difficulties involved when the unloved child attempts to separate from his or her objects:

> During the course of analysis, such an individual provides the most striking evidence of conflict between an extreme reluctance to abandon infantile dependence and a desperate longing to renounce it; and it is at once fascinating and pathetic to watch the patient, like a timid mouse, alternately creeping out of the shelter of his hole to peep at the world of outer objects and then beating a hasty retreat. (39)

Fairbairn's work needs little translation when applied to patients, as it is so close to human experiences. The efforts of many borderline individuals to escape the power of their dependency on their bad objects are far more heroic than Fairbairn's analogy would suggest, yet few succeed. Their strivings for autonomy are usually thwarted by their pressing needs, their narrow focus on a single object, and the absolute nature of their dependency. This is illustrated in case 5.10 (Celani 2005),

---

CASE 5.10

Richard, a young man in his mid-twenties, attempted to separate from his parents by taking an epic bicycle trip across the continent with a group of other young adults. He described his mother as a meticulous and mechanical house cleaner who ignored him except when he interfered with her cleaning, and his father as a barely controlled perfectionist. When his father tried to help him learn how to hunt, he would become so enraged with his son's age-appropriate difficulties that he would begin to clap his hands rhythmically behind his son's head until Richard fled the woods in a frenzy of shame. For instance, if Richard stepped on a twig that snapped, or if his father spotted the game before Richard did, the hand clapping would begin, and the hunting trip would be terminated. The bicycle trip was an attempt to get away and find a new part of the country to live in, as well to provide relief from his daily life with his parents. The tour went across the width of Canada, down the West Coast of the United States, and back through the South, then up the East Coast, terminating in New England. Soon after he returned, he bought a house next door to his parents!

---

which illustrates the power of dependency and the inability of the neglected child to separate from the objects he or she depends on. The greater the failure of the objects, the more persistent and destructive is the child's attachment to them.

RESISTANCE TO CHANGE FROM THE BORDERLINE PATIENT'S POOR DIFFERENTIATION

Fairbairn cited the schizoid's "identification" (lack of differentiation) from the object as a powerful factor that made separation from his or her objects difficult, if not impossible. The developing child requires the help of his or her object to achieve a separate identity. Without the active help and cooperation of the object, success is highly unlikely. Fairbairn noted that the emotionally undernourished child remains far more identified with the frustrating/exciting object and directs more attention toward the object than toward him- or herself. For example, Connie, the nurse discussed in case 5.9, experienced a peculiar but frequent form of empathy for her father, who was often suffused with murderous rage toward her. She reported worrying that he would die of a heart attack in the middle of a hateful tirade against her. She was so undifferentiated from him, and so needy of his (assumed) emotional supplies, that any distress on his part, regardless of whom it was directed toward, caused her anxiety. This extreme lack of differentiation from the rejecting object also plays a large role in the crushing guilt experienced by borderline individuals if they even contemplate leaving their objects. Doing so would be like leaving behind a part of themselves, as well as abandoning an infantile object whom they have helped to function. As noted previously, many dependent borderlines have a dual view of their abandoning and abusive object. They often act as if they were their parents' parent. They are forced to sacrifice their emotional development in order to allow their (infantile) parent to function, while their own dependency needs are put on hold. They are actually waiting for the parent to grow up and assume the parental role. This mixup of self and object, based on a lack of differentiation, continues indefinitely because psychological separation requires that the parental object support the child's developmental needs.

One of the worst outcomes when working with an undifferentiated patient is for the therapist to make a premature interpretation regarding the symbiotic relationship between the patient and his objects, with the result that the patient then returns to the parental object and repeats the whole interpretation. There is no contest between the therapist's opinion of the patient and the bad object's opinion, simply because the patient has been focused on the bad object for his or her entire life. The impact that a new, unknown object can make on an infantile patient is limited, at least until there has been some internalization of the good-object therapist.

Fairbairn also saw a lack of differentiation as the key to understanding shame. He recognized that the child of bad objects becomes an unwilling partner, but a partner nonetheless, to the parent's brutality or libidinal badness. He explored this in his 1943 paper, as part of the prelude to explaining the moral defense: "That a relationship with a bad object should be shameful can only be satisfactorily explained on the assumption that early in childhood all object-relationships are based on identifications" (64). The child is ashamed of himself because he is not being cared for by the person who should be doing so, and he is also ashamed of his own self because it is now the repository of the parental object's contempt. Simultaneously, the child is ashamed of his object because he is undifferentiated from, and therefore part of, his faulty object. Private shame is one thing, but to be exposed publicly to the view of others as being hopelessly attached to a demeaning parental object is simply mortifying, as a number of my patients demonstrated. Several of my patients reported that their enraged mothers had scratched their faces. These children's greatest fear was not the brutalization at the hands of their mothers but the possibility that the source of the scratches would be known to their teachers. Many borderline patients have, by necessity, become masters of deceit in order to reduce their overwhelming shame and at the same time protect their dependency relationship on their bad objects. Consider case 5.11.

Borderline individuals feel that the shame inherent in associating with bad objects is amplified when others see them as victims of neglect, for they will then think less of them. This stems directly from the borderline's antilibidinal ego's experience of feeling demeaned by being neglected by the rejecting object. I experienced an example of obvious shame based on a lack of differentiation from bad objects when I went to mail a package at the post office. I had to leave the post office without accomplishing my task, because a loud argument erupted between an unruly and aggressive woman and the postal employees. Upon exiting, I noticed an old, rusty car in the post office parking lot with a number of unkempt children inside. A young boy, no older than ten, had the hood open and was pouring oil into the engine when he caught me observing him. The young boy glared at me with

---

CASE 5.11

Garry arrived for a consultation regarding his inability to leave his promiscuous and physically violent wife. In describing his history, he reported that his depressed mother had slept on the living room couch all morning throughout his childhood. When he grew older, his job was to get his brother ready for school while his mother slept. He was never aware of being neglected or ashamed of himself or his mother, until the morning when his fourth-grade teacher came to his door to pick him up for a school field trip. Upon opening the door, he realized that his sleeping mother was exposed to his teacher's view. Overcome with shame, he slammed the door and refused to leave his house.

unabashed hatred, for he was publicly exposed as being involuntarily associated with a bad object. He had to take care of his parental object and the car, and he seemed to be acutely aware of the badness that was enveloping him.

Another source of shame in rejected children comes from the disparagement of the love they express toward their object. Very often, children express their love by attempting to help their distressed object by relieving some of their burden. A former patient described an incident she inadvertently caused when she tried to ease her mother's depression by cleaning the house while her mother was out doing errands. She was filled with a sense of anticipated appreciation and love as she scrubbed floors, dishes, and bathrooms. When her mother returned, she saw the newly cleaned house and went into a blind rage, knocking over furniture and emptying food from the cabinets onto the kitchen floor. She screamed at her daughter that if she was so eager to clean the house, she should clean up the new mess. Her mother was enraged by the implication that she was not a good housekeeper (which was true) and by the incorrect assumption that her daughter was criticizing her. In Fairbairn's (1944) words, my patient had discharged her libidinal feelings into a vacuum, which resulted in her experiencing severe shame and humiliation. Her humiliation was so vivid and painful that the patient reported that the next day, she made a shoe box into a symbolic coffin and placed her mother's name on it. She then went outside and held a mock funeral service for her rejecting maternal object. Despite this valiant effort to bury her attachment to her rejecting object, she returned to he mother's home time and time again during adulthood.

HOSTILE TRANSFERENCES TOWARD SAFE OBJECTS

Fairbairn understood that rage toward the rejecting object cannot be discharged directly, as this action would further endanger the borderline's perilous dependency. The rage is temporarily suppressed and then discharged on other objects who do not pose as great a threat to the borderline's security. Fairbairn (1951b) addressed this issue of the inhibition of aggression toward the frustrating object: "The risk involved in his expressing aggressive feelings towards her is that it will make her reject him more and love him less, i.e. will make her seem more real for him as a bad object and less real as a good object" (172). This common clinical observation contradicts theorists who describe borderline patients as absolutely unable to contain their aggression. As noted earlier in this chapter, clinical experience, as well as the experience of authority figures from all walks of society, attest to the reality that many borderline individuals inhibit direct aggression toward their needed objects and conversely direct it toward "safe" objects who do not endanger their dependency relationships. Alternatively, the aggression toward the rejecting object is disguised, as in the example of the young man whose "accidents" wrecked his father's car, sunk the family sailboat, and ruined the rowing shell. Case 5.12 illustrates the remarkable ability of borderline

CASE 5.12

Thomas was referred as a patient by a local Employment Assistance Program for having stolen from his employer. He worked for a large beverage distributor and had been observed, for more than a year, stealing expensive wines that he then sold, as if they were unadvertised specials, to his restaurant customers. The whole affair mystified his employer, who waited until he was absolutely sure of Thomas's involvement before confronting him. Thomas, who was the most successful of seven salespersons employed by the firm, could not verbalize what motivated his behavior when his employer confronted him. Most remarkable was that Thomas had developed an affectionate son-like relationship with his employer, who, understandably, could not fathom why he had been betrayed by an employee whom he had emotionally "adopted." Thomas proved to be a difficult patient because of his extreme lack of psychological mindedness and the resistance of the dissociated material in his unconscious. Over a number of months, exploration revealed that his apparently "normal" childhood was normal for his four siblings, but not for him. The family was divided by gender; his mother had exclusive hegemony over the three daughters, and his father was exclusively concerned with the two boys. He recalled that his father favored his brother as he grew up, and eventually his brother joined the father's trade and they were currently working together in the family business. Thomas's abandonment would have been less enraging if his mother had taken some interest in him, but she was exclusively preoccupied with her daughters. He reported that in adolescence he had become a gifted athlete, but he found himself walking home alone after high school baseball games and noticing that other parents had been there supporting their children. Worse, as he passed his father's automobile-repair shop, he could hear his father and brother working late together. Thomas was completely unaware of any conscious resentment toward his father, though he did remember a number of instances when he deliberately hid tools in his father's shop, which exasperated and enraged his father. Further exploration revealed that Thomas's acting out against his good-object employer was motivated by dissociated rage at an object that was less dangerous than his original parent. Had he acted out in a similar manner against his original object, his abandonment would have been complete. His employer, notably, did not fire him but instead urged him to come for therapy and also accepted gradual restitution for the losses he had suffered.

individuals to deflect rage away from their frustrating objects, who would certainly abandon them completely were they exposed to such hostility.

The example of the patient, Thomas, again emphasizes the primacy of dependency on frustrating objects over all other alleged sources of borderline psychopathology. Not only was Thomas's acting out a consequence of his dependency, but his unconscious choice of the displaced object also reflected his need to protect himself from becoming aware of the source of his anger while also protecting his frustrating parental object from his anger. He had a clear though unconscious understanding that his father was uninterested in him in the first place and would not tolerate rebellion from a son in whom he was not emotionally invested.

THE BORDERLINE PATIENT'S USE OF TRANSITIONAL OBJECTS TO PROVOKE LIBIDINAL FANTASIES

The inner emptiness of the central ego in severely neglected and dependent borderline patients, which results from early and repeated abandonment, leaves an enormous desire for transitional objects that are used to trigger their libidinal egos. Many borderline individuals contain few remembered internal representations of comfort and support, thus lending disproportionate power to external objects symbolic of the family. Adler (1985) notes that adults' use of transitional objects suggests they are relying on "recognition memory" as opposed to "evocative memory." Recognition memory occurs at a stage prior to the solid introjection of internalized good objects. Children (or deprived adults) require some form of actual external stimulus to recall those fragmentary introjects that they contain. Conversely, individuals with abundant and secure introjects—internalized ideal objects—can rely on "evocative memory," which Adler describes as the ability to access internalized good objects without external aids. Many borderline individuals try to assuage the pain of their unmet dependency needs by clinging to physical remnants of the original unsatisfying objects. Consider case 5.13.

CASE 5.13

The patient described a family scene in which her father brought out items of clothing worn by her now deceased mother and "auctioned" them off to the daughter most willing to serve his needs. The longed-for mother had been spectacularly inept (as was the father) and therefore was strongly sought after by the three deprived daughters. During the development of the narrative of her childhood, this patient described a prototypical event between herself and her mother that had occurred when she was nine years old. She had run home from the playground with a badly cut knee. When her mother caught sight of the blood, she screamed and ran into the woods behind the house and refused to come out. My patient, who was bleeding profusely, tried to coax her mother out of the woods to help her with the wound, and her efforts attracted the attention of a neighbor who was deeply concerned about her untreated knee. She then reacted to her unrecognized shame by lying about the situation, minimizing her obvious injury, and refusing treatment from the neighbor. She realized that she would be punished were she to expose her mother's failures to people outside the family. Twenty years later, she was willing to offer her father unlimited dinners that she prepared and delivered to his home in exchange for her mother's nightgowns. These transitional objects were essential for this patient to gain access to her libidinal ego, which was undersupplied with memories based on reality. The touch of the clothing her mother once wore was an effective libidinal-ego stimulus for this patient. In effect, it was the only "part" of her mother that she really had.

CASE 5.14

Donald, a successful graphic artist, described a childhood in which he was systematically discriminated against by his mother, who favored his younger sister. His father, a minister, took refuge from his family in his study and left his son entirely in his wife's care. His mother used Donald as a target for all her frustrations toward her powerful and indifferent husband. She abused her son for his maleness, saying that he, like all boys, was selfish, cruel, and insensitive, while praising his sister for her feminine attributes. His mother would spend long hours combing his sister's hair or shopping with her. Donald recalled his recurrent wish to wake up a female so he could join the club from which he felt painfully excluded. He recalled that during his childhood he became fascinated with his mother's clothes and began to wear them at every opportunity. It was apparent to him as a child that his mother knew about his behavior and approved of it. She began leaving clothing around for him to wear. On one occasion, he remembered a brief discussion between them regarding which of them would be the first to wear new clothes she had purchased. This habit, along with chronic depression, eventually brought him into therapy. Donald was using women's clothes as transitional objects to provoke his libidinal ego and thus provide him with the only memories of closeness he had with the exciting aspect of his mother. His mother, without question, was a frustrating and hateful object, and yet her rejection of him produced an equivalently large need for closeness in his libidinal ego. She was also the better object of the two he had, and his attachment continued because the chronic maternal neglect made any fragment of closeness with her so potent.

When a patient relies on transitional objects, the clinician can assume that the patient has very weak introjects and that extensive prodding is needed for them to emerge. It also indicates, obviously, that the relationship is with an internal rather than an external object. Case 5.14 demonstrates just how long lived and potent transitional objects can be when they are used to bring back the few attenuated comfort-giving memories that were available to the child. The habit of the patient, Donald, of dressing in women's clothing continued throughout his life, as relationships with internalized objects are as stubborn as those with external objects. This example also supports Adler's model of recognition versus evocative memory. Donald needed specific props to provoke his memory, as he had so few memories of closeness with his object.

DISSOCIATION OF THE REJECTING ASPECTS OF THE BAD OBJECT

As demonstrated in the preceding discussion, the Fairbairnian point of view cannot separate the act of splitting from dependency on bad objects. The "obstinate attachment" to bad objects could not occur if the individual could remember all the incidents of rejection, disappointment, and abuse that are split off in the antilibidinal ego. Working with many borderline patients throughout my career convinced me that Fairbairn discovered a psychological phenomenon so large and powerful that there simply is no interpersonal power in the world that can force a split patient to see the truth about her needed object. Defensive splitting can be otherworldly in its power, and as long as splitting prevents access to antilibidinal memories, the individual will be able to return to the exciting part of the bad object filled with hope, as described in case 5.15.

The patient, Howard, was an educated, well-read, and urbane man, yet no amount of confrontation could break through his rigid libidinal-ego position regarding his mother. I have noted that confrontation of the patient's libidinal-ego fantasy is almost always futile, because the very presence of the libidinal ego indicates that the patient is holding on to his object with all his psychic might, and Howard was one of the patients who reinforced the truth of this observation. Considerable psychological understanding by the therapist is required to accept that a sixty-year-old, worldly man with children of his own, and a long history of academic scholarship, could be absolutely blind to the reality of his abusive, manipulative, and pathetic mother. However, dependency and unmet needs plus the power of dissociation trump logic every time. In therapy, Howard maintained that his mother was a heroic survivor of harsh city life who provided for him and who loved and supported him. Occasionally, after one of Howard's weekly sessions,

---

CASE 5.15

Howard was a sixty-year-old retired college professor who had been raised in New York City by a manipulative, controlling, and inadequate mother. During his childhood, she repeatedly sent him to neighbors or distant relatives to stay overnight. He would arrive with this expectation, only to discover that his mother had not bothered to call ahead to his hosts; she simply wanted to get rid of him for a day or two. The little suitcase he carried became a focus of shame and rage. He was always "invited" to stay overnight after his hosts realized the situation, but he experienced waves of betrayal and humiliation in the process. This scenario was repeated again and again, and his abandonment panic would build whenever he was sent off to visit. Not surprisingly, as he got older, he was unable to differentiate from his mother and was frequently called on for financial support by both his mother and his sister. He was also called on to rescue his sister, who would have "breakdowns" in restaurants or other public places. His adult life was filled with periodic returns to his now elderly mother's home to take care of affairs for both her and his sister, who never developed enough central ego to allow her to separate from their mother. His mother would demand that he transport her around the city (despite adequate public transportation) or pay small debts. Howard brought her a clock, a calculator, and subway schedules during one of his visits, in a vain attempt to "teach" her to be more independent of him. This attempt to stop her incessant demands for transportation and money from him, not unexpectedly, failed totally.

I would receive a bulging envelope reframing the session and recasting his mother as a vicious, manipulative predator who had used him unmercifully for her own needs. When confronted with his own letter in the next session, Howard would blithely refuse to listen to his own words, sweeping them away with a grand gesture and describing his mother in beatific terms. The most striking aspect of Howard's psychological functioning was this uncanny lack of integration, which allowed the two separate views of his object to live in his inner world side-by-side without influencing each other. Howard required many years of work before his central ego could accept all the years of dissociated negative experiences with his frustrating/exciting object.

Splitting of this severity is common in individuals who received the least amount of early support and who remain eternally dependent on the original object. The dependency on the exciting/frustrating object can last forever if the firmly rooted and protected bad object is not challenged by a new attachment between the patient's central ego and the ideal-object therapist. Howard also demonstrated the need for transitional objects by wearing his mother's wedding ring on his small finger in lieu of his own wedding ring. He, like so many introjectively empty individuals, needed tangible items to prop up his inner void. Splitting and introjective insufficiency often show up in the same person, since each is an aspect of interpersonal deprivation

THE BATTERED WOMAN

During my career as a clinician, I worked with many borderline women in the 1970s and many of them mentioned, in passing, that they were currently, or had been, in battering relationships. It was remarkable how straightforwardly they mentioned this reality, without emphasizing it in any way, as if it were a normal part of life. In 1979, Lenore Walker published *The Battered Woman*; suddenly victims of abuse had a strong advocate, and domestic violence was a topic of conversation on television. As I read *The Battered Woman*, it became clear that Walker's three-part "Cycle Theory of Violence" could be understood by using Fairbairn's model of splitting. The battering scenario is perhaps the clearest demonstration of splitting, as it requires the abuser to shift from his identification with his rejecting object back to his libidinal ego, while the female victim shifts from her libidinal ego to her antilibidinal ego and then back to her libidinal ego, all during the three-part scenario. Neither the abuser nor the victim has a strong central ego, so they continually split from one extreme subego (or are identified with the internalized rejecting object) to another, without being able to maintain an integrated, central-ego view of the other. Patients who come to therapy because of a battering scenario also offer the most appalling demonstration of the self-destructive and obstinate attachment to the exciting/rejecting bad object.

Like all severe borderline patients, battered women come from emotionally impoverished and abandoning families. Notably, none of my patients witnessed violence in her family of origin; rather, they all developed powerful libidinal and antilibidinal structures in relation to their objects based on deeply dissociated emotional deprivation. Frequently, my middle-class battered women patients were involved with lower-class men (Celani 1998) in order to find an object who could enact the extreme emotionality and rage-filled violence that validated their inner structures. Many of these patients reported that the only time they felt "real" and alive was when interacting with their abuser, who, because of the extreme swings in his behavior, was able to engage both their unrealistic libidinal ego and their self- and object-hating antilibidinal ego. Much of the following material comes from my book *The Illusion of Love: Why the Battered Woman Returns to Her Abuser* (Celani 1994).

PHASE ONE: TENSION BUILDING

The first phase of Walker's (1979) Cycle Theory of Violence is called the "tension-building phase" and is characterized by minor battering events that the victim either minimizes or denies. In this first phase, the empty, enraged batterer has identified with his rejecting object and is pouring out his historical resentment on his object, whom he sees as worthless and deserving of abuse. The victim puts up with mild abuse and fights to stay in her libidinal ego and see her object as exciting, but it is an enormous strain. The abuser is dominated by his identification with his rejecting object either because of frustration at his job or because his partner did not meet some aspect of his infantile needs. In this early phase, the abuser becomes hostile and verbally demeaning, and may begin to physically push or otherwise bully the victim. The victim is appropriately fearful of her abuser and assumes, using the rationalizations of the moral defense, that she has done something wrong or has somehow provoked him. The moral defense motivates the victim to focus on a personal "failing," often one that her partner has pointed out as the reason for his abusive behavior. For instance, the battering victim may rationalize that if she had cooked a better meal, then her partner would not have overturned the dining room table in a rage. This rationalization originally protected her parents, and now it protects her partner from appearing as "bad" as he really is.

During the first phase, the victim tries to mollify the abuser and retain a libidinal-ego view of him as an exciting object. She fears that he will further identify with his rejecting object and abuse her once again. She is not eager (at least consciously) to derepress her antilibidinal ego and pour out all her resentment toward him, as her antilibidinal ego also contains the memory of abandonment, *an eventuality that she dreads more than the physical abuse.* The victim utilizes the mechanisms of her childhood and believes that with a little more effort on her part her object will see her goodness, and this will release the love that she assumes is hidden behind his negativity.

PHASE TWO: ACUTE BATTERING INCIDENT

The first phase can continue for only so long before the victim splits into her antilibidinal ego, because the intensity of the abuse turns to all-out physical violence and her libidinal ego is dissociated and replaced by her engorged antilibidinal ego. The battering scenario is characterized by physical violence (Walker 1979), which is the extreme enactment of the relationship between the batterer as a rejecting object and the victim, who is now completely dominated by her antilibidinal ego. The full fury of a lifetime of frustration within the batterer's internalized rejecting object is now discharged against his weaker partner. As the batterer's rage is unleashed, splitting cuts off all memories of his partner as an exciting object, the person he longs for and loves. The batterer's attack is motivated by primitive, pre-ambivalent frustration, based on a childhood filled with unmet needs and abuse that could not be actualized against the original objects and now is discharged toward his partner, often causing enormous physical damage. During the battering event, the victim's antilibidinal ego is also free to attack her partner with all the hate and rage stored up in her unconscious, though typically she is completely overwhelmed

One of the most notable aspects of the battering scenario that Walker (1979) mentions is that the victim of abuse frequently attacks the police who have come to her aid: "Police also complain of being attacked by the women themselves if they attempt to intervene during a phase two incident. They become understandably indignant when the very person they set out to help turns on them" (64). This is not surprising, given Fairbairn's model, since abandonment is the greatest fear of the psychologically underdeveloped individual. The police are a threat to the ongoing relationship because they can arrest the abuser and remove him from the home. The danger of physical abuse is less significant to the battered woman than is abandonment, as it was for the children whom Fairbairn treated in Edinburgh who were temporarily removed from their homes. Those children wanted desperately to return home despite the threat of continuing violence from their parents. The antilibidinal ego is amazingly fearless, and a number of my battered women patients who refused to back down from their far stronger abusive partners told me that they hoped they would be able to "teach him a lesson." This is the logic of the antilibidinal ego, which is in an intense and lifelong struggle to reform or defeat the rejecting object.

PHASE THREE: "KINDNESS AND CONTRITE LOVING BEHAVIOR"

The third phase of the battering scenario, which Walker (1979) calls "Kindness and Contrite Loving Behavior," begins after the batterer has discharged his rage

THE BORDERLINE PATIENT AND THE BATTERED WOMAN ■ 183

from his rejecting object onto his partner. Walker describes (without the benefit of the splitting model) the batterer's sudden shift from one ego structure to another, which in Fairbairn's model is the dissociation of his identification with his rejecting object, and the reemergence of his previously unconscious libidinal ego: "The third phase follows immediately on the second and brings with it an unusual period of calm. The tension built up in phase one and released in phase two is gone. In this phase, the batterer constantly behaves in a charming and loving manner. He begs her forgiveness and promises her that he will never do it again" (65).

After the abuser finishes his violent assault, he is left in a relatively neutral state. The torrent of rage in his internalized rejecting object is fully discharged, and his partner may be badly injured. It then occurs to the abuser that he might be abandoned by his partner because of his brutality toward her. This realistic fear of abandonment, which is just as powerful in the abuser as it is in his victim, reactivates his libidinal ego and once again he sees her as an alluring and exciting object. He is faced with a distinct problem: that his abused, physically injured, and still enraged partner is still in her antilibidinal ego, seething with hate and recriminations. He tries everything in his power to reactivate her libidinal ego, which often seems absurd to the observer, given that his partner may even be hospitalized and severely injured. The abuser who has split back into his libidinal ego will work feverishly to induce his partner to see him as an exciting object once again. If the victim of abuse has sought help, the abuser will work to counter all the efforts of social workers and workers at the battered women's shelter who will likely urge her to remain separate from him. Walker (1979) illustrates the extent of the batterer's efforts to stimulate the derepression of his partner's libidinal ego and thus make him appear to be an exciting object:

> These women were thoroughly convinced of the desire to stop being victims, until the batterer arrived. I always knew when a woman's husband had made contact with her by the profusion of flowers, candy, cards and other gifts in the hospital room. By the second day, the telephone calls and visits intensified, as did his pleas to be forgiven and promises never to do it again. He usually engaged others in his fierce battle to hold on to her. His mother, father, sisters, brothers, aunts, uncles, friends, and anyone else he could commandeer would call and plead his case to her. (66)

The batterer is like many others who have learned how to stimulate splitting in the borderline individual. The batterer is usually "genuine" in his promises to discontinue his abuse; because he no longer has access to the rage in his now dissociated rejecting object, his protestations of a new start are, as far as he can tell, real. Indeed, these tactics often work to split the victim back into her libidinal ego, as the batterer appears to be a larger-than-life example of a person who contains unlimited love, as Walker (1979) notes: "The battered woman wants to believe that she will no longer have to suffer abuse. The batterer's reasonableness supports her belief that he really can change, as does his loving behavior during this phase" (67).

In some ways, the batterer's behavior is a "dream come true" for the abused woman because her object is begging forgiveness for his failings, something her parents never did. Thus there is a powerful "match" between the illusions of the libidinal ego and the exciting-object behavior of the contrite batterer, and frequently the battered woman will split back into that unrealistic ego structure. That the "cycle of violence" is repeated again and again without any learning or understanding on the part of either participant indicates that neither partner has an integrated central ego that can see both aspects of the other and that both use the splitting defense and have the ability to dissociate huge amounts of reality, thus allowing the scenario to continue endlessly.

CHAPTER 6

A STRUCTURAL ANALYSIS OF OBSESSIONAL AND HISTRIONIC DISORDERS

FAIRBAIRN'S STRUCTURAL MODEL PROVIDES a clearly reasoned analysis of the linkage between specific childhood relational patterns and the development of internal structures that are unique to each specific diagnostic group. Each diagnostic group has relatively similar developmental experiences that, in turn, create ego structures with similar contents and styles, and these structures then engage the interpersonal world through repetition compulsions, transferences, and perceptual distortions to re-create new versions of the patient's inner world with a new cast of objects. Fairbairn's model also implies that there are systematic and repeatable differences in the patterns of object relationships in the ego structures (and internalized objects) of mutually exclusive diagnostic groups. For example, an analysis of the contents and relational patterns of the pathological structures characteristic of a hysteric's libidinal and antilibidinal egos will be similar to those of other hysterics, and these patterns will differ compared with the contents and patterns within the ego structures found in obsessional disorders. Thus each specific disorder has different relational patterns embedded in the subegos and internalized objects. Chapter 5 demonstrated that the borderline individual has a libidinal ego that relies on the illusory hope that by effort he will succeed in charming and winning over the exciting object, while his antilibidinal ego is intent on modifying, reporting on, or destroying the rejecting object. This chapter will demonstrate that there are clear differences between this configuration and that of the hysteric, including the gender of the primary rejecting object and, most important, the absence of

---

Certain material in this chapter originally appeared in "A Structural Analysis of the Obsessional Character: A Fairbairnian Perspective," *American Journal of Psychoanalysis*, 67(2) (2007): 119–140, reprinted by permission of *The American Journal of Psychoanalysis*; and in "Working with Fairbairn's Ego Structures" in the journal *Contemporary Psychoanalysis*, 2001, 37:391–416. All rights reserved.

a sexual agenda in the relationship between the borderline patient's antilibidinal ego and the rejecting part of the paternal object. The hysteric and the borderline diagnostic groups do have one major similarity in that they display two subegos that allow them to act out both hope and hate toward the very same object. Conversely, the obsessive displays little or no libidinal interest in exciting objects and, in fact, does not even appear to have a libidinal ego because developmentally he did not perceive his objects as containing the potential for love.

Fairbairn's model also assumes that there is a relatively linear relationship (though major variations can occur) between the traumatic events in the interpersonal environment and the toxicity of the internalized structures that are created. The intensity of the "badness" of the memories of the internalized rejecting objects (and therefore of actual early developmental experiences) can vary from parental sarcasm to indifference, mockery, and humiliation, and on to physical violence and inappropriate sexuality. Children with extremely aggressive or extremely abandoning parental objects will tend to have more enraging and frightening experiences in their antilibidinal egos that require more thorough dissociations, and thus create more powerful structures. Consequently, the pathological structures in these children will be more powerful and exert more influence over them than will those of children raised in less developmentally frustrating environments. This accounts for the variance in the severity of the disorder within diagnostic groups.

A STRUCTURAL ANALYSIS OF THE OBSESSIONAL DISORDER

The first ego structure that appears to be damaged by families that produce obsessional children is the central ego, that part of the self that relates to the objects when they are gratifying and behaving in an appropriate manner. The central ego's relationship with the ideal object is relaxed and calm, as opposed to the internalized relationships between the angry and cowed antilibidinal ego and the punitive and uncompromising rejecting object, or the passionate pressure experienced by the libidinal ego for its exciting object. Pine (1985) has commented on the importance of quiet contact between the child and his objects in the development of the central ego:

> For the child with optimal developmental opportunities, there are innumerable periods of quiet play, quiet object contact, and quiet bodily experience that provide low-keyed pleasure in unthreatening doses. I believe that this underlies some of what later appears as comfortable self-feeling and object contact, as resourcefulness and the ability to overcome pain, as positive mood—overall, the underpinnings of healthy functioning. These are "background" experiences, so to speak, not of high intensity; but they are omnipresent in the day-to-day life of the child at home. (5)

Unfortunately, relaxed contact with good objects is almost never the case in the histories of obsessionals raised in critical, opinionated, and "highly verbal" families (Adams 1973:61), in which language is used in a punitive and contradictory manner. The constantly changing meanings and prohibitions keeps the developing child in an uneasy state of tension and emotional flux, never knowing which rules will (or will not) apply, as Sullivan (1956) notes:

> No matter what aggression anyone perpetrates on another—no matter what outrages the parents perpetrate on each other, or the elder siblings perpetrate on each other, on the parents, or on little Willie—there is always some worthy principle lying about to which appeal is made. And the fact that an appeal to an entirely contradictory principle was made 15 minutes earlier does not seem to disturb anybody.   (230–231)

Children raised in this atmosphere have enormous difficulty knowing what emotions mean, what they feel, what is prohibited and what is accepted. The result is a profound confusion in the central ego, as their object(s) change their position(s) so frequently that the central ego cannot build a consistent view of themselves or their parents. This results in a feeling of unreality in children and a lack of integration between words and feelings. The consequences of this type of repeated family interactional pattern leads to a child's "mystification," as Winckler (1995) describes: "The concept of mystification of experience refers to a person's losing both the ability to know his own experience and the ability to know another. Mystification implies that the individual's experience is actively (unconsciously) intentionally clouded by another person; it is not merely a byproduct of anxiety" (470). Mystification allows the parents to punish and condemn their children freely, using principles that they proclaim to be important yet change unexpectedly from time to time. The confused child, who is trying desperately to play by the rules, assumes that his parents are motivated by goodwill, since they strenuously claim that they are innocent: "Families in which the parents are harsh, critical and arbitrary—yet deny the impact of such behaviors—evoke a panoply of perplexing responses in the child . . . not only do parents of obsessionals tend to prohibit the direct expression of anger, resentment or retaliation, they also portray such behavior as unrelated to any conceivable precipitant" (Winckler 1995:471).

Confusion and mystification are aided by the child's need, fueled by dependency, to continue misperceiving his parents as good objects. Thus there is a powerful synergy between the parents' unconscious strategies and the child's need to keep his objects blameless. His parents strengthen his use of the rationalization provided by the moral defense by specifying a never-ending set of principles that they claim the child has violated. Often parents define their child's transgressions as being tainted with universal "badness." In other words, their child is deemed to have violated sacred moral, religious, or ethical principles, which further over-whelms and shames the child, as Adams (1973) notes:

> A fifth attribute of the parental ethos lay in the parents *adherence to an instru-mental morality*, to goodness not as a goal but as a means of reaching heaven, or achieving conquest, or of asserting moral superiority. . . . Over-goodness as a way of control was very much in evidence in these households. Likewise, there was strongly articulated examples of what might be called the parent's "narcis-sistic morality"—meaning the equation of what gratifies the parent with what is right and sacred, and conversely "what bugs Mother is plain wicked." (63)

Thus the family of the obsessional undermines, confuses, and mystifies (and therefore weakens) the child's central ego. The child is burdened by guilt because of the bewildering number of violations he has, in all innocence, accrued, and is over-whelmed by the accusations that his moral transgressions are offenses in the eyes of God or society. The child uses the splitting defense and the rationalizations of the moral defense to protect himself from being aware of the badness of his objects, a position that is actively supported and amplified by his parents' enumeration of his transgressions. Ironically, as Fairbairn noted, the moral defense is a source of comfort, as it reassures the child that he is being appropriately corrected by loving objects. Kopp (1978), an existential psychologist, described his own central-ego con-fusion as a young man in regard to locating the source of "badness" that he felt to be within himself: "I had emerged from adolescence believing that I was an awful, inadequate human being who went around making other people unhappy. It was the only way I could account for being condemned by people as honest and good as my parents. I entered therapy to be cured of whatever failings had warranted their condemnation" (86). Kopp illustrates both the rationalizations of the moral defense and the attachment to bad objects. The illusion that the child is securely attached to good objects prolongs his hope that his unmet developmental needs have a chance of being satisfied and that the feeling of abandonment will be avoided.

A second way that parents of obsessives hinder the development of their child's central ego is to frustrate her appropriate developmental needs, thus starving the child of the types of interactions that would allow her central ego to mature and thus foster the process of differentiation. The obsessional patient, at first glance, seems excessively mature (if not old) for her age. As a young adult, she may appear highly conventional, over- rather than under-controlled and interested in "mature" topics, including the sciences and technology. Appearances do not reveal the whole story, as the obsessional is likely to be socially timid, overly dependent, and passive-aggressive in her personal relationships as a result of a developmental his-tory that ignored her needs while simultaneously requiring her to perform well in the external world, as noted by Barnett (1969):

The child is simultaneously infantilized in regard to interpersonal skills and instrumental competence within the home, while considerable demands are made for him to achieve outside the home in school, work or sports. Consequently, he seeks to verify his significance by performances of ever increasing perfection in the impersonal world outside the home, which then entitle him to the attention and applause he has no other means of winning. His insignificance to family life and the low premium put on his own needs and development as a person foster dependency, [and] feelings of insignificance and incompetence in intimate situations, even in the face of success in the larger world. The preoccupation with achievement, performance, and perfectionism resulting from this split type of dependency leads to the aggressive competitiveness so typical of many areas of the obsessional's life. Within the family this often manifests itself in severe sibling rivalry, and in the frequent hostile competitiveness that exists between the child and the parent of the same sex. (49)

This family pattern accounts for the disjunction between the apparent maturity that one sees in the outer world of the obsessional and the private expression of unmet dependency needs, cynicism, hypersensitivity to criticism, and ambivalence toward his love objects. A healthy central ego is fundamental in all relationships with adult partners, which require mutual affection, cooperation, and commitment. Sadly, the central ego of the obsessive is not suffused with enough memories of love and trust in objects to freely enter into a cooperative relationship with another individual. Despite enormous ambivalence, the obsessional individual cannot avoid attachments to others because his unmet dependency needs drive him toward partners who promise to compensate him for his developmental emptiness. Despite the initial romance of a new relationship, the obsessional's powerful unmet needs, coupled with the transferences emanating from the unconscious relational templates of self and other, soon change loving relationships into those rife with adversarial contests. In short, his powerful inner structures cause him to misperceive his love object either as a rejecting object, whom he responds to with his cynical and passive-aggressive antilibidinal ego, or as a weak, complaining, and undermining antilibidinal object, whom he responds to by identifying with his uncompromising rejecting object. In either case, his response will be based on the roles around which his inner world was originally constructed, as Mallinger (1982) has noted: "Eventually, the d.s. [demand sensitive] obsessional might view his marriage, or any committed relationship, as essentially an adversary relationship. Thus, even in his closest relationships, he may feel unloved and unloving" (422).

Thus the early unmet needs of the obsessive individual makes her feel that she is being forced into a relationship with an object whom she sees as either powerfully malevolent or hopelessly inferior, and her destructive childhood relational patterns are reenacted with this new object. This is the tragedy of so many obsessionals who are highly competent in terms of instrumental behaviors yet have internal structures that turn potentially loving partners into opponents. The attachment between the antilibidinal ego and the rejecting internalized object, which is the attachment based on hate and the desire for one structure to overpower the other in the inner world, becomes the template of many obsessional marriages.

DAMAGE TO THE CENTRAL EGO'S SENSE OF VOLITION

The central ego is the seat of volition in Fairbairn's model, and the obsessional disorder is perhaps the best example of distortion of this essential part of the self. Shapiro (1965) originated the focus on volitional problems of the obsessive. Although he worked within a classical analytic framework, Shapiro's timeless descriptions of this disorder appear to be uninfluenced by any given model, and, most notably, he does not speculate on developmental or interactional antecedents of the adult pathology that he so beautifully describes. Mallinger (1982), however, sees many connections between the specifics of the childhood experiences of individuals who later display obsessional pathology and issues of self-direction. Mallinger (1982) notes that the criticism to which the child is exposed creates a great hesitancy in him to take independent action, which then leads him to adopt the defensive fiction that his actions are dictated by external sources of authority:

> His sense of adequacy, general competence, and acceptability to important others may become seriously impaired. Unsure of himself, and exaggeratedly frightened of disapproval, the pre–d.s. [demand sensitive] obsessive child may become increasingly fearful of taking risks associated with initiative, decisions and action. . . . Rather than be held accountable for decisions, feelings and actions that emanate from him, he represses or disowns these focusing intently upon the apparent salvation provided by real or self-manufactured external directives and expectations. (415)

The obsessive's chronic reliance on external sources of authority to guide his actions leads to the erosion of his sense of autonomy. The reward for the obsessional individual is that these sources of authority relieve him of the task of decision making (Shapiro 1965:43). However, this apparent solution to his childhood experience of having all his decisions criticized by his external objects costs him dearly in terms of his ability to fully experience the world. Over time, his central ego's confidence becomes eroded because it overly relies on external directives to the point that the obsessional individual loses his sense of conviction about reality, as Shapiro (1965) notes:

> A sense of conviction about the world—a sense of truth, in other words—involves a breadth of attention, an interest in and sensitivity to the shadings and

proportions of things, and a capacity for direct response to them for which the obsessive-compulsive person is not geared. Instead, he concerns himself with technical details, indicators which he interprets according to authoritative rules and principles. (51)

The result of this specific family pattern of abuse weakens the central ego of the obsessional person and leaves him mystified, alienated from his feelings, fearful of direct action unless mediated by external fiat, and unsure of consensual reality. As mentioned, Fairbairn saw the inner world in terms of shifting territories, wherein the obsessional individual's attenuated central ego becomes secondary to the relationship between his antilibidinal ego and the rejecting object, who outstrips the central-ego–ideal-object relationship in size and intensity. This antilibidinal-ego–rejecting-object relationship is a consequence of the numerous harshly critical exchanges between his antilibidinal ego and his rejecting-object parents.

A commonly seen compensatory mechanism that the obsessional individual uses to rid himself of a sense of confusion and weakness is to develop a narrow sense of expertise that his eroded central ego uses as a tool or weapon to deal with the world. He becomes an expert in some specialized esoterica on which he focuses exclusively while simultaneously ignoring larger issues in life that overwhelm and confuse him:

> The sense of inner weakness makes him feel insubstantial, vulnerable to being easily influenced, swayed or overpowered by external forces, especially the wishes of others. In addition, he feels as if both his identity and his sense of autonomy, unanchored as they are, can at any moment be obliterated or swallowed up by these perceivedly more powerful outside forces. (Mallinger 1982:418)

Thus the obsessive defends himself from this sense of vulnerability by learning more and more about less and less, and he uses this narrow knowledge base to protect and bolster his weakened central ego. This compensatory technique allows him to appear strong and knowledgeable and, most important, helps him from becoming submissive to others by dismissing interest in all areas of life except his own narrow path.

TYPICAL DEVELOPMENTAL HISTORIES THAT STRENGTHEN THE OBSESSIVE'S INTERNALIZED ANTILIBIDINAL-EGO AND REJECTING-OBJECT STRUCTURES

The preceding discussion of parental criticism does not do justice to parents' intense and pervasive hostility toward children who later develop obsessional personality disorders. Many writers have reported that parental hostility is the most common factor in the developmental histories of obsessional patients, as Kainer (1979) points out:

> Among my obsessional patients I noted certain similarities of background, especially in what I call the parental style. Although there were variations, each patient had at least one harshly critical parent. The criticism started early in life and had a flailing, arbitrary ring to it from which the child could not escape. . . . The criticism persisted, often over school performance (although the children performed well), and ranged over all aspects of the child's "beingness." (276–277)

Kainer's description illustrates the impossible position of the child who is unconditionally dependent on parents who spout unending criticism and hostility. Sullivan wrote extensively on the development of the obsessional individual, and he used even stronger language when describing the cruelty evident in the childhood histories of his obsessional patients. The following is one of Sullivan's (1956) several observations on parental cruelty:

> The recitations of the obsessional neurotic about the past gradually come to reflect rather singular brutality toward the patient by a significant person, usually the parent. If this rather brutal recital includes some thin disguise which the parent wore, I think you may always accept the account as being reasonably close to the truth. In other words, in a very considerable number of cases these patients have been subjected to really severe cruelty by a parent, but always the parent had a little mask to conceal the sheer brutality of what was going on. (267–268)

The child must deal with the bluntness of the hostility emanating from the needed objects by erecting defensive barriers to protect her illusion of a continuing attachment to a good object. Sullivan (1953:318–319) described "substitutive processes" that children use that involve a suspension of awareness to the obvious rejection or abandonment, which, if experienced directly by the child, would produce massive anxiety. This Sullivanian defense and Fairbairn's splitting defense are functionally equivalent.

The obsessional child's dissociated antilibidinal ego has defended itself against the worst attacks by the rejecting parts of the parental objects. This structure is engorged with rage, self-loathing, and vindictiveness. The type of critical and demanding formative experience to which the obsessional is exposed creates a particularly caustic and passive-aggressive antilibidinal self, described by Schimel (1972): "The ironic, the sardonic, the mocking and contemptuous view of self and others can be regularly observed in the obsessional and teased out of his verbalizations and fantasies as well as his dreams" (27). Thus the antilibidinal ego in the obsessional individual contains a massively caustic and shameful view of itself along with a passive-aggressive stance toward the rejecting object. The obsessive will eagerly identify with his rejecting-object structure when he finds a weaker individual with whom to relate, and he will adopt the same techniques that his parents once used to attack him to destroy this new external object. In this way, he will become a rejecting object toward weaker objects and condemn them with self-righteous appeals to rules and universal truths. An extreme example of a patient dominated by his antilibidinal ego was a former patient of mine, William, who consulted me because of his increasing isolation (Celani 2005), as described in case 6.1.

The highly verbal, hypersensitive, and argumentative antilibidinal ego in this patient was strong enough and hostile enough to carry out a battle with his rejecting-object parent, with neither individual able to fully dominate the other. William knew just how far he could go with his sarcastic and hostile appraisals of his father's responses so as not to overstep and cause his father to reject him completely (by demanding that he leave the house). Even when William won the "debates," his father would retain the dominant rejecting-object position and would physically demonstrate his ascendancy by pushing or shoving William. This external stalemate between my patient and his father characterizes the endless battles fought in the internal world of many obsessional individuals between the antilibidinal ego and the rejecting object.

CASE 6.1

Like many severe obsessional individuals, William had been exposed to intense, withering, and unremitting criticism from his frustrated and socially impotent immigrant parents, who had suffered setbacks after moving to America. They regarded his talents as a musician as a threat to their sense of superiority and because it attracted the support of his teachers who encouraged him to go to music school, which opened up the possibility of his eventually separating from them. Despite the impact of his good-object teachers, William's massive inferiority and developmental fixation on his bad objects won out, and he ended up living in a basement apartment at home while attending a community college. During these years, he and his father became involved in a repeated morning battle in which his father would wake him up in a derisive manner, pointing out that he (the father) was going to work while William was still sleeping. William had perfected the same style of argumentation and debate that had been used to undermine him during his childhood. He would ask his father an entrapping question such as, "Are you first and foremost a Christian, an American, or a man?" His father, who loved debate but was less skilled than his clever and enraged son, would answer, and William would systematically destroy his father's responses. These debates often ended with his father pushing or slapping William and leaving in a rage. This intense acting out of the relationship between the rejecting object and the antilibidinal ego was typical of the transference–countertransference relationship that this patient developed toward me in our work.

These two opposing sub-selves account for the often contradictory observations made about the obsessive. When the individual is faced with an object that he sees as powerful and rejecting, his antilibidinal response will be half-hearted and hesitant, though compliant. Whenever the obsessional person displays compliance in a relationship, he is dominated by his antilibidinal ego, which is not willing to risk a full battle with the rejecting object, as that might lead either to abandonment or to a humiliating defeat. The meager cooperation that the obsessive displays is just enough to appease the rejecting object and is simultaneously satisfying to his own need for some sense of power (via withholding). Mallinger (1982) notes the development of passive-aggressive thwarting behaviors as a consequence of the child's perception that his parents were not to be trusted, yet were too powerful to defy openly:

> He learns eventually, though, that he dare not resist openly. After all, not only might he doubt the strength and sincerity of his parents' allegiance to him; he also maintains an awareness of his relative helplessness, a sincere desire to please, a desperate need for approval, a fear of forcing his mistrust to the surface, and memories of prior painful experiences (of his own or those of his siblings) whenever open opposition was tried. . . . He may equate automatic acquiescence with death itself. (412)

Thus the obsessive is trying to appease the (external) rejecting object while maintaining his own positive self-regard (by not giving in completely). Conversely, a very different "obsessive" appears on those occasions in which the individual identifies with the rejecting object role such as when the other person with whom he is in a relationship appears to be weak. In these situations, the obsessive will identify with the role of the rejecting object and boldly criticize every aspect of the other. The shift from the antilibidinal ego to identifying with the rejecting object, both of which are organized sub-selves, accounts for these two poles of obsessional behavior. When given power, the obsessional eagerly takes on the role of rejecting object and forces others into an antilibidinal position, as Schimel (1972) has noted: "The incorrigible person does not attack the really strong. Others are fair game. Authority is anathema to him. To authority that is exercised with any uncertainty, the incorrigible, as with inferiors, is intolerant and inexorable. He manifests what amounts to a compulsion to punish" (9). The "compulsion to punish" is a good description of the obsessional individual taking on the role of his original rejecting objects and treating weaker objects as he once was treated. Thus Fairbairn's structures seamlessly account for the puzzling and contradictory observations of obsessional behavior.

The internal relational struggle between the condemning rejecting object and the enraged, passive-aggressive, and self-righteous antilibidinal ego can be the source of both symptoms and transferences. A particularly clear clinical example of this struggle was expressed in symptoms (that had occurred years before) exhibited by one of my patients, a talented computer-chip designer. He had come for help because of his inability to finish any given work assignment on time, which caused constant conflict with his superiors, a battle he seemed to relish. As a teenager, his exacting and tyrannical father demanded that he paint a rowboat at their summer cottage. His father, who worked in a nearby city, was due back to the summer cottage on the weekend, but my patient passively resisted doing the assigned task and had painted only the top row of planking by the time his father returned. His father met this act of defiance by unhesitatingly and thoroughly beating his son. Soon after that incident, my patient discovered that he was having difficulty walking through rooms if he was not exactly in the center. He pressed his hands together as a guide to help him align himself with the exact center of the room. Often it took as many as fifteen attempts before he was satisfied that he was perfectly centered. A structural analysis of this symptom sees it as the acting out of the relationship between his internal rejecting object, who demanded perfection and submission, and his defiant yet cowed antilibidinal ego, which "tried" to comply with this arbitrary demand but was simultaneously subverting it in order to sustain some semblance of pride. His symptom managed to symbolically defeat his father's demands by complying in a manner that used up so much time with his bizarre performance that it (probably) frustrated the internalized rejecting object. Shapiro (1965) sees ritualistic behavior as an extension of his observation, noted earlier, on the obsessive's loss of a sense of truth: "Ritualistic *behavior* conforms in a very clear way to the description of obsessive-compulsive activity as mechanical, effortful, and as though in the service of an external directive. . . . The ritualistic act, as such, must ultimately seem absurd to one whose sense of reality and interest in truth are not impaired, no matter how appropriate the symbolic significance of its content may be" (52).

Fairbairn pointed out just how powerful the emotionally damaged individual's inner world was and how the split-off subegos can motivate the individual in ways not easily understood. Shapiro's point that the obsessive individual looks as if he were following an "external directive" fits right into Fairbairn's structural theory. The obsessive is actually following the demands of an internalized rejecting object, one that was originally external but now lives on in the internal world. Many seemingly odd obsessional symptoms become comprehensible when viewed as a dialogue between the incompletely repressed antilibidinal ego and the dominant and demanding rejecting object, while the individual is ostensibly in his central-ego state. This often makes the obsessional patient feel "crazy," because the central ego "knows better" than to behave in this manner. But the struggle of the powerful antilibidinal ego with the internalized rejecting object dominates the patient's inner world, and this battle spills out of the unconscious and becomes known to the relatively weaker central ego. The central ego impotently stands by and observes but is unable to stop the unwanted proceedings of these larger and more powerful structures.

ATTACHMENT IN THE OBSESSIONAL PATIENT

If it is true that the obsessional patient has enormous unmet dependency needs because of her fixation on objects who refused to nurture her, an antilibidinal ego bursting with memories of being criticized, and one that struggles endlessly with a demanding and hostile rejecting object, then why is the obsessional individual not psychopathic? The answer lies in the central ego's early experience of attachment to one or more ideal object(s), an attachment that was just strong enough to prevent the child's collapse into sociopathy. Often, in the histories of obsessional individuals, there is a good object, a grandparent or a mentor, outside the family with whom the child develops a central-ego–ideal-object emotional attachment, or, alternatively, the child experienced just enough early emotional support to create a bond with small parts of one or the other parent when he or she was behaving as an ideal object. These good experiences with the ideal object are abundant enough to preclude reliance on a fantasy-based libidinal ego that creates an exciting object for itself. Frequently, the pathway to the ideal-object–central-ego relationship is through performance at school, which allows the child to develop attachments outside the family with supportive teachers. Sometimes children are fortunate enough to find adult tenderness inadvertently, as Sullivan (1956) has described:

> She announced very early in the work with me that her trouble descended directly, unalterably from very, very early in life and was the work of an exceedingly hateful mother who never had any use for her. . . . That the mother was hateful, ye gods, how well I knew by the end of six months! But then, apropos of some little clue a little too elusive for the patient to see it in advance, I did get to what had kept her alive, which had been a vast mystery. It happened to be an old woman who did sewing for the whole family; she worked in an attic room in the house, and the little girl liked to go up and talk with her when she came, which was quite often. This old woman, who was somewhat in the role of a servant, showered the little girl with tenderness. (282)

This is precisely the kind of early experience that you will find in the histories of many obsessional adults. Somewhere, often outside the immediate family, the child finds a good object who offered just enough attachment to keep her from becoming indifferent to object relationships or overly dominated by her revenge-seeking antilibidinal ego. Many papers in the literature on obsessional patients cite similar histories; for example, Kainer (1979) described a patient who was deliberately conceived by his parents for the sole purpose of allowing his father to avoid the military draft. This patient's almost completely indifferent parents hired his grandmother to take care of him during the week, and he witnessed many scenes in which his mother and grandmother quibbled about the amount of pay his grandmother was due, a humiliation that lived on in his inner world. His parents ridiculed his high performance in school, and he looked forward to the respite of being with his loving grandmother:

> He was often witness to discussions of the amount of the payment, which varied in terms of the length of time and other expenses that his mother felt affected what she owed her mother for his care. . . . His mother (and to some extent his father) were experienced by him as harsh, critical and arbitrary, with very little capacity for tender parenting. He was intellectually gifted, but his 95's and A– were ridiculed. His compositions were torn apart and rewritten by both his parents. . . . He would spend the week with his simple, undemanding and loving grandmother, and dread the weekend with his tormentors and attackers.   (Kainer 1979:278)

Within Fairbairn's framework, this example suggests that the development of the obsessional personality disorder occurs in individuals who experienced at least one central-ego–ideal-object attachment during their development that they could rely on, although most of the time they resided in a sea of hostility and indifference. Sadly, the overwhelming criticism and humiliation that the child experiences during his development tends to overwhelm this smaller covert attachment to a good object, thus ensuring that generosity, a fluid ability to commit emotionally to others, and the easy display of tender emotions are all impossible for the obsessional individual to display. However, the small but important central-ego attachment that the child experienced during his development is strong enough to keep him in the orbit of other humans. Unfortunately, his unmet childhood needs, coupled with his powerful internal structures, including his cynical antilibidinal ego and his occasional identification with his aggressive rejecting object, make him an unappealing romantic partner. Many obsessional individuals display a paradoxical discontinuity between their high performance in the world and their passivity and passive-aggressive dependency within their marriages. The unfortunate circumstances of the obsessional individual's original interpersonal experiences are endlessly re-created in his adult world, and he tends to live a life of emotional penury, even toward those who were once willing to love him.

COMMON TREATMENT ISSUES WITH THE OBSESSIONAL PATIENT

One of the many benefits of working with Fairbairn's model is that a description of the structures and the family history that typically produce the disorder simultaneously offers the clinician guidance regarding the type of transferences the clinician will face. In my experience, the obsessive individual's desire to look normal and well modulated, his fear of being dominated by others, and his absolute avoidance of "crazy" dissociated material in his unconscious are all sources of resistance to both his cooperating in the therapeutic process and the uncovering of repressed material. The very act of asking for help, of revealing himself to another person, as well as accepting a submissive position in relation to the therapist's superior knowledge and authority are *very* difficult obstacles for the obsessive patient to surmount.

The style of the obsessive person is almost the very opposite of that of the open, dramatic, and anguished borderline individual, who cannot speak fast enough to say all that she wants to and who does not want the session to end because she has so much more to say. The obsessive patient, however, does not reveal his inner world easily and defends his positions at all costs as if the therapist were a new version of his critical, rejecting-object parents. He will defend himself from assumed criticism with logic, debate, and outright argumentation concerning nearly everything the therapist says. The most extreme example I encountered during my years of practice was a socially isolated, fifty-year-old single man who spent part of his free time reading and copying over his graduate school notes from a Ph.D. history program he had attended twenty-five years earlier (and from which he failed to graduate because of passive rebelliousness). During the interviews, he would wave his hands crosswise when I tried to voice *any* comment during his formidable, session-long monologues. It was amusingly clear that this patient did not want to hear *anything* that contradicted his personal model of the world or any interpretation that would suggest that I knew something of which he was unaware, which would place him in a submissive position in the relationship.

Despite the superficial affability of obsessive individuals, the long history of criticism during their development makes these patients extremely touchy and resistant to any interpretation, for almost any observation from the therapist sounds like an attack from a rejecting object. My solution to this clinical problem was to intervene with a transference interpretation only when the patient's transformation of me into a bad object was too great to ignore. Very often, the aftermath of a transference interpretation would result in an endless debate about my observation, which was *never acceptable* to the patient, simply because the individual refused to "give in" to a facsimile of the bad object. As already noted, borderline patients are also wary and hypersensitive, but the key difference between these two groups is that the borderline diagnostic group faces every session with a new issue and with little memory of past sessions. Conversely, the focused and easily hurt obsessive patient will return to past issues and rehash them endlessly until he either defeats or exhausts his opponent. Rather than involve myself with many interpersonally tangle-prone relational interpretations with obsessive patients,

I would focus on cooperation by means of the co-creation of a narrative of a patient's developmental history and, whenever possible, avoid transference interpretations. The cooperatively arrived at understandings of how, and by whom, the patient was deprived tended to offer a relatively safe avenue for discussion. I would offer patients nonthreatening parts of Fairbairn's model and allow them to draw their own conclusions about their developmental history with an absolute minimum of interventions. In some ways, my style of working with obsessive patients was an attempt to develop the "quiet object contact" described by Pine (1985) earlier in this chapter, in the hope that it would foster development in the patient's central ego. My lack of intrusiveness allowed these hypersensitive patients to maintain the fantasy that they were working alone and were not capitulating to the demands of an external object. Over time, I would offer more complex explanations from the model as well as transference interpretations, and most of my obsessive patients gradually accepted this procedure and would begin to see me as a cooperative partner—a completely new relational experience for their central ego. Over time, this approach often yielded good results, with the improvements coming slowly and without drama. As a group, obsessive patients appear to lack gratitude because they are unwilling to credit others, an act that would demean their fragile central ego by drawing attention to how badly they needed help in the first place.

THE HISTRIONIC PERSONALITY DISORDER

Fairbairn (1954) wrote specifically about the histrionic personality disorder, and his paper contains the beginnings of his analysis of patient material in terms of ego structures. Hysteria is an interesting disorder, as the child is exposed to a very different type of rejection from her maternal object compared with the rejection she experiences from her paternal object; as a consequence, the antilibidinal "strategy" she develops is sharply different for each gender of objects. This contrasts with the obsessive patient, who often is exposed to criticism from both parental objects and thus requires only one antilibidinal strategy.

Fairbairn examined clinical material in a way that only *implied* structural analysis, as he did not specify that the view of the object was either libidinal or antilibidinal. The following is Fairbairn's (1954) analysis of a dream related to him by his patient Louise:

> In front of each door stood a figure of her father facing her with what appeared to be a stick in his hand. One of these figures held his stick in front of his genitals pointing toward her in such a manner as to indicate clearly that it symbolized an erect penis, whilst the other figure was holding his stick above his head like

a whip with which he was about to punish her. . . . Meanwhile she saw through the window a procession of couples of men and women, who cast superior and scornful glances upon her as they passed by and observed her predicament. Their glances conveyed to her the impression that they regarded her as just "a silly little thing"; and this was exactly what she felt about herself, overwhelmed as she was by a sense of utter helplessness and hopeless inferiority as she stood immobilized between the two figures of her father in the passage.   (109)

Fairbairn goes on to say that her father had "manic-depressive characteristics" and at times treated Louise with indifference and at other times was sexually provocative. Her dream displays two unambiguous antilibidinal views of her father as a rejecting object, one as a physical abuser and the other as a sexual abuser. Her dependency on her father as her only object prevented her from experiencing these views of him consciously, as they would threaten, if not destroy, her needed attachment to him, even in adulthood. In the same dream, Louise sees couples, symbolizing normal families, looking at her scornfully, and this feeds her sense of inferiority. This aspect of the dream is another facet of her antilibidinal view of herself, one in which she sees herself in a diminished and shameful relationship compared with "normal" others because she is unconditionally dependent on objects who do not love her and from whom she cannot flee. Fairbairn's clinical example of Louise describes the same interpersonal relationships that we see today in patients with hysterical character structures.

FAMILY DYNAMICS AND THE DEVELOPMENT OF UNIQUE INTERNAL STRUCTURES

A common family dynamic found in the histories of patients suffering hysteria is a hostile relationship between a female child and her mother, whereas her relationship with her father is inappropriately sexualized (Celani 1976). This dynamic was described first by Hollender (1971) and then by Slipp (1977). Hollender noted that the developmental histories of many hysterics is one in which a female child was severely rejected by her maternal object and consequently turned to her slightly less frustrating paternal object, who offered her a greater amount of nurturance. Unfortunately for the young girl, the paternal attention is mixed with, or contingent on, the child's display of sexuality:

The mothers of hysterical personalities are depicted as cold, preoccupied or detached, and their daughters complain of being deprived of love. . . . When children lose hope of obtaining emotional sustenance they crave from their mothers, they turn to their fathers for it. Attractive little girls soon find that coyness is effective in capturing and holding their father's attention. Closeness is sustained "by a subtle mutual sexual interest." (Hollender 1971:22)

This dynamic is easily understood by Fairbairn's model of development, as it assumes that the child is unconditionally dependent on her objects and that emotional deprivation from the maternal object motivates the child to actively pursue the paternal object, who is preferable to the more rejecting maternal object. Slipp (1977) arrived at the same conclusion from a slightly different angle. He sees the pattern in families that produce hysterics as originating in the behavior of narcissistic men (as opposed to depressed withholding mothers) who exploit both their wives and their children. Over time, the husband's narcissistic demands on his wife for constant tribute exceed his partner's ability to cope. The narcissistic man then splits his wife and sees her as a rejecting object and simultaneously sees his daughter as a new exciting object partner. The spouse is often unable to defend herself and accepts the devaluation, thus allowing a sexualized alliance between her husband and her daughter from which she is excluded. This family configuration deprives the daughter of an enhancing attachment to her now devalued mother, which devalues her as well because she, too, is female. It also sets into motion competition between the mother and the daughter for the father's affection and attention, a relational pattern that persists in hysterics throughout their lives. In both Hollender's and Slipp's views of the dynamics, the developmental consequences of the relationship with the two faulty parental objects damages the child's personality structure, even though the child has taken the best pathway toward the only developmental support available.

The structural consequence of this relationship scenario is that the developing young girl will perceive women as competitors for men's attention. Women are also seen as non-nurturing and unimportant, and men will be viewed in two opposite ways: first, as the only source of nurturance (exciting object) and, second, as sexually exploitative, rejecting objects. These perceptions become "structural" (dissociated) when the sexuality between father and daughter becomes too much for the child's central ego to integrate. The combination of nurturance and sexual exploitation from the same needed object is the "intolerable" aspect of the paternal object that must be dissociated by the child in order for her to remain attached to him. The female child's antilibidinal ego is suffused with bitter, almost unendurable disappointment because of the paternal object's demand for displays of sexuality and flirtation as *payment* for the empathy and attention he offered. On the other side of the split, the hysteric's libidinal ego seeks her paternal object as the primary parent, since he offered a form of closeness that gave the libidinal ego hope, particularly since the intolerable aspects of their relationship were dissociated in her unconscious. Notably, clinical experience suggests that splitting of the maternal object does not occur. This conclusion is based on the observation that hysterics do not have sudden exciting/rejecting shifts in their perceptions of women; rather, females appear to be permanently devalued and contain no promising (exciting object) facets. Thus it appears that the female hysteric gives up her attachment to her maternal object in favor of an attachment to the exciting part of her paternal object. This, as already noted, is the differential response to the parental objects. It produces two separate strategies and transference patterns in the antilibidinal egos of hysterics to external objects, based on the gender of the object, which is clinically significant and plays a major role in the treatment process.

During clinical interviews, hysterics generally minimize discussion of their mothers and produce far more material indicating that they see their fathers, or displaced paternal objects, as both extremely exciting and rejecting. The exciting aspect of the paternal (or displaced) object contains an intense promise of love and nurturance for her unmet childhood needs. The intensity of the attachment stems from a chronic deprivation of maternal love and because the paternal love she did receive was tainted by sexual exploitation that had to be dissociated and thus deprived her of a potential central-ego–ideal-object relationship. The attachment to the exciting object father is not a self-generated fantasy (as it can be in borderline patients) but is fueled by the actual paternal object, who actively promotes a sexualized relationship between himself and his daughter. In borderline individuals, exciting objects do very little (if anything) to promote themselves. It is the child's extreme deprivation that motivates her to see hope and the potential of love in the object, even when that object is emotionally unavailable. This is not the case with fathers of hysterics, as they deliberately stimulate their daughters' libidinal ego by dressing them up and taking them out on "dates" or by taking them to clothing stores and admiring them as they try on different dresses. These behaviors heighten the child's libidinal-ego hope that her paternal object actually contains love and that her father will choose her over her excluded and devalued mother. Perhaps the most extreme example in my clinical work was a female patient whose father had built a small plywood stage in the basement of their house, complete with a curtain and spotlights, and had his preteen daughter entertain him by singing and dancing, dressed in a dance costume, while his wife fumed in impotent fury upstairs. Fairbairn (1954) noted the intensity of the hysteric's hope and despair when he spoke about the female hysteric's view of her paternal object: "So far as the hysteric is concerned, a characteristic feature of the basic endopsychic situation which I have just outlined is that the exciting object is excessively exciting, and the rejecting object excessively rejecting; and from this it inevitably follows that the libidinal ego is excessively libidinal, and the antilibidinal ego is excessively persecutory" (18).

The intensity of the structures in many hysterics suggest that, as children, they did experience some longed-for gratification in relation to their paternal objects, but much of the relationship had to be dissociated because it was tainted by unendurable disappointment from the co-occurring sexual demands. On the antilibidinal side of the split, the rejecting part of the object is experienced as extremely rejecting because the developing child knows that she should never have to trade her sexuality for her father's love. Individuals suffering from obsessive, paranoid, and phobic disorders are *extremely* unlikely to have had histories of intense sexualized emotionality with the opposite-sex parent, and therefore this specific relational pattern is unique to this diagnostic group.

In adulthood, hostility toward sexuality almost always is expressed toward "safe" objects. A long-standing example is the "castration" scene (Celani 1976), which occurs when an attractive woman approaches a man seductively and engages him animatedly in a conversation. The male object frequently assumes that the woman's liveliness, apparent interest in him, and sexualized dress all translate into an interest in sexuality. When he responds with a sexual proposal, the woman is outraged and storms away. When this scenario is understood in terms of Fairbairn's metapsychology, we see that it begins with the female hysteric dominated by her libidinal ego as she approaches an exciting-object man. Her approach is motivated by the need for attention and involvement, which she experiences as nurturance, and she assures herself of attracting the object's attention by displaying apparent sexual availability. Her overt sexualized behavior, however, is completely dissociated from her awareness. When the male object responds to the hysteric's sexual message, it immediately transforms him from an exciting parental object into a rejecting object. This provokes the hysteric's antilibidinal ego to emerge from her unconscious while simultaneously her libidinal ego is dissociated, and she then express outrage or disgust. Thus the castration scene is simply a variant of splitting, and Fairbairn's hypothetical constructs offer an explanation for the "how" and the "why" of this once common interpersonal event.

THE CONTINUUM OF PSYCHOPATHOLOGY
WITHIN THE HISTRIONIC DIAGNOSTIC GROUP

Fairbairn's model predicts that adult hysterics with the least amount of developmental deprivation will have conscious, as opposed to dissociated, conflicts about their paternal objects as well as about displaced versions of that object. These conflicts can be verbalized and will be laced with ambivalence, as they were not originally disruptive enough to require dissociation. In these hysterics, the central ego develops sufficient strength to tolerate ambivalence, because the frustrating relational events in the family were not so severe that they had to be dissociated for the child to stay attached to her objects. The resulting adult woman from a family with a mild version of the standard family dynamics that produce hysteria might be a flirtatious career woman who is well integrated but envious of men and who uses sexuality as a weapon but tolerates disappointment without retaliating, splitting, or abandoning her partner.

At the next level on the continuum of the hysterical dynamic, we expect to find individuals who have the same patterns in their inner worlds as the less developmentally deprived members of the same group, but splitting replaces ambivalence because parental failure (by both objects) was too severe to be tolerated consciously by the central ego. This less integrated level of the disorder is the histrionic personality disorder, and as a group the individuals with this disorder display an increased intensity of need, a greater fantasy component in the libidinal ego, and an engorged antilibidinal ego that may contain actual memories of sexual abuse. The central ego is also weaker, and reenactments of the original trauma are expected, because the central ego cannot preclude one or the other of the subegos from becoming the dominant ego.

Below this level, but in the same histrionic diagnostic group, are hysterics who are more antilibidinal than libidinal, and their behavior seems to be a primitive vendetta against all objects who are of the same gender as their original rejecting paternal object. An early patient of mine was a clear example of this level of disorder (Celani 2001). She was a sexually attractive young woman who lived a chaotic life and was involved in a series of affairs with married men who were far more educated and successful than she. She complained bitterly of their indifference to her needs and was acutely aware of the status and power differential between her and her lovers. During one session, she described the following dream:

> She was lying naked in a muddy corral engaged in intercourse with a cowboy. Along the corral fence sat a number of other men all entranced by her sexuality and eager for their turn. She felt both enormous contempt for them while simultaneously enjoying the power that her sexuality gave her. When she was finished with her partner she threw him off her with a movement of her hips and signaled for the next cowboy to begin having intercourse with her. Later in the same dream she was walking through the barn and came across a cardboard box with three newly born kittens in it that were walking in circles, searching for their mother.
>
> (Celani 2001:412)

This patient was engaged in a continual acting out of her inner structures, which were engorged with rage. The dream material clearly demonstrates that her antilibidinal rage was stronger than her libidinal ego's hope. In other words, within her inner world men had lost their ability to be exciting objects (to offer her nurturance) and were reduced to the status of slaves by their need for her sexuality. In her dream, and in her actual life, she transformed herself into the bad object, with both exciting and rejecting components, and the men with whom she was involved were placed in the dependent (libidinal and antilibidinal) position, where she could both excite and reject them at her whim. This is a *stunning reversal* of the developmental dynamics of all rejected children whose legitimate developmental needs place them in a dependent position in relation to their objects, which allows the bad-object parent to enslave them with occasional gratification and, alternately, devastate them with rejection. My patient was enslaving others with their needs, as she had once been enslaved.

That the sexuality was taking place in the mud indicates that it is a "dirty" act, and this suggests that her unconscious saw the original relational configuration with her father in the same way. But this patient could not hide from her maternal need, which appears bluntly in the dream in her vision of the motherless kittens. This view is from her antilibidinal ego, which sees herself as an abandoned, lost infant with no maternal object present, a view similar to, but stronger than, Fairbairn's patient Louise, who saw herself as contemptible and unimportant.

Fairbairn's model also predicts that patients in whom the splitting defense is severe will have relational patterns encapsulated in their ego structures that will be increasingly potent and intrusive, because the structures will be heavily suffused with rage and fantasies of hope. This particular patient contained features of both the histrionic personality disorder and the borderline personality disorder, a diagnostic combination that has been described by Marmour (1953), Easser and Lesser (1965), and Zitzel (1968). The diagnostic difference between these two disorders is based on the presence or absence of the specific hysterical pattern (split and eroticized paternal object, non-split but devalued maternal object) in the subegos rather than on the degree of splitting. As previously noted, the borderline personality is characterized by great intensity of need and rage in the subegos, but the exciting and rejecting object for the borderline individual can be of either gender. In female hysterics the bad (exciting/rejecting) object is always the paternal object. Fairbairn's model also predicts that the structural pattern for the relatively rare male hysteric (Luisada, Peele, and Pittard 1974) would be a split maternal object and non-split and devalued paternal object.

WORKING WITH THE HISTRIONIC PATIENT

The hysteric is easier to work with than the obsessive because she is unperturbed by the submissive position that the framework requires, and she is eager for the (male) therapist's attention. As the discussion here clearly implies, the transferences to which the therapist will be exposed will vary by gender, with hysterics experiencing female therapists as unimportant and cold. Conversely, male therapists will be approached with a libidinally based sexualized interpersonal display that can split into antilibidinal rage and despair the moment that the patient feels exploited. The patient's initial interviews with a male therapist will contain exaggerated emotionality, excitement about coming to sessions, constant references to romance, and numerous themes involving disappointment in male objects. I have also experienced an undisguised desire in a number of my hysterical patients to break the frame so they could "get to know me" in an informal social situation, thus transforming me into a familiar exciting object that they could deal with through a preexisting relational template from their unconscious.

During the treatment process, the hysterical patient will not overtly disagree with the therapist, yet this seeming acceptance of interpretations is usually followed by the continuation of self-destructive involvements. In short, the hysterical patient, like most patients, pays far more attention to her inner structures than she does to external objects. Transference interpretations are often accepted on a cognitive level, but the same transformations of the therapist will be seen even after the patient allegedly "knows" what she is doing. I have previously mentioned "preemptive interpretations," and I often used them with hysterics who were actively splitting. I would suggest that a perceptual shift of me from an important and exciting person to an exploitative and destructive man, who is "just like all the others," is a signal that progress was occurring. This tended to diffuse the hostile emotionality in the antilibidinal perception when it did arrive as well as involve the central ego.

The co-construction of the narrative of the patient's developmental history and the internalization of the therapist as a non-exciting and non-rejecting ideal object in relation to the patient's central ego lead once again to the pathway to change. Initially, the hysteric tends to show less interest in the co-construction of a narrative of her history, as it is tedious, repetitive, and lacking in "glamour." However, the therapist's leadership, which focuses on the task of reconstructing the patient's developmental history, almost universally succeeds in involving the hysteric, and, once committed to the task, the patient will work just as diligently as one from any other diagnostic group. In terms of the therapist's gender, the gradual development and internalization of a central-ego relationship with a female therapist as an ideal object allows the hysteric to develop a relationship with a woman who is not incompetent and unloving. Conversely, the relationship between the patient's central ego and the ideal-object male therapist (and the internalization of this relationship) allows the patient's central ego to discover that men can be trusted to provide nurturance and are not out to exploit them sexually. Once the patient has internalized the ideal-object therapist as a supportive alternative to her original objects, the hysterical patient will have full access to an integrated view of her parents. The grief and despair that results in this integrated view of her objects will produce real emotionality as profound as it is in any other diagnostic group, and the growth of the central ego will lead ineluctably to higher levels of functioning.

CHAPTER 7

THE LEGACY OF FAIRBAIRN'S CONTRIBUTION TO PSYCHOANALYSIS

JAMES S. GROTSTEIN WROTE a short chapter at the end of *Fairbairn and the Origins of Object Relations* (1994) that begins with an emphasis on the impact of Fairbairn's thought as a modification of preexisting psychoanalytic ideas regarding both the innocence of the child as a nonsexual being and the legitimacy of children's developmental needs. He then moves into the larger issue of Fairbairn's influence in developing a whole new interactional view of human functioning:

> In stressing the fundamental importance of the object's (caretaking person's) meeting the infant's needs, he became, along with Ian Suttie, the first "infant advocate" in psychoanalysis and as a consequence, one of the first formulators of the principle of "infantile innocence" and "entitlement." In this regard, he also anticipated Bowlby's work on bonding and attachment. His emphasis on the relational rather than the hedonic aspects of the object-seeking drives challenged the primacy of Freud's pleasure principle and substituted for it the primacy of the reality principle—a concept that has been affirmed by infant developmental research. He thus introduced and formalized the interactional perspective of psychoanalysis and anticipated the intersubjective dimension. (319)

Thus Grotstein elevates Fairbairn's work from that of a modifier of a preexisting philosophical model of human behavior to that of an innovator and creator of a whole new way of looking at the psychological functioning of humankind.

Despite Fairbairn's fundamental importance to the field, his work remains relatively unknown to the average practitioner. The problem lies, as noted previously, both in the difficulty of Fairbairn's writing and in his "timing." His original papers are very difficult to follow because of the numerous digressions and philosophical debates that permeate his writing. He also used few clinical examples to illustrate the application of his theory in the clinical setting, so the interested mental health professional has few guidelines to follow. His "timing" was unfortunate in that he published in an era in which psychoanalysis was completely closed to the possibility of replacing drive theory with any other model. Drive theory, with all the attendant speculation about id-based fantasy, formed the very core of psychoanalysis. Classically trained analysts assumed that their "deep" analysis of the drives set them apart from practitioners who used "lesser" models of psychoanalysis (in terms of status within the confines of the field), such as Sullivan's Interpersonal Psychoanalysis. Had Fairbairn published his work in the 1970s, it would likely have met with a very different reception. Not surprisingly, the publication of his book of collected papers in 1952 produced almost no reaction from his colleagues in the British Psycho-Analytical Society:

> There was relatively little notice taken of Fairbairn's work in the British Psycho-Analytical Society following the appearance of his book. Melanie Klein was not enthusiastic about it, though valuing his observations, while Anna Freud gave no indication that she had noticed it, and they each exerted a powerful inhibiting brake on any of their associates wasting time on unorthodox theory. . . . Miss Freud's exclusive investment in the classical principles of her father, theoretical and practical, also had its inhibiting effect in the USA because of her status amongst the European analysts who had moved there. Klein was for many years kept as taboo there by a much more active campaign. Fairbairn scarcely merited a "campaign"; he was merely ignored.   (Sutherland 1989:144)

Despite being ignored by his colleagues who were not invested in divergent views that challenged drive theory, Fairbairn's model remained alive, though dormant. In terms of the historic shift away from the drive model, Fairbairn's model played an absolutely pivotal role. It was akin to a Trojan horse: accepted inside the fortress of classical psychoanalysis as an innocent digression, only to be set off in a corner and ignored for forty years. Although the process was less dramatic than the metaphor might suggest, the outcome was the same. Fairbairn's model was "acceptable" (in a limited sense) to classical psychoanalysis for several reasons. First, Fairbairn was an analyst and a member of the British Psycho-Analytical Society, and his work was published in the *International Journal of Psycho-Analysis* and the *British Journal of Medical Psychology*. His papers constantly referred to Freud's model, and they described a new version of the unconscious, a model of transference, resistance, and repetition compulsion, all central issues in the analytic enterprise. As noted, his work was seen as a relatively nonthreatening philosophical exercise on the periphery of the field, and, consequently, the average analyst did not take it seriously. However, within the obscurities of Fairbairn's prose was his emphasis on the central importance of individually constructed meanings based on *unique relational experiences*, a complete repudiation of Freud's notion of universal, instinctually based meanings. Fairbairn, effectively, was one of the two originators of the philosophical position that brought the greatest changes to classical analytic thought in the past thirty years. Drive theory was not based on unique relational events but on the assumption that humankind was subject to universal biologically based expectancies, as noted by Odgen (1990):

> Freud's theory of psychological development is built upon the notion of an inborn expectancy of particular constellations of meanings (including dangers specific to each phase of development) *where expectancy does not depend on actual experie*nce. The universality of castration anxiety, for example, is not simply the product of environmental factors; rather, experience serves as a trigger for inborn expectation of a specific form of bodily damage. Further, the Oedipus complex as a whole is understood by Freud as a universal mode of organizing and responding to experience, and not simply as a feature of the family environment to which the child responds. (20)

Fairbairn recognized, as I have already pointed out, that the emotionally deprived, intensely needy child longs for attention and support from *either* parental object. The children Fairbairn treated in the University Psychological Clinic for Children in Edinburgh had no need for the Oedipal conflict; instead, they needed a loving object (of either gender) to whom they could feel securely attached and thus continue their psychological development. Fairbairn recognized, and boldly rejected, universal inherited meanings, and he elevated the importance of what actually happened to the child in the relationship to his parental objects as the source of his unconscious and of his personality as a whole. Mitchell (1988) has commented on Fairbairn's emphasis on the primacy of unique and individualized relational patterning as the building blocks of the personality:

> Within the relational model, psychological meanings are not regarded as universal and inherent; bodily experiences and events are understood as evoked potentials which derive meaning from the way they become patterned in interaction with others. From this viewpoint *what is inherent is not necessarily formative*; it does not push or shape experience but is shaped by the relational context. The mind employs what anatomy and physiology supply, but the *meanings* of those body parts and processes, the underlying structure of experience and its deeper meanings, derive from relational patterns—their role in the struggle to establish and maintain connections with others. (4)

This new emphasis on the importance of interpersonally created meanings is the basis for the relational approach to psychoanalysis, a movement initiated by Fairbairn's insistence that the most important source of personality development is what actually happens between the child and his or her objects. Fairbairn's model, as I have suggested, was politely ignored as a fragmentary offshoot of classical analysis that was seen as an interesting metapsychological challenge that did not constitute a threat to Freud's theory. Mitchell (2000) has also noted that a number of theorists who challenged Freudian drive theory, including Fairbairn, survived direct attack from the classical analytic establishment because their work was not accessible: "Sullivan was a tortured, blocked writer. Fairbairn was tedious and difficult. Winnicott was poetic and elusive. Loewald was extremely subtle and often obscure" (80).

Mitchell was the first to cite Fairbairn's complex, obscure, and tedious writing style as a factor contributing to the scant attention the model received. To return to the metaphor of the Trojan horse, Fairbairn's model sat silent and unmolested by critics within classical psychoanalysis until the changing world of psychoanalysis could tolerate his philosophical perspective, and then his model reappeared and the walls of classical drive theory were breached. When the modern era of constructed meaning began, Fairbairn's model was there, waiting to be acknowledged for the very first time. Modern relational psychoanalysis and classical psychoanalysis are mutually exclusive models, and analysts as well as other clinicians who use analytic models in their work must choose between the two views of human psychological functioning: "Either interaction is viewed in the context of the expression of preformed forces or pressures, *or*, mental content is viewed as expressed and shaped in the context of the establishment and maintenance of connections with others. Psychological meaning is either regarded as inherent and brought to the relational field, *or* as negotiated through interaction" (Mitchell 1988:5).

Fairbairn's model is one of the two early psychoanalytic models (the other is Sullivan's) that hold that psychological development, both conscious and unconscious, is formed from individualized relational events with the child's caregivers and that these events are organized, sorted, and stored in the child's unconscious. Each individual's personality is formed from the unique experiences and relational patterns encountered by the child in his or her developmental history from being loved and cherished to being raped and beaten. There are no universal meanings in relational psychoanalysis but universal techniques for protecting the self from external threats. The danger is not from inherited drives and primitive motives contained in the interior of the personality but from destructive, malicious, or indifferent caregivers on the outside. Thus Fairbairn, a modest man who worked in virtual isolation in Scotland, far from the center of psychoanalytic thought, produced a model too obscure to be considered threatening in his time, and yet, when the field matured, his model acted as a catalyst for sweeping changes in the world of psychoanalytic thought.

Clearly, Fairbairn understood that his model had been passed over and that he had made no tangible impact on psychoanalytic theory of his time. Toward the end of his life, he had frequent and long-lasting bouts of influenza that incapacitated him for periods of up to six months (Sutherland 1989:157). He knew that his time was limited, and his final paper (1963), written in his last period of declining health (he died on December 31, 1964), is a curiosity, as it is merely a single page composed of seventeen numbered declarative statements, the first six reading as follows:

1. An ego is present at birth.
2. Libido is a function of the ego.
3. There is no death instinct; and aggression is a reaction to frustration and deprivation.
4. Since libido is a function of the ego and aggression is a reaction to frustration or deprivation, there is no such thing as an "id."
5. The ego, and therefore libido, is fundamentally object seeking.
6. The earliest and original form of anxiety, as experienced by the child, is separation anxiety. (224)

This exceedingly unusual paper strikes me as his attempt to leave a reminder to future generations of analysts about the existence of his work and, perhaps more striking, to post a notice analogous to Martin Luther's "Ninety-five Theses" against the Catholic Church. Effectively, Fairbairn, a man with extensive philosophical and religious training, was leaving his psychoanalytic thesis on the "door" of the *International Journal of Psycho-Analysis*, the analytic equivalent of Luther's use of the church door of the Castle Church in Wittenberg in 1517. His seventeen "positions" contradicted and challenged the fundamental tenets of classical drive theory. Unlike Luther, whose influence spread rapidly, Fairbairn's protest, like his work, was largely ignored by his contemporaries.

The real issue regarding Fairbairn's legacy is its current prevalence in the field of psychoanalytic practice. Odgen (1990) has noted that all models contain ineffable truths and unique perspectives on the human condition, and if any given model falls into disuse, then the field will lose an important view of human functioning:

Different psychoanalytic perspectives are much like different languages. Despite the extensive overlap of semantic content of the written texts of different languages, each language creates meaning that cannot be generated by the other languages now spoken or preserved in written form. The interpreter is not merely a passive carrier of information from one person to another; he is the active preserver and creator of meaning as well as the retriever of the alienated. (1)

Thus the existing literature that describes Fairbairn's model, as well as the texts and papers that apply it to the clinical enterprise, is actively preserving a specific point of view that has something to offer that is missing in other models. Unique about Fairbairn's model is the awareness of the imperatives of attachment for the developing child; the view of human personality as a set of different selves that relate to various internal objects, selves that are dissociated from one another and can overpower the central ego; the idea of the interior world of humans as one dominated by the splitting defense; and, finally, the concept of a longing, needy, empty self that creates a need-satisfying object out of bits of reality enhanced with fantasy.

The legacy of Fairbairn's work, in terms of preserving his original writing as well as commentary on his theory, is robust, and a number of texts are essential to students of his work. Fairbairn's only book, *Psychoanalytic Studies of the Personality* (1952), is still in print, and it contains his most significant papers, except for "On the Nature and Aims of Psycho-Analytical Treatment" (1958). Interest in Fairbairn has been sufficient enough to stimulate the creation of an extensive research literature, developed by David E. Scharff and Jill Savege Scharff. In 1994, David Scharff and Ellinor F. Birtles (Fairbairn's daughter) edited a two-volume set of Fairbairn's papers, *From Instinct to Self*, which offers the interested reader access to many of his lesser-known papers as well as commentary on his work. In addition, John D. Sutherland has written a biography of Fairbairn, *Fairbairn's Journey into the Interior* (1989), and Jill Savege Scharff has edited a collection of Sutherland's papers, *The Autonomous Self* (1994), which support and extend Fairbairn's work.

Another major resource on Fairbairn's metapsychology are the books of Stephen A. Mitchell, who co-authored, with Jay R. Greenberg, the first widely read reappraisal of Fairbairn's work: *Object Relations in Psychoanalytic Theory* (1983). This was the first "commentary" on Fairbairn's work, and Mitchell and Greenberg place his model in the keystone position in the historic shift away from drive theory and toward relational theories that has occurred in the past twenty-five years. Mitchell, the stronger supporter of Fairbairn, went on to publish a number of other commentaries on Fairbairn's work, which began the process of integrating his work into the new field of "relational psychoanalysis." Mitchell's *Relational Concepts in Psychoanalysis* (1988) is a detailed metapsychological analysis of the merits of relational models (largely Fairbairn's relational model) compared with drive theory. A later text by Mitchell, *Relationality* (2000), also contains valuable insights and commentary on Fairbairn's model, particularly regarding the problem of the internalization of good objects.

A number of significant books of collected essays and papers comment and expand on Fairbairn's work, in terms of his metapsychology and application to issues in practice. The first is James S. Grotstein and Donald B. Rinsley's *Fairbairn and the Origins of Object Relations* (1994), which has been quoted extensively in this text. When read alongside Fairbairn's original work, it illuminates large parts of his model through essays and commentary by fourteen authors in the field. The second book of collected papers, *Fairbairn, Then and Now* (1998), edited by Neil

J. Skolnick and David E. Scharff, is a collection of papers presented in 1996 at the Fairbairn Conference in New York. It is a valuable resource for those interested in Fairbairn's work. The third, and most recent, edited book of short papers on Fairbairn's work is *The Legacy of Fairbairn and Sutherland* (2005), edited by Scharff and Scharff, and it includes essays on the application of Fairbairn's model by authors from Europe and South America as well as the United States. These three books offer the interested reader a wide range of approaches to working with Fairbairn's model in various settings.

A second important group of texts focuses on the application of Fairbairn's model to clinical issues, as opposed to explanations of his theory. These include the works of Jeffrey Seinfeld: *The Bad Object* (1990), *The Empty Core* (1991), *Interpreting and Holding* (1993), and *Containing Rage, Terror, and Despair* (1996). Each book focuses on a different aspect of Fairbairn's model as applied to specific clinical issues. An even larger cache of texts exists on the application of Fairbairn's model to the clinical dyad (as well as to couples, sexual issues, and family treatment) that originates from the work of David E. Scharff and Jill Savege Scharff, authors and editors of The Library of Object Relations. This series of books contains at least a dozen volumes describing Fairbairn's model and its application to the treatment process. These authors integrate Fairbairn's model with key concepts from Klein, Winnicott, and Bion, and apply this integrated object relations model to various treatment issues. Many of their texts are intended for teaching and are specifically designed to clarify the relationship between theory and practice. Three of these texts form a valuable triptych: Scharff and Scharff's basic *Primer of Object Relations Therapy* (1995), which is written in a question-and-answer format and is meant for beginning students; *Object Relations Theory and Practice* (1996), edited by David Scharff, which contains sixty short excerpts from classic papers in object relations theory from Fairbairn, Klein, Winnicott, Bion, and others, and offers the student of object relations theory the most salient parts of the original papers that have become the mainstream of relational psychoanalytic thought; and Scharff and Scharff's *Object Relations Individual Therapy* (2000), which provides many clear examples of working with object relations theory with patients in the clinical setting, with an emphasis on transference–countertransference interpretation. Thus the legacy of Fairbairn is well established within the field of relational theory, and it appears that his original work will influence psychoanalytic thought for many years to come.

REFERENCES

Adams, P. L. (1973). *Obsessive Children: A Sociopsychiatric Study*. New York: Bruner/Mazel.

Adler, G. (1985). *Borderline Psychopathology and Its Treatment*. New York: Jason Aronson.

Armstrong-Perlman, E. M. (1991). The allure of the bad object. *Free Association, 2*, 343–356.

Barnett, J. (1969). On aggression in the obsessional neuroses. *Contemporary Psychoanalysis, 6*, 48–57.

Beattie, H. J. (2003). The repression and the return of bad objects: W. R. D. Fairbairn and the historical roots of theory. *International Journal of Psychoanalysis, 84*, 1171–1187.

——. (2005). Revenge. *Journal of the American Psychoanalytic Association 53*(2), 513–524.

Birtles, E. F. (1996). Comment at the Fairbairn Conference, October 4, 1996, New York.

Birtles, E. F., and D. E. Scharff (Eds.). (1994). *From Instinct to Self: Selected Papers of W. R. D. Fairbairn*. Vol. 2. Northvale, N.J.: Jason Aronson

Bollas, C. (1998). Figures and their functions: On the Oedipal structure of psychoanalysis. In O. Renick (Ed.), *Knowledge and Authority in the Psychoanalytic Relationship* (pp. 3–22). Northvale, N.J.: Jason Aronson.

Celani, D. (1974). An interpersonal approach to hysteria. *American Journal of Psychiatry 133*(12), 1414–1418.

——. (1993). *The Treatment of the Borderline Patient: Applying Fairbairn's Object Relations Theory in the Clinical Setting*. Madison, Conn.: International Universities Press.

——. (1994). *The Illusion of Love: Why the Battered Woman Returns to Her Abuser*. New York: Columbia University Press.

——. (1998). Structural sources of resistance in battered women. In N. J. Skolnick and D. E. Scharff (Eds.), *Fairbairn, Then and Now* (pp. 235–254). Hillsdale, N.J.: Analytic Press.

——. (1999). Applying Fairbairn's object relations theory to the dynamics of the battered woman. *American Journal of Psychotherapy, 53*, 60–72.

——. (2001). Working with Fairbairn's ego structures. *Contemporary Psychoanalysis, 37*, 391–416.

——. (2005). *Leaving Home: The Art of Separating from Your Difficult Family*. New York: Columbia University Press.

——. (2007). A structural analysis of the obsessional character: A Fairbairnian perspective. *American Journal of Psychoanalysis, 67*(2), 119–140.

Clarke, G. (2005) The preconscious and psychic change in Fairbairn's model of mind. *International Journal of Psychoanalysis, 86*, 61–77.

Davies, J. M. (1996). Linking the "pre-analytic" with the postclassical. *Contemporary Psychoanalysis*, 32(4), 553–576.

——. (1998). Repression and dissociation—Freud and Janet: Fairbairn's new model of unconscious process. In N. J. Skolnick and D. E. Scharff (Eds.), *Fairbairn, Then and Now* (pp. 53–69). Hillsdale, N.J.: Analytic Press.

Davies, J. M., and M. G. Frawley. (1991). Dissociative processes and transference-countertransference paradigms in the psychoanalytically oriented treatment of adult survivors of childhood sexual abuse. *Psychoanalytic Dialogues*, 2(1), 5–36.

Druck, A. (1989). *Four Therapeutic Approaches to the Borderline Patient: Principles and Techniques of the Basic Dynamic Stances*. Northvale, N.J.: Jason Aronson.

Easser, B., and S. Lesser. (1965). Hysterical personality: A reevaluation. *Psychoanalytic Quarterly*, 34, 390–405.

Fairbairn, W. R. D. (1927). Notes on the religious phantasies of a female patient. In W. R. D. Fairbairn, *Psychoanalytic Studies of the Personality* (pp.183–196). London: Routledge & Kegan Paul, 1952.

——. (1931). Features in the analysis of a patient with a physical genital abnormality. In W. R. D. Fairbairn, *Psychoanalytic Studies of the Personality* (pp. 197–222). London: Routledge & Kegan Paul, 1952.

——. (1940). Schizoid factors in the personality. In W. R. D. Fairbairn, *Psychoanalytic Studies of the Personality* (pp. 3–27). London: Routledge & Kegan Paul, 1952.

——. (1941). A revised psychopathology of the psychoses and psychoneuroses. In W. R. D. Fairbairn, *Psychoanalytic Studies of the Personality* (pp. 28–58). London: Routledge & Kegan Paul, 1952.

——. (1943). The repression and the return of bad objects (with special reference to the "war neuroses"). In W. R. D. Fairbairn, *Psychoanalytic Studies of the Personality* (pp. 59–81). London: Routledge & Kegan Paul, 1952.

——. (1944). Endopsychic structure considered in terms of object relationships. In W. R. D. Fairbairn, *Psychoanalytic Studies of the Personality* (pp. 82–132). London: Routledge & Kegan Paul, 1952.

——. (1951a). Addendum. In W. R. D. Fairbairn, *Psychoanalytic Studies of the Personality* (pp. 133–136). London: Routledge & Kegan Paul, 1952.

——. (1951b). A synopsis of the development of the author's views regarding the structure of the personality. In W. R. D. Fairbairn, *Psychoanalytic Studies of the Personality* (pp. 162–179). London: Routledge & Kegan Paul, 1952.

——. (1952). *Psychoanalytic Studies of the Personality*. London. Routledge & Kegan Paul.

——. (1954). Observations on the nature of hysterical states. *British Journal of Medical Psychology*, 27, 105–125.

——. (1958). On the nature and aims of psycho-analytical treatment. *International Journal of Psychoanalysis*, 39, 374–385.

——. (1963). Synopsis of an object-relations theory of the personality. *International Journal of Psychoanalysis*, 44, 224–225.

Giovacchini, P. (1984). *Character Disorders and Adaptive Mechanisms*. New York: Jason Aronson.

Greenberg, J. R. (1991). *Oedipus and Beyond: A Clinical Theory*. Cambridge, Mass.: Harvard University Press.

Greenberg, J. R., and S. A. Mitchell. (1983). *Object Relations in Psychoanalytic Theory*. Cambridge, Mass.: Harvard University Press.

Greenson, R. R. (1978). A dream while drowning. In R. R. Greenson, *Explorations in Psychoanalysis* (pp. 415–423). Madison, Conn.: International Universities Press.

Grotstein, J. S., and D. B. Rinsley (Eds.). (1994). *Fairbairn and the Origins of Object Relations*. New York: Guilford Press.

Guntrip, H. (1971). *Psychoanalytic Theory, Therapy, and the Self.* New York: Basic Books

Hamilton, N. G. (1988). *Self and Others: Object Relations Theory in Practice.* Northvale, N.J.: Jason Aronson.

Harrison, K. (1997). *The Kiss.* New York: Random House.

Havens, L. (1976). *Participant Observation.* New York: Jason Aronson.

Hollender, M. (1971). Hysterical personality. *Comments on Contemporary Psychology*, 1, 17–24.

Hughes, J. M. (1989). *Reshaping the Psychoanalytic Domain: The Work of Melanie Klein, W. R. D. Fairbairn, and D. W. Winnicott.* Berkeley: University of California Press.

Kainer, R. G. (1979). The critical voice in the treatment of the obsessional. *Contemporary Psychoanalysis*, 15, 276–287.

Kernberg, O. (1966). Structural derivatives of object relationships. *International Journal of Psychoanalysis*, 47, 236–253.

——. (1967). Borderline personality organization. *Journal of the American Psychoanalytic Association*, 15, 641–685.

——. (1984). *Severe Personality Disorders: Psychotherapeutic Strategies.* New Haven, Conn.: Yale University Press.

Klein, M. (1946). Notes on some schizoid mechanisms. In M. Klein, *Envy and Gratitude and Other Works, 1946–1963* (pp. 1–24). London: Hogarth Press, 1975.

Kopp, S. (1978). *An End to Innocence: Facing Life Without Illusions.* New York: Bantam Books.

Langs, R. (1973). *The Technique of Psychoanalytic Psychotherapy.* Vol. 1. Northvale, N.J.: Jason Aronson.

Levenson E. A. (1991). *The Purloined Self: Interpersonal Perspectives in Psychoanalysis.* New York: Contemporary Psychoanalysis Books.

Liotti, G. (1992). Disorganized/disoriented attachment in the etiology of the dissociative disorders. *Dissociation*, 5(4), 196–204.

Loewald, H. (1960). On the therapeutic action of psychoanalysis. *International Journal of Psychoanalysis*, 41, 16–33.

Luisada, P., R. Peele, and E. Pittard. (1974). The hysterical personality in men. *American Journal of Psychiatry*, 131(5), 518–522.

Mallinger, A. E. (1982). Demand sensitive obsessionals. *Journal of the American Academy of Psychoanalysis*, 10(3), 407–426.

Marmor, J. (1953). Orality in the hysterical personality. *Journal of the American Psychoanalytic Association*, 1, 656–671.

Mitchell, S. A. (1981). The origins and nature of the "object" in the theories of Klein and Fairbairn. In J. A. Grotstein and D. B. Rinsley (Eds.), *Fairbairn and the Origins of Object Relations* (pp. 66–87). New York. Guilford Press, 1994.

——. (1993). *Hope and Dread in Psychoanalysis.* New York: Basic Books.

——. (1997). *Influence and Autonomy in Psychoanalysis.* Hillsdale, N.J.: Analytic Press.

——. (1998). Fairbairn's object seeking: Between paradigms. In N. J. Skolnick and D. E. Scharff (Eds.), *Fairbairn, Then and Now* (pp. 115–135). Hillsdale, N.J.: Analytic Press.

——. (2000). *Relationality: From Attachment to Intersubjectivity.* Hillsdale, N.J.: Analytic Press.

Odgen, T. H. (1983). The concept of internal object relations. In J. S. Grotstein and D. B. Rinsley (Eds.), *Fairbairn and the Origins of Object Relations* (pp. 88–111). New York: Guilford Press, 1994.

——. (1990). *The Matrix of the Mind: Object Relations and the Psychoanalytic Dialogue.* Northvale, N.J.: Jason Aronson.

Pine, F. (1985). *Developmental Theory and Clinical Process.* New Haven, Conn.: Yale University Press.

Porter, K. A. (1948). The necessary enemy. In *The Collected Essays and Occasional Writings of Katherine Anne Porter* (pp. 182–186). Boston: Houghton Mifflin, 1970.

Rayner, E. (1991). *The Independent Mind in Psychoanalysis.* Northvale N.J.: Jason Aronson.

Rubens, R. (1984). The meaning of structure in Fairbairn. *International Review of Psycho-Analysis,* 11, 429–440.

——. (1994). Fairbairn's structural theory. In J. S. Grotstein and D. B. Rinsley (Eds.), *Fairbairn and the Origins of Object Relations* (pp. 151–173). New York: Guilford Press.

Schafer, R. (1998). Authority, evidence, and knowledge in the psychoanalytic relationship. In O. Renick (Ed.), *Knowledge and Authority in the Psychoanalytic Relationship* (pp. 227–244). Northvale, N.J.: Jason Aronson.

Scharff, D. E. (1989). An object relations approach to sexuality in family life. In J. S. Scharff (Ed.), *Foundations of Object Relations Family Therapy* (pp. 399–417). Northvale, N.J.: Jason Aronson.

—— (Ed.). (1996). *Object Relations Theory and Practice: An Introduction.* Northvale N.J.: Jason Aronson.

Scharff, D. E., and E. F. Birtles. (1997). From instinct to self: The evolution and implications of W. R. D. Fairbairn's theory of object relations. *International Journal of Psychoanalysis,* 78, 1085–1103.

—— (Eds.). (1994). *From Instinct to Self: Selected Papers of W. R. D. Fairbairn.* Vol. 1. Northvale, N.J.: Jason Aronson.

Scharff, J. S. (Ed.). (1994). *The Autonomous Self: The Work of John D. Sutherland.* Northvale, N.J.: Jason Aronson.

Scharff, J. S., and D. E. Scharff. (1995). *The Primer of Object Relations Therapy.* Northvale, N.J.: Jason Aronson.

——. (2000). *Object Relations Individual Therapy.* Northvale, N.J.: Jason Aronson.

—— (Eds.). (2005). *The Legacy of Fairbairn and Sutherland: Psychotherapeutic Applications.* New York: Routledge.

Schimel, J. L. (1972). The power theme in the obsessional. *Contemporary Psychoanalysis,* 9, 1–28.

Searles, H. F. (1965). *Collected Papers on Schizophrenia and Related Topics.* New York: International Universities Press.

Seinfeld, J. (1990). *The Bad Object: Handling the Negative Therapeutic Reaction in Psychotherapy.* Northvale, N.J.: Jason Aronson.

——. (1991). *The Empty Core: An Object Relations Approach to Psychotherapy of the Schizoid Personality.* Northvale, N.J.: Jason Aronson.

——. (1993). *Interpreting and Holding: The Paternal and Maternal Functions of the Psychotherapist.* Northvale, N.J.: Jason Aronson.

——. (1996). *Containing Rage, Terror, and Despair: An Object Relations Approach to Psychotherapy* . Northvale, N.J.: Jason Aronson.

Shapiro, D. (1965). *Neurotic Styles.* New York: Basic Books.

Skolnick, N. J., and D. E. Scharff (Eds.). (1998). *Fairbairn, Then and Now*. Hillsdale, N.J.: Analytic Press.

Slipp, S. (1977). Interpersonal factors in hysteria: Freud's seduction theory and the case of Dora. *Journal of the American Academy of Psychoanalysis*, 5(3), 359–376.

Sullivan, H. S. (1953). *The Interpersonal Theory of Psychiatry*. New York: Norton.

——. (1956). *Clinical Studies in Psychiatry*. New York: Norton.

Sutherland, J. D. (1989). *Fairbairn's Journey into the Interior*. London: Free Association Books.

Szasz, T. S. (1957). On the theory of psycho-analytic treatment. *International Journal of Psycho-Analysis*, 38, 166–182.

Walker, L. E. (1979). *The Battered Woman*. New York: Harper & Row.

Winckler, M. M. (1995). Obsessionalism. In M. Lionells, J. Fiscalini, C. H. Mann, and D. B. Stern (Eds.), *Handbook of Interpersonal Psychoanalysis* (pp. 469–490). Hillsdale, N.J.: Analytic Press.

Winnicott, D. W. (1986). *Home Is Where We Start From: Essays by a Psychoanalyst*. New York: Norton.

Winnicott, D. W., and M. Kahn. (1953). A review of Fairbairn's *Psychoanalytic Studies of the Personality*. *International Journal of Psychoanalysis*, 34, 329–333.

Youngerman, J. (1995). Borderline conditions. In M. Lionells, J. Fiscalini, C. H. Mann, and D. B. Stern (Eds.), *Handbook of Interpersonal Psychoanalysis* (pp. 419–434). Hillsdale, N.J.: Analytic Press.

Zetzel, E. (1968). The so-called good hysteric. *International Journal of Psychoanalysis*, 49, 256–261.

INDEX

Adams, P., 187–188
Adler, G., 167; on recognition memory, 177
ambivalence: avoidance of, using splitting defense, 78; destruction of attachment and, 8
antilibidinal ego: characteristics of, 8, 86–91; desire for revenge and, 88–89; extreme example of, 81, 89; Fairbairn's patient with, 86; integrating dissociated memories and, 105–110; as "internal saboteur," 52; in obsessional patient, 192; patient's dream of being poisoned and, 45; resistance of, to treatment, 12; revenge against rejecting object and, 145; sabotage of treatment for, 111; strategies against rejecting object and, 56, 60; struggle with rejecting object and, 87; as therapeutic ally, 90; transferences to external objects and, 64, 101–102
Armstrong-Perlman, E., 96, 170
Autonomous Self, The (Sutherland), 212

"badness": internalized objects and, 32; obsessional child and, 188; of self, 11, 38, 156
bad object: acting out against safe, 156; assessment of attachment to, 44, 154–155; borderline patient's return to, 171–172; continuing need for, 139–140; fear of release of, 6, 48; power of, over child, 44
Bad Object, The (Seinfeld), 213
Barnett, J., 188

Battered Woman, The (Walker), 180
battered women, 180–184
Beattie, H.: on Fairbairn's childhood, 17; on Fairbairn's creative period, 25; on Fairbairn's relationship to his father, 70; on influence of "shell-shocked" officers on Fairbairn, 18; on "The Repression and the Return of Bad Objects," 34–35; on revenge against rejecting objects, 88, 111
Bollas, C., 97
borderline personality disorder, 153–180
British Journal of Medical Psychology, 208
British Psycho-Analytical Society, 74, 82–83

Celani, D., 26, 57, 61, 65, 68–69, 86, 117, 181, 203
central ego: definition of, 52; example of improvement of, 149–150; Fairbairn's lack of interest in, 53; impoverishment of, 57; impoverishment of, in obsessional patient, 188–189, 191; maturity of, 146; "mystification" of, 187; relationship of, to ideal object, 54, 186; relationship of, to subego, 9, 55–56; strengthening of, 11, 46, 65, 141, 144–145; supporting gains of, 147–148
child: assumption of, that love is worthless, 4; attachment of, to frustrating objects, 28; fear of, of expressing hate toward object, 67; fear of, of expressing need toward object, 69–70; focus of, on

child (*continued*)
   partial objects, 6, 27; hate of objects by, 29–30; need of, for bad objects, 44; need of, for love, 32, 56; sexuality as substitute satisfaction for, 33; unconditional dependence of, on objects, 34
Containing Rage, Terror, and Despair (Seinfeld), 213

Davies, J.: on averagable and irreconcilable representations, 120–121; on constructivism, 119; on dissociative models, 23; on "inviting" technique, 130
Davies, J., and M. Frawley, on projective/introjective processes of psychotherapy, 122–123
dreams: dissociated perceptions in, 47; as reflecting parts of self, 59
Druck, A., 141, 153

Easser, B., and S. Lesser, 205
Empty Core, The (Seinfeld), 213
"Endopsychic Structure Considered in Terms of Object Relationships" (Fairbairn), 6, 51–71
exciting object, 96–97; transference of, toward therapist, 104–105

Fairbairn, Then and Now (Skolnick and Scharff), 212
Fairbairn, W. R. D.: childhood of, 17; early papers of, 24; education of, 17–18; errors of, on internalization, 29; influence of children's clinic on, 19, 36; influence of Klein on, 25, 35; influence of "shell-shocked" officers on, 18; lack of influence of, in psychoanalysis, 19–20, 72, 208; Martin Luther protest and, 211; neurotic symptom of, 16; at Royal Edinburgh Hospital, 18. *See also individual papers*
Fairbairn and the Origins of Object Relations (Grotstein and Rinsley), 212
Fairbairn's Journey into the Interior (Sutherland), 212
framework: challenges to, 134; patient violations of, 206; vacation disruptions to, 136

Freud, S.: on death instinct, 22; on inherited drives, 24
From Instinct to Self (Fairbairn), 212

Giovacchini, P., 128–129
good object: encountering, in the real world, 134; in Fairbairn's model, 45; influence of, 150–151; reliance on, during stress, 130
Greenberg, J., and S. Mitchell: on attachment to neglectful parents, 22; on Fairbairn's inconsistency, 20; on Fairbairn's lack of good objects, 140; on Fairbairn's relational model, 15–16; influence of, 21; on repetition compulsion, 23; on self-defeating characteristics of psychopathology, 21–22
grief, 10, 139; integration of dissociated structured and, 146
Grotstein, J., and D. Rinsley: on attachment to bad objects, 19; on "demonic" view of child, 67; on Fairbairn's character, 16–17; on impact of Fairbairn's work, 207
guilt: abandonment of abusive object and, 156–157; separation and, 172
Guntrip, H.: on function of analytic innovators, 24; visit of, to orphanage, 19

Hamilton, N., 69, 142
Harrison, K., 33
Havens, L., 154
histrionic personality disorder, 199–206; continuum of, 204; family patterns of, 13, 201–203; sexual exploitation and, 200–201
Hollander, M., 200
Hughes, J., on Guntrip's analysis with Fairbairn, 19

Illusion of Love, The (Celani), 12, 49, 181–184
inner world: as closed system, 73, 78, 79; structuralization of, 141–142; therapist's attempt to breach, 81–82; therapist's lack of impact on, 167
internalization: of bad objects, 37; of fragments of good objects, 40; of objects,

"Synopsis of an Object-Relations Theory of the Personality" (Fairbairn), 54

Szasz, T., 71

transference: confusion of therapist and, 122; fury of rejecting object and, 92; futility of interpretations, 79; patterns of, 9, 98, 121–130

Treatment of the Borderline Patient, The (Celani), 1, 47

unconscious: competing models of, 77; reciprocal relationship of, to conscious-ness, 54–55; source of, 35; unacceptable memories in, 36

Walker, L., 12; on "Cycle Theory of Violence," 12, 181–183

Winckler, M., on "mystification" of child, 12, 187

Winnicott, D., 139, 143

Winnicott, D., and M. Kahn, 72

Youngerman, J., 117

Zitzel, E., 205